D0408496

The Oxford Guide to
Word Games

The Oxford Guide to
Word Games

TONY AUGARDE

Oxford   New York

OXFORD UNIVERSITY PRESS

1984

Ref
GV
1507
W8
A84
1984

Oxford University Press, Walton Street, Oxford OX2 6DP

London New York Toronto
Delhi Bombay Calcutta Madras Karachi
Kuala Lumpur Hong Kong Tokyo
Nairobi Dar es Salaam Cape Town
Melbourne Auckland

and associated companies in
Beirut Berlin Ibadan Mexico City Nicosia

Oxford is a trade mark of Oxford University Press

© *Tony Augarde 1984*

All rights reserved. No part of this publication may be reproduced,
stored in a retrieval system, or transmitted, in any form or by any means,
electronic, mechanical, photocopying, recording, or otherwise, without
the prior permission of Oxford University Press

British Library Cataloguing in Publication Data
Augarde, Tony
The Oxford guide to word games.
1. Word games
I. Title
793.73 GV1507.W8
ISBN 0-19-214144-9

Library of Congress Cataloging in Publication Data
Augarde, Tony.
The Oxford guide to word games.
Bibliography: p.
Includes index.
1. Word games. 2.. Word games — History. I. Title.
GV1507.W8A84 1984 793.73 83-25140
ISBN 0-19-214144-9

Set at the University Press, Oxford
Printed in Great Britain by
Billing & Sons Ltd.
Worcester

To my family

Contents

Introduction

One of the more lovable characteristics of human beings is their persistent tendency to find new and often frivolous uses for things. Words were designed for the serious business of communication but humans constantly devise novel uses for them.

Babies play with the sound of words. Young children delight in rhyme, revelling in the fact that one word sounds like another. All poetry—indeed, all writing—is a kind of word play: slotting words into appropriate (or inappropriate) places, shifting words around like the pieces of a jigsaw puzzle and choosing those that make up a particular pattern.

With glorious perversity, human beings insist on finding similarities between entirely different words, or double meanings in the same word, thus creating puns and riddles. In the same way, they use words as the raw material for innumerable games. Often the words serve very much as raw material: pulled to pieces and rearranged in strange, surprising sequences (as in anagrams and palindromes). In other cases the words are linked together in diagrams or patterns (as in acrostics, crosswords, Scrabble, and word squares). Sometimes people play about with the individual letters of words (in Beheadments and chronograms), their shape (in concrete poetry), or their sounds (in rebuses and tongue-twisters). At other times words have to be guessed (as in charades, Dumb Crambo, Hangman, and many other games).

Word games can be organized events for several people but they can also be amusing—or infuriating—pastimes in which one or more people wrestle with words: trying to write a sentence containing all the letters of the alphabet (a pangram) or a piece of writing that avoids a particular letter of the alphabet (lipograms and univocalics).

It is difficult to draw a line between word games as such and various types of word play, which are generally included in this book if they have some of the characteristics of a game. For example, puns are admitted because they are virtually the only kind of jokes which essentially depend upon verbal manipulation.

Games can teach us much about ourselves and the times we live in. The social life of the present and the past is mirrored in the games people play. The enduringly popular games are restyled by each generation to fit the prevailing mood and interests. This book is unusual in that it not only describes games but also outlines their history and places them in their social context. Of particular interest are the occurrences of games in literature, in the work of Thackeray and Jane Austen, for example. As far as possible, contemporary descriptions of games are used to give the flavour of the times when they were popular. Spellings have generally been modernized, except where they are an intrinsic part of the game. To save the reader constantly having to turn to the back of the book, answers to puzzles are given alongside each game. Sources to quotations, when not given in the text, will be found in the Acknowledgements or Select Bibliography.

Word games may seem trivial but they reflect some truths about humanity. The same impulse which drives poets, playwrights, and artists also moves us to play with words: to find order in what we are given, to make new sense (or nonsense) by playing with the basic elements of our language, as well as for pure entertainment and enjoyment. Word games can never compete with the arts but perhaps they are the foothills of literature, involving the same sort of creativity with language, although at a humbler, more approachable level.

I am very grateful to Fleur Augarde for her typing and understanding; to Judith Luna, Iona Opie, and Henry Hardy for their useful comments; to John Sykes and Richard Palmer for solving some problems; and to the almost invariably helpful staff of the Bodleian Library for access to their invaluable resources.

A. J. A.

Note on Proprietary Terms

This book includes some names which are or are asserted to be proprietary names or trade marks. Their use does not imply that they have acquired for legal purposes a non-proprietary or general significance, nor is any other judgement implied concerning their legal status.

Riddles

The RIDDLE is the oldest and the most widespread type of word game. Riddles are found at every period of history and in every part of the world.

The American expert on riddles, Archer Taylor, says that 'the oldest recorded riddles are Babylonian school texts which show no literary polish'. For example: 'Who becomes pregnant without conceiving, who becomes fat without eating?' The answer is probably *a rain-cloud*. Another Babylonian riddle refers mysteriously to a chest of silver and a casket of gold. The answer is *an egg*, reminding us of a better-known riddle about an egg, beginning 'Humpty Dumpty sat on a wall . . .'

Humpty Dumpty and the first of these Babylonian riddles use a common device in riddle-making: describing a thing as if it were a person. Personification is typical of the imagery which is at the heart of many riddles. Aristotle noted the fact that riddles develop from the natural human tendency to create metaphors—seeing similarities between things and describing one thing as if it were another:

Most smart sayings are derived from metaphor, and also from misleading the hearer beforehand. For it becomes more evident to him that he has learnt something, when the conclusion turns out contrary to his expectation, and the mind seems to say, 'How true it is! but I missed it.' . . . And clever riddles are agreeable for the same reason; for something is learnt, and the expression is also metaphorical.

An anonymous writer in the *Cornhill Magazine* of November 1891 used this connection with metaphor to draw a comparison between riddles and literature:

It is not an accident that times of literary revival have been prolific in riddles. For it may be said generally that the powers of language which are exercised in riddle-making are the selfsame powers that are exercised in the art of literature, only that in making riddles those powers are drawn upon more continuously which in general literature are exercised with less intensity and effort. Metaphors, secondary meanings, adroit groupings which alter significations, all the powers that make words elastic, these are the faculties by which language is rendered plastic for the writer, and these are they that are brought into action by the riddle-maker with a more laboured accumulation of effects.

There are few, if any, countries where riddles have not been found. And the same subjects for riddles occur in widely different places. For example, a bell in a tower is the subject of riddles in the following countries:

Scotland: What is it that hangs high, and cries sore, has a head and no hair?

Wales: I saw some object near to a town, in a very finely made palace between earth and heaven. It has a fine tail which almost reaches to the ground, and its tongue hangs in a very large skull. It spends most of its time in silence, but sometimes it calls its friends together.

France: The more one pulls it, the more it cries out.

Lithuania: A horse with a silver tail neighs on a high hill.

Serbia: A dead mare doesn't neigh, but when somebody pulls it by the tail, it neighs so that all men can hear it!

Newfoundland: Round as a hoop, deep as a pail;
                  Never sings out till it's caught by the tail.

Chile: Señora Carolina likes to live in a high house, and if they pull her feet, she disturbs the inhabitants.

Modern riddles usually take the form of a question, as in 'What is black and white and red all over?' (Answer: *a book*). But the riddles quoted above take the form of enigmatic statements, and that was generally the style of the oldest riddles. It was the form of the famous riddle which Samson asked at his wedding, as recounted in the Book of Judges:

Samson said to them, 'Let me ask you a riddle. If you can guess it during the seven days of the feast, I will give you thirty lengths of linen and thirty changes of clothing.' . . . 'Tell us your riddle,' they said; 'let us hear it.' So he said to them:

> 'Out of the eater came something to eat;
> Out of the strong came something sweet.'

Samson's wife persuaded Samson to tell her the answer, which was that he had a seen a swarm of bees making honey in the carcass of a lion. She treacherously told the answer to the Philistines, who were thus enabled to present Samson with the reply: 'What is sweeter than honey? What is stronger than a lion?'

It is interesting that this answer itself sounds like a riddle (to which the answer could have been *love*) and that, in his reply, Samson used yet another metaphor: 'If you had not ploughed with my heifer, you would not have found out my riddle.'

Another testimony to Solomon's skill in riddles occurs in the first Book of Kings:

The Queen of Sheba heard of Solomon's fame and came to test him with hard questions . . . Solomon answered all her questions; not one of them was too abstruse for the king to answer.

The Bible fails to tell us what the questions were, but a Hebrew text by Yachya Ben Sulieman dating from much later—1430—lists some of the Queen's riddles:

'A woman said to her son, thy father is my father, and thy grandfather my husband; thou art my son, and I am thy sister.' 'Assuredly,' said he [Samson], 'it was the daughter of Lot who spake thus to her son.' 'There is something which when living moves not, yet when its head is cut off it moves.' 'It is the ship in the sea' [the living tree has no motion, the trunk from which the crowning branches have been severed supplies the material for the moving vessel]. (*Folk-Lore*, 1890)

Riddle-contests are a familiar feature of folk-tales from many countries. They are found in the ancient Hindu Vedas, and in the Old Norse Eddas of the twelfth century. In these contests, a person might have to forfeit his life if he failed to answer a riddle.

In *The Golden Bough*, J. G. Frazer describes how riddles were exchanged in various communities at important ceremonies such as weddings and funerals, and at harvest-time: 'In Brittany after a burial, when the rest have gone to partake of the funeral banquet, old men remain behind in the graveyard and . . . ask each other riddles.' Frazer could not understand why riddles were used at such times of crisis, but it was probably thought that the solving of riddles might provide a stimulus to solving the greater problems of life and death.

Riddles were also important to the ancient Persians and Arabs. From Persia came the story of Turandot and her three riddles (also leading to death for anyone who could not solve them). Through the *Arabian Nights*, the Turandot story reached Italy where Puccini turned it into his last opera.

The Greeks, who valued scepticism and mental ingenuity, invented many riddles. Oedipus saved Thebes by solving the riddle of the Sphinx. Here is Thomas De Quincey's retelling of the story:

The riddle proposed by the Sphinx ran in these terms: 'What creature is that which moves on four feet in the morning, on two feet at noon-day, and on three towards the "going down of the sun"?' Oedipus, after some consideration, answered that the creature was *Man*, who creeps on the ground with hands and feet when an infant, walks upright in the vigour of manhood, and leans upon a staff in old age. Immediately the dreadful Sphinx confessed the truth of his solution by throwing herself headlong from a point of rock into the sea; her power being overthrown as soon as her secret had been detected. Thus was the Sphinx destroyed; and, according to the promise of the proclamation, for this great service to the state Oedipus was immediately recompensed. He was saluted King of Thebes, and married to the royal widow Jocasta. (*The Theban Sphinx*, 1849)

The Sphinx's riddle has survived ever since that time. It is the first riddle in the collection made by the Holme family of Chester about 1640 ('What creature is that in the world that first goes on 4 foot then 2 foot then 3 foot and then with 4 foot again?'). Iona and Peter Opie found the riddle recited by twentieth-century schoolchildren in Kirkcaldy ('Walks on four feet On two feet, on three, The more feet it walks on The weaker it be').

Solving the Sphinx's riddle had unfortunate consequences for Oedipus, as Jocasta turned out to be his mother. Another riddle with dire effects was the one which Homer could not solve. Some authorities say that he died of frustration at being unable to answer it. He had asked some fishermen what they had caught and they replied: 'What we caught, we left behind, and we carried away all that we did not catch.' The answer was: *fleas or lice.*

The Romans were less prolific inventors of riddles than the Greeks but they had riddle-contests at the Saturnalia, the December festival of unrestrained merrymaking. And one Roman writer, Symphosius, who probably lived in the late fourth or early fifth century AD, wrote a hundred riddles which had a great influence on subsequent riddle-writers. Here are two of them:

Letters have nourished me, but I know not what letters are. I have lived in books, but am no more studious thereby. I have devoured the Muses, and yet so far have not myself made progress. (Answer: *a bookworm*)

I do not straightway die while breath departs; for repeatedly it returns, though often too departs again: and now my store of vital breath is great, now none. (Answer: *bellows*)

Symphosius' influence is apparent in the work of Bishop Aldhelm of Sherborne (640–709), who borrowed the Roman author's idea of writing a hundred riddles.

The most famous medieval riddles are those found in the *Exeter Book*, a manuscript dating from about 1000 but including riddles which were probably written two hundred years earlier. This example, translated by Michael Alexander, describes a rake:

> She feeds the cattle, this creature I have seen
> In the houses of men. Many are her teeth
> And her nose is of service to her. Netherward she goes,
> Loyally plundering and pulling home again;
> She hunts about the walls in hope of plants,
> Finding always some that are not firmly set.
> She leaves the fair fast-rooted ones
> To stand undisturbed in their established place,
> Brightly shining, blossoming and growing.

The first printed collection of English riddles was the *Demaundes Joyous*, published in 1511 by Wynkyn de Worde, who had learned printing from Caxton. This consists of fifty-four riddles, of which twenty-nine were taken from a French book called *Demandes joyeuses en maniere de quolibets*. De Worde omitted most of the obscene riddles from the French book. According to the Shakespearian actor Robert Armin, Henry VIII's jester—Will Sommers—used obscene riddles to cure the King of 'extreme melancholy' and they are found in various riddle books of Elizabethan times. They depended upon a *double entendre*, whereby the listener was led to believe the answer was obscene and was then surprisingly told that the answer was something innocuous like a broom-handle or an eye. Such riddles may have been unsuited to Wynkyn's character, for he opens his *Demaundes Joyous* with a religious riddle:

Who bare the best burden that ever was borne? That bare the ass when Our Lady fled with Our Lord into Egypt.

Other riddles in this collection have survived to the present day. For instance, Wynkyn de Worde's 'How many calves' tails behoveth to reach from the earth to the sky? No more but one, and [if] it be long enough' survives in the modern riddle: 'How many balls of string would it take to reach the moon?' Wynkyn's 'What thing is that that is most likest unto a horse? That is a mare' is echoed in a riddle from *Wit Revived* (1655): 'What is likest to a cat in a hole? A cat out of a hole', and another in *The Puzzle* (1745): 'What is most like a cat looking out of a window? A cat looking in at a window'.

Wynkyn de Worde takes delight in the same sort of simple humour that pleases modern schoolchildren:

Wherefore set they upon church steeples more a cock than a hen?—If men should set there a hen, she would lay eggs, and they would fall upon men's heads.

He even asks the familiar question 'Which was first, the hen or the egg?' His answer is the hen, when God created it.

The popularity of riddles in Elizabethan times is indicated by a reference in *The Merry Wives of Windsor*. The ineffectual Slender is trying to impress Anne Page with his conversation, and wants to use some riddles to show what a humorous person he is. Slender asks his servant Simple: 'You have not the Book of Riddles about you, have you?' and Simple replies 'Book of Riddles! why, did you not lend it to Alice Shortcake upon All-Hallowmas last, a fortnight afore Michaelmas?'

It is uncertain if the book referred to is the same as *The Book of Merry Riddles* which appeared in many editions around this time. It contained numerous riddles which have since become classics, as well as such venerable problems as how to transport a lamb, a wolf, and a load of hay across a river one at a time. Some of its solutions are almost as long as the questions, as in this familiar riddle:

Two legs sat upon three legs, and had one leg in her hand; then in came four legs, and bare away one leg; then up start two legs, and threw three legs at four legs, and brought again one leg. *Solution*: That is a woman with two legs sat on a stool with three legs, and had a leg of mutton in her hand; then came a dog that hath four legs, and bare away the leg of mutton; then up start the woman, and threw the stool with three legs at the dog with four legs, and brought again the leg of mutton.

Another common riddle in this book is the following:

He went to the wood and caught it,
He sat him down and sought it;

Because he could not find it,
Home with him he brought it.

Solution: That is a thorn: for a man went to the wood, and caught a thorn
in his foot . . .

Three centuries later, this riddle appeared in Gaelic in a collection
published by Alexander Nicolson (1938). And the scholarly journal
Notes and Queries for 8 October 1864 included a riddle on 'a thorn
in the hand' which the contributor claimed to have written:

I went to the wood, and I caught it:
Then I sat me down and sought it:
The longer I sought,
For what I had caught,
The less worth catching I thought it.
I would rather have sold it than bought it:
And when I had sought,
Without finding aught,
Home in my hand I brought it.

One further riddle from the 1631 edition of *The Book of Merry
Riddles* will strike a chord of recognition for anyone familiar with
Beatrix Potter's *Squirrel Nutkin*:

Hitty pitty within the wall,
And hitty pitty without the wall,
If you touch hitty my toy,
Hitty pitty will bite the boy.

As Iona and Peter Opie explain:

Squirrel Nutkin sang this riddle as he danced up and down tickling old Mr
Brown with a *nettle*. Had he been Scottish he might have sung of 'Heg-beg',
'Hobbity-bobbity', or 'Robbie-Stobbie', had he been German 'Kripple die
Krapple' or 'Peter Krus', but had he lived in England three centuries ago he
would probably still have sung of 'Hitty Pitty'.

Another Squirrel Nutkin riddle—about 'Hickamore, Hackamore, on
the King's kitchen door' (i.e. *a sunbeam*)—dates back to at least the
middle of the nineteenth century.

The 'hitty pitty' riddle reappears in 'The Holme Riddles' of *c*.1640.
As well as the Sphinx riddle mentioned above, this collection includes
many classic riddles such as 'There is a thing that goes round about
the house and leaves his gloves in the window' (Answer: *snow*) and

'I have a little boy in a white coat, the bigger he is the lesser he grows' (Answer: *a lighted candle*).

This last riddle is a perennial. Similar riddles are found in Hungary ('A queen sits on her chair. She wears a white gown, her tears fall in her lap') and Nova Scotia ('Nibby come nabby ko, with a red nose. The longer she stands, the shorter she grows'). *Tom Thumb's Royal Riddle Book* (1788) gives it as:

> Nancy with the white petticoat and the red nose,
> The longer she stands, the shorter she grows.

In *Lancashire Legends* (1873) by John Harland and T. T. Wilkinson, it occurs as follows:

> Little Nancy Netticoat
> Has a white petticoat;
> The longer she stands
> The shorter she grows;
> Now cross both your hands,
> And tell me who knows.

Iona and Peter Opie found the rhyme still current in the 1950s at schools in Shropshire, Aberystwyth, Birmingham, and Market Rasen.

Tom Thumb's Royal Riddle Book also included a puzzle of a recurrent type:

> As I went to a feast, I met with a beast,
> With ten heads, and ten tails,
> Forty feet, and fourscore nails.

The answer is *a sow with nine pigs*. Another riddle like this is the one about a man and woman on horseback, described in *A New Collection of Enigmas* (1810):

What creatures are those which appear closely connected, yet upon examination are found to be three distinct bodies, with eight legs, five on one side, and three on the other; three mouths, two straight forwards, and the third on one side; six eyes, four on one side, two on the other; six ears, four on one side, and two on the other?

Of course, the lady must be riding side-saddle! A similar riddle of Stuart times describes an eight-legged animal with two hands and wings, which is a man on horseback, carrying a hawk.

Such riddles attempt to bemuse the listener with an alarming total, like the 'St Ives' riddle, which dates back to the early eighteenth century:

> As I was going to St Ives,
> I met a man with seven wives,
> Each wife had seven sacks,
> Each sack had seven cats,
> Each cat had seven kits:
> Kits, cats, sacks, and wives,
> How many were there going to St Ives?

The answer is either *none* or *one*.

The Riddles of Heraclitus and Democritus (1598) has this:

> The miller, and the miller's wife,
> That they might merry make,
> Were set down with a dish of fruit,
> A cake, and half a cake,
> The parson of the town with them,
> His sister and no more:
> Now have you heard of all the guests,
> And of their bread the store.
> Yet did they use the matter with
> Such cunning, skill, and art,
> That every one ate half a cake,
> Before they did depart.

The author explains that 'the miller's wife was the parson's sister: and so the division not hard to make'.

Even more puzzling is the following:

> Twelve pears hanging high,
> Twelve knights riding by;
> Each knight took a pear,
> And yet left eleven there.

Many solutions have been suggested—for example, that each knight took the same pear, or that 'pear' should be read as 'pair'—but the most likely answer is that only one knight took a pear and his name was *Eachknight*. This answer is supported by the evidence of a similar riddle in a French book, *Les Adeuineaux amoureux*, published in 1478:

> Trois moines passoient
> Trois poires pendoient

> Chascun en prist une
> Et s'en demoura deux.
>
> L'explication—L'un des moines avoit nom Chascun.

That is:

> Three monks were passing
> Three pears were hanging
> Each took one
> And that left two.
>
> Answer: One of the monks was named 'Each'.

Such versified riddles now largely survive in nursery rhymes, like 'Humpty Dumpty', 'Hickamore Hackamore', and 'Long legs, crooked thighs, Little head, and no eyes' (*a pair of tongs*). Most modern riddles are actually CONUNDRUMS—that is to say, riddles which depend on a pun (q.v.). The pun is usually in the answer ('When is a door not a door?' 'When it's *ajar*') but it may be in the question ('Which is the greatest *Friday* in the year?' 'Shrove Tuesday').

Nowadays conundrums are considered childish, suitable only for the playground or for times when adults let their hair down, as when pulling a Christmas cracker (although conundrums also survive on the back of match-boxes). However, in the nineteenth century they seem to have been more acceptable. In Jane Austen's *Emma* (1816), Harriet Smith collected riddles and conundrums:

The only literary pursuit which engaged Harriet at present, the only mental provision she was making for the evening of life, was the collecting and transcribing all the riddles of every sort that she could meet with into a thin quarto of hot-pressed paper, made up by her friend, and ornamented with cyphers and trophies. . . . Mr Elton was the only one whose assistance she asked. He was invited to contribute any really good enigmas, charades, or conundrums, that he might recollect; and she had the pleasure of seeing him most intently at work with his recollections; and at the same time, as she could perceive, most earnestly careful that nothing ungallant, nothing that did not breathe a compliment to the sex, should pass his lips. They owed to him their two or three politest puzzles.

On an expedition to Box Hill, Mr Weston compliments Emma by devising a conundrum:

'What two letters of the alphabet are there that express perfection?'
'What two letters—express perfection? I am sure I do not know.'

'Ah! you will never guess. You (to Emma), I am certain, will never guess. I will tell you. M and A. Emma. Do you understand?'

Understanding and gratification came together. It might be a very indifferent piece of wit, but Emma found a great deal to laugh at and enjoy in it.

Being dependent on puns, conundrums are often liable to make the hearer groan at the answer. Here are some examples from Frederick Planche's *Guess Me* (1872):

When is coffee like the soil? When it is *ground*.

If you stumble over your new mat in the passage, what science are you shown to have neglected? *Pneumatics*.

Why is a thought like the sea? Because it's *a notion* (an ocean).

When does a sculptor explode in strong convulsions? When he *makes faces* and *busts*.

Why does a puss purr? For an obvious *purr-puss*.

Peter Puzzlewell's *Home Amusements* (1859) includes several conundrums that are still known today:

Why is the Desert of Arabia the best place for a picnic? Because of the *sand which is* there.

Why do ducks put their heads in the water? For *divers* reasons.

Why does a chicken three weeks and two days old walk across the road? To get to the other side.

The last of these riddles is perhaps the best known of all, although nowadays the question is usually: 'Why did the chicken cross the road?' It illustrates another common form of riddle, in which the answer is so obvious that the solver does not think of it. Others of this kind are:

Where was Moses when the light went out? In the dark. [Sometimes expanded to 'under the bed looking for the matches' or 'under the bed in his nightshirt'.]

> Pease porridge hot,
> Pease porridge cold,
> Pease porridge in the pot
> Nine days old.
> Spell me *that* in four letters.   T, H, A, T.

Why does a miller wear a white hat? To cover his head. [This is the 1745 version of a riddle which, among modern schoolchildren, takes the form: 'Why does the Duke of Edinburgh wear red, white, and blue braces? To keep his trousers up.']

What is the difference between a rhododendron and a cold apple-dumpling?
The one is a rhododendron and the other is a cold apple-dumpling.

The last of these comes from *Drawing-Room Amusements* (1879)
by 'Professor Hoffmann', who adds: 'You surely wouldn't wish for
a greater difference than that.' Many conundrums take the form
'What is the difference between . . .', often with a clever switch
between two words:

What is the difference between an engine-driver and a schoolmaster? One
minds the train, and the other trains the mind.
What is the difference between an accepted and a rejected lover? One kisses
his missus, the other misses his kisses.
What is the difference between an elephant and a flea? An elephant can
have fleas, but a flea can't have elephants.
What is the difference between a cat and a comma? A cat has its claws at
the end of its paws, and a comma has its pause at the end of its clause.

Yet another category of riddle is the one involving a letter of the
alphabet:

What letter of the alphabet would be of more service to a deaf woman than
a patent ear trumpet? The letter A, because it would make *her* he*ar*.
Why is Paris like the letter F? It is the capital of France.
Why is the letter T like Easter? Because it comes at the end of Lent.

The French have similar riddles:

> Je suis à la tête de l'armée,
> Et je suis toujours en garde contre l'ennemi,
> Et sans moi Paris serait pris.   (Answer: *the letter A*)

La lettre S, pourquoi est elle plus heureuse que la lettre T? Nous disons
Richesse mais *Pauvreté*.

Lewis Carroll combined a 'letter' riddle with the French language
when he asked his friend Agnes Hull 'Why is Agnes more learned in
insects than most people?' and answered 'Because *she* is so deep in
entomology.' He explained the answer as follows:

Of course you know that 'she' is '*elle*'? (At least, if you don't, what's the
good of your having French lessons?) 'Well!' you will say. 'And why is
"*elle*" deep in entomology?' Oh, Agnes, Agnes! Can't you spell? Don't you
know that 'L' is the 7th letter of 'entomology'? Almost exactly in the middle
of the word: it couldn't be well deeper (unless it happened to be a *deeper
well*, you know).

In *Alice in Wonderland*, Lewis Carroll set a riddle for which he had no answer: 'Why is a raven like a writing-desk?' So many people demanded a solution that Carroll eventually made one up: 'Because it can produce a few notes, tho' they are *very* flat; and it is never put with the wrong end in front!' The American puzzle-expert Sam Loyd proposed some other answers: 'The notes for which they are noted are not noted for being musical notes'; 'Bills and tales are among their characteristics'; and 'Poe wrote on both'.

Queen Victoria was amused by riddles, as 'One of Her Majesty's Servants' described in *The Private Life of the Queen* (1897):

Her Majesty takes delight in a clever riddle or rebus, but on one occasion she was very angry at having been hoaxed over a riddle which was sent to her with a letter to the effect that it had been made by the Bishop of Salisbury. For four days the Queen and Prince Albert sought for the reply, when Charles Murray (Controller of the Household) was directed to write to the bishop and ask for the solution. The answer received was that the bishop had not made the riddle nor could he solve it.

However, the popularity of riddles was already waning by the end of the nineteenth century, as a writer noted in *Chambers's Journal* for 29 July 1893:

Luckily for this generation, the tyranny of the English riddle is overpast. Familiarity with such a conversational kill-joy has long been reckoned the reverse of a social accomplishment.

The riddle became almost entirely the preserve of schoolchildren, who still take great delight in riddles and conundrums, many of which are much older than themselves. The majority of the jokes supplied by children for *The Crack-a-Joke Book* (1978) took the form of riddles:

Why do people go to bed? Because the bed won't come to them.
Which is the fastest, heat or cold? Heat, because you can catch cold.
What's worse than raining cats and dogs? Hailing taxis.
What's the difference between a lion with a toothache and a rainstorm?
    One roars with pain and the other pours with rain.
Why did the owl 'owl? Because the woodpecker woodpecker.
How can you tell if an elephant has been in your fridge? Footprints in the
    butter.

The last of these is obviously modern—and a typical example of the craze for 'elephant' jokes which existed in the 1970s. But the first three of these riddles date from the nineteenth century or earlier.

Riddles may no longer be used in rituals or on ceremonial occasions such as those described in J. G. Frazer's *Golden Bough*. However, by their continuing delight in exchanging riddles, children are perpetuating a very old custom which might otherwise die out. As the American folklorist Charles Potter recalled in 1950:

I have sat by the stove of a winter night and given the answers to the riddles my father and mother alternately asked me as they went through the catechism their parents had taught them. It was part of my education, and much more interesting than the lessons in grammar school. (*Funk and Wagnalls' Standard Dictionary of Folklore*)

Enigmas

The ENIGMA in its narrowest sense is simply a kind of riddle in verse. Although riddles have often been versified (q.v.), they have seldom made good poetry. But for a period, particularly in the eighteenth and nineteenth centuries, the enigma developed into a genre in which the poetry became as important as the riddle.

Perhaps the first enigmas of this kind were written by Sir Thomas Wyatt (?1503-42), an English poet at the court of Henry VIII. One of his enigmas—on the name *Anna*—was probably dedicated to Anne Boleyn:

> What word is that, that changeth not
> Though it be turned and made in twain?
> It is mine answer, God it wot,
> And eke the causer of my pain.
> A love rewardeth with disdain,
> Yet is it loved. What would ye more?
> It is my health eke and my sore.

Another of Wyatt's enigmas is the following, to which the answer could be *a kiss*:

> A lady gave a me a gift she had not,
> And I received her gift I took not.
> She gave it me willingly and yet she would not,
> And I received it albeit I could not.
> If she give it me I force not,
> And if she take it again she cares not.
> Consider what this is and tell not,
> For I am fast sworn I may not.

Samuel Danforth, an English printer who emigrated to America in the seventeenth century, published enigmas in his almanacs, such as the following which describes the ships that brought supplies to the settlers:

> The wooden birds are now in sight,
> Whose voices roar, whose wings are white,

> Whose maws are filled with hose and shoes,
> With wine, cloth, sugar, salt and news,
> When they have eased their stomachs here
> They cry, farewell until next year.

The enigma was well established by the beginning of the eighteenth century, as is shown by this extract from *Delights for the Ingenious* (1711):

A well-penned enigma, artfully contrived, wherein truth walks in masquerade, and where a delicacy of thought and beauty of expression shines throughout, is one of the most agreeable and delightful entertainments that I known of; and no less pleasant is the explication, when it falls into the hands of an ingenious answerer. An instance or two of each I shall here present my reader, the better to explain my meaning.

An Enigma

> I'm thick, I'm thin, I'm short and long,
> And loved alike by old and young;
> I make diseases, and I heal,
> And know what I shall ne'er reveal.
> The fairest virgin, fraught with pride,
> No beauty from my view can hide.
> I rack the miser, cure the sot,
> And make, and oft detect a plot:
> No lover that would happy be,
> Desires his mistress more than me:
> Yet though a thousand charms I have,
> Next step from me is to the grave.

The Explication

> A *bed* may be little or great, short or long,
> The strong it makes weak, and the weak it makes strong,
> Oppressed with his load, the sot there finds relief,
> And the miser is racked with the fears of a thief:
> The lady's there gentle, and free to her lover,
> And what might it not, could it tell us, discover!
> There plots are oft hatched, and as often detected,
> And things well contrived that are never effected:
> There dreaming of peril and pleasures we lie,
> And wretched and happy, we are born and we die.

Several collections of enigmas were published in the eighteenth century and even more in the early nineteenth century. Jonathan Swift and his friends took pleasure in composing them:

> Ever eating, never cloying,
> All devouring, all destroying,

Never finding full repast,
Till I eat the world at last. (*Time*)

We are little airy creatures,
All of different voice and features,
One of us in glass is set,
One of us you'll find in jet,
T'other you may see in tin,
And the fourth a box within,
If the fifth you should pursue
It can never fly from you. (*vowels*)

As in some of the versified riddles in Anglo-Saxon, many enigmas describe a thing as if it were a person. Such is the case in this enigma by Swift, on a typically low subject:

Because I am by nature blind,
I wisely choose to walk behind;
However, to avoid disgrace,
I let no creature see my face.
My words are few, but spoke with sense:
And yet my speaking gives offence:
Or, if to whisper I presume,
The company will fly the room . . . (*'The Posteriors'*)

Horace Walpole attributed the following enigma to Sir Isaac Newton:

Four people sat down at a table to play;
They play'd all that night, and some part of next day:
This one thing observ'd, that when they were seated,
Nobody played with them, and nobody betted:
Yet when they got up, each was winner a guinea;
Who tells me this riddle, I'm sure is no ninny. (*musicians*)
(*Letters*, 1773)

This is called a 'riddle' and it is often difficult to draw the line between riddles and enigmas. The main distinction is that the latter should have some pretension to poetic quality instead of being mere doggerel verse. The difference might be exemplified by two puzzles on letters of the alphabet. The first is from *A New Collection of Enigmas, Charades, Transpositions, etc.* (1810):

Pray ladies, who in seeming wit delight,
Say what's invisible, yet never out of sight. (*the letter 'I'*)

The second has more poetic quality and it is found in W. M. Praed's *Poems* (1864):

Through thy short and shadowy span
I am with thee, Child of Man;

> With thee still, from first to last,
> In pain and pleasure, feast and fast,
> At thy cradle and thy death,
> Thine earliest wail, and dying breath.
> Seek not thou to shun or save,
> On the earth, or in the grave;
> The worm and I, the worm and I,
> In the grave together lie.   (*the letter 'A'*)

One of the most famous enigmas has a similar theme. It has often been attributed to Lord Byron but was actually written by Catherine Fanshawe about the year 1814. Her original version had as its first line 'Twas in heaven pronounced, and twas muttered in hell' but Horace Smith changed this to its more familiar form:

> 'Twas whisper'd in heaven, 'twas mutter'd in hell,
> And echo caught faintly the sound as it fell;
> On the confines of earth 'twas permitted to rest,
> And the depths of the ocean its presence confess'd;
> 'Twill be found in the sphere, when 'tis riven asunder;
> 'Tis seen in the lightning, and heard in the thunder;
> 'Twas allotted to man from his earliest breath,
> It assists at his birth, and attends him in death;
> Presides o'er his happiness, honour and health,
> Is the prop of his house, and the end of his wealth;
> In the heaps of the miser 'tis hoarded with care,
> But is sure to be lost in his prodigal heir;
> It begins every hope, every wish it must bound;
> It prays with the hermit, with monarchs is crown'd;
> Without it the soldier and seaman may roam,
> But woe to the wretch that expels it from home!
> In the whispers of conscience 'tis sure to be found,
> Nor e'en in the whirlwind of passion is drown'd;
> 'Twill soften the heart, but, though deaf to the ear,
> 'Twill make it acutely and constantly hear;
> But, in short, let it rest; like a beautiful flower,
> Oh! breathe on it softly, it dies in an hour.   (*the letter 'H'*)
>
> (C. M. Fanshawe, *Literary Remains*, 1876)

Famous people such as Lord Chesterfield, the actor Garrick, and William Cowper the poet tried their hands at writing enigmas. Cowper used the same subject as Thomas Wyatt had employed more than two centuries earlier:

> I am just two and two, I am warm, I am cold,
> And the parent of numbers that cannot be told.

I am lawful, unlawful, a duty, a fault,
I am often sold dear, good for nothing when bought.
An extraordinary boon, and a matter of course,
And yielded with pleasure when taken by force.
Alike the delight of the poor and the rich,
Though the vulgar is apt to present me his breech.   (*a kiss*)

Enigmas were equally popular in other parts of Europe. The German poet Schiller wrote several, and Mrs Piozzi in a letter of 4 May 1819 quotes a French enigma which may have been written by Rousseau:

Enfant de l'art, enfant de la nature,
Sans prolonger la vie j'empêche de mourir;
Plus je suis vrai, plus je suis imposteur,
Et je deviens plus jeune à force de vieillir.

which Mrs Piozzi translates as:

Art's offspring, whom nature delights here to foster,
Can death's dart defy, tho' not lengthen life's stage;
Most correct at the moment when most an impostor,
Still fresh'ning in youth, as advancing in age.   (*a portrait*)

Enigmas were also written in prose. One of the most complex was 'printed for private circulation' in 1866 by Lewis Carroll:

Enigma

I have a large box, with two lids, two caps, three established measures, and a great number of articles a carpenter cannot do without.—Then I have always by me a couple of good fish, and a number of a smaller tribe,—besides two lofty trees, fine flowers, and the fruit of an indigenous plant; a handsome stag; two playful animals, and a number of a smaller and less tame herd:—Also two halls, or places of worship; some weapons of warfare; and many weathercocks:—The steps of an hotel: the House of Commons on the eve of a dissolution; two students or scholars, and some Spanish grandees, to wait upon me.

All pronounce me a wonderful piece of mechanism, but few have numbered up the strange medley of things which compose my whole.

Explication of the Enigma

The whole,—is MAN.

The parts are as follows.

A large box—the chest.
Two lids—the eye lids.

Two caps—the knee caps.
Three established measures—the nails, hands, and feet.
A great number of articles a carpenter cannot do without—nails.
A couple of good fish—the *soles* of the feet.
A number of a smaller tribe—the muscles (mussels).
Two lofty trees—the palms (of the hands).
Fine flowers—two lips (tulips) and irises.
The fruit of an indigenous plant—hips.
A handsome stag—the heart (hart).
Two playful animals—the calves.
A number of a smaller and less tame herd—the hairs (hares).
Two halls, or places of worship—the temples.
Some weapons of warfare—the arms, and shoulder blades.
Many weathercocks—the veins (vanes).
The steps of an hotel—the insteps (inn-steps).
The House of Commons on the eve of a dissolution—Eyes and nose (ayes
    and noes).
Two students or scholars—the pupils of the eye.
Some Spanish grandees—the tendons (ten Dons).

Like many other kinds of versified game, enigmas have now died
out, although they may be considered to survive in children's rhyming riddles which are mostly survivals from earlier centuries. To end
this survey of enigmas here is a verse from Charles Dickens's magazine *All the Year Round* (16 December 1876) which makes an enigma
out of the nursery rhyme 'Jack and Jill':

> 'Twas not on Alpine snow or ice,
> But honest English ground,
> 'Excelsior' was their device;
> But sad the fate they found.
> They did not climb for love or fame,
> But follow'd duty's call;
> They were together in their aim,
> But parted in their fall.

Charades

Most people think of CHARADES as a game in which scenes are acted which contain each syllable of a word, followed by the whole word. However, the charade probably started life as a written, not acted, game.

The written charade developed from the enigma (q.v.), in which a word was suggested by an enigmatic verse. As early as 1711 we find an enigma which gives clues to the syllables as well as to the whole word:

> From the mate of the cock, winter-corn in the ground
> The Christian name of my friend may be found:
> Join the song of a cat, to the place hermits dwell in,
> Gives the surname of him who does music excel in.

This is from *Delights for the Ingenious* (1711), which gives the answer thus:

Here the mate of a cock is a *hen*: the winter-corn is either wheat or ry; but because it is to make up a name, it is the latter that is meant: so the Christian name is *Henry*. Then the song of a cat is what we call the *pur* of a cat; and the place a hermit dwells in is called a *cell*; so the surname is *Purcell*: so that this rebus is upon the name of M. Henry Purcell, the late famous Master of Music, perhaps the best that ever England bred.

Charades were certainly well known by the time of Richard Sheridan's *School for Scandal* (1777), in which Crabtree says to Sir Benjamin Backbite:

Repeat . . . the charade you made last night extempore at Mrs Drowzie's conversazione. Come now; your first is the name of a fish, your second a great naval commander.

This was the form often taken by written charades: a verse or sentence beginning 'My first is a . . .' Peter Puzzlewell's *Choice Collection of Riddles, Charades, Rebusses, etc.* (1796) contains many charades in this form, such as:

My first, is a stream which meandering glides
Through meadows with verdure fresh crown'd;
My second's, a path which your footsteps oft guides,
And near to my first may be found!
My whole, is a seat where the muses retire,
And Apollo has taken his station;
Where aided by science, they jointly conspire
To form brilliant men for this nation!

The answer is *Cam-bridge*.

Other collections of charades from this period suggest that they were very popular at the end of the eighteenth century. Horace Walpole, in a letter of 29 October 1786 to H. S. Cowley, wrote:

Lady Ossory has sent me two charades made by Col. Fitzpatrick: the first she says is very easy, the second very difficult. I have not come within sight of the easy one; and though I have a guess (spelling-book) at the other, I do not believe I am right . . .

In concert, song, or serenade,
My first requires my second's aid.
To those residing near the pole
I would not recommend my whole.

Charades of all things are the worst,
But yet my best have been my first.
Who with my second are concern'd
Will to despise my whole have learn'd.

Walpole adds: 'Had I anything better, I would not send you charades, unless for the name of the author.' Suggested solutions to the first of the above charades have included the unsatisfactory *lute-string*, while the second has been explained either as *plain-song* or *hard-ships*.

A New Collection of Enigmas, Charades, Transpositions, etc. (1810) includes sixty-one charades, such as the following:

What I do, what I do not, and what you are.   (*love-ly*)
My third is under my second, and surrounds my first.   (*waist-coat*)
My first's a prop, my second's a prop, my third's a prop.   (*foot-stool*)

My first I hope you are,
My second I see you are,
My third I know you are.   (*wel-come*)

My first doth affliction denote,
Which my second was born to endure;

My third is a sure antidote
That affliction to soften and cure.   (*wo-man*)

The last of these charades is quoted by Jane Austen a few years later in *Emma*, where she calls it 'that well-known charade'. A charade plays an important part in the plot of *Emma*, when Mr Elton writes one which Emma assumes is directed at her friend Harriet Smith (when it is really directed at Emma herself):

My first displays the wealth and pomp of kings,
Lords of the earth! their luxury and ease.
Another view of man, my second brings,
Behold him there, the monarch of the seas!

But, ah! united, what reverse we have!
Man's boasted power and freedom, all are flown;
Lord of the earth and sea, he bends a slave,
And woman, lovely woman, reigns alone.

Thy ready wit the word will soon supply,
May its approval beam in that soft eye!

Emma's reaction to this is to think:

Very well, Mr. Elton, very well indeed. I have read worse charades. *Courtship*— a very good hint. I give you credit for it. This is feeling your way. This is saying very plainly—'Pray, Miss Smith, give me leave to pay my attentions to you. Approve my charade and my intentions in the same glance.'

The naive Harriet Smith has more trouble guessing it, asking, 'Is it Kingdom? . . . Can it be Neptune? . . . Or a trident? or a mermaid? or a shark? Oh, no! shark is only one syllable.'

If charades seemed a childish amusement for the leisured classes of the nineteenth century, they could be justified by pointing to the skill used in concealing the word, or the poetic quality of the writing. In a letter of 29 January 1813 to her sister Cassandra, Jane Austen wrote:

We admire your Charades excessively—but as yet have guessed only the 1st. The others seem very difficult. There is so much beauty in the versification, however, that the finding them out is but a secondary pleasure.

Serious poets as eminent as W. M. Praed (1802–39) and C. S. Calverley (1831–84) indulged in long poems with enigmatic meanings. This is one by Praed on the word *bride-groom*:

Morning is beaming o'er brake and bower;
Hark to the chimes from yonder tower!
Call ye my First from her chamber now,
With her snowy veil, and her jewelled brow.

Lo, where my Second in gallant array
Leads from his stable her beautiful bay,
Looking for her, as he curvets by,
With an arching neck, and a glancing eye.

Spread is the banquet, and studied the song;
Ranged in meet order the menial throng;
Jerome is ready with book and stole;
And the maidens fling flowers:—but where is my Whole?

Look to the hill; is he climbing its side?
Look to the stream; is he crossing its tide?
Out on him, false one; he comes not yet!
Lady, forget him! yea, scorn and forget!

Charades probably developed from a written pastime into an acted one during the nineteenth century. Maria Edgeworth, in a letter to her sister on 12 November 1821, wrote:

We acted *words*—charades last night—
   Pillion. Excellent—M. F. H. little dear pretty Bertha—and Mr Smith the best hand and head at these diversions imaginable. First we entered swallowing pills with great choking—Pill—next on all fours roaring lions— Fanny and Harriet roaring devouring lions much clapped—Next as to my tout—Enter Bertha riding on Mr Smith's back *pillion*.
   Coxcomb. Mr Smith. Mr Ricardo—F—H—and M crowing. Ditto—ditto ditto combing hair. Mr Ricardo solus—strutting coxcomb very droll.
   Sinecure. Not a good one.

This description suggests that the earliest acted charades were mimed, not spoken. Only later did it become common to use dialogue in which each syllable of the word and then the whole word were hidden.

Acted charades seem to have come to Britain from France. The derivation of the French word *charade* is uncertain. It probably comes from Portuguese *charrado* meaning 'conversation' or *charra* meaning 'chatter', but Skeat compares the Spanish word *charrada* which means 'the speech or action of a clown' and 'a showy thing made without taste'. W. M. Thackeray, in *Vanity Fair* (1848), wrote that: 'At this time the amiable amusement of acting the charades had come among us from France; and was considerably in vogue in this country, enabling the many ladies among us who had beauty to display their charms, and the fewer number who had cleverness to exhibit their wit.' In one of the charades he described, the first scene features a 'Turkish dignitary' (the *Aga*); the second scene contains 'an enormous Egyptian head' (the statue of *Memnon* at Thebes); and the third scene portrays the murder of *Agamemnon*.

At about the time when Thackeray was writing *Vanity Fair*, J. C. Maitland published his *Historical Charades* (1847) which were designed to help people learn history in an entertaining way. Maitland describes the game of charades as follows:

The players divide themselves into two parties, who take it in turn to act and to guess the word. If grown-up people join in the game, the children generally act, leaving the pappas and mammas to look on and guess. The actors go out of the room, and choose a word of two or more syllables, each syllable or division of the word having a separate meaning. For instance: Improbability, Imp-Rob-Ability, Rail-Way, Ram-Pant, Miss-Fortune. Each having arranged the part that every person is to take, they return to the company, and represent each syllable in its turn, and lastly the entire word.

In his *Parlour Pastime for the Young* (1857), 'Uncle George' suggests the following words as suitable for acting: *air-gun*, *arch-bishop*, *dice-box*, *fag-end*, *game-cock*, *Jack-pudding* [a kind of clown], *jew-el*, *king-craft*, *love-apple*, *mad-cap*, *mend-i-cant*, *night-cap*, *pack-cloth*, *quarter-staff*, *sauce-box*, *Vat-i-can*, and *zeal-ot*.

The list of recommended words in *Cassell's Book of Indoor Amusements* (1881) repeats *jewel* and *madcap* and adds many others, including *bellman*, *bondmaid*, *bridewell*, *exciseman*, *highgate*, *hornbook*, *illwill*, *jonquil*, *kneedeep*, *loveknot*, *quarto*, *ragamuffin*, *sparerib*, *stucco*, *ticktack*, *tractable*, and *yokemate*.

One variant of charades is DUMB CRAMBO, which developed from a very popular game called CRAMBO. Samuel Pepys recorded as early as 1660 in his diary playing a game of Crambo in a wagon on the way to The Hague. Joseph Strutt, in his *Sports and Pastimes of the People of England* (1801), describes Crambo as 'a diversion wherein one gives a word, to which another finds a rhyme'. Patrick Beaver describes the game in more detail:

One player leaves the room while the rest select a word. The guesser is then called in. He or she is told a word that rhymes with the chosen one and must go on to guess, *without naming them*, other words that rhyme with the chosen word until the latter is discovered. For example, let us suppose the chosen word is *play* and the clue given to the guesser is *hay*. The game might then continue as follows:

> *Guesser*: Is it a month in Spring?
> *Omnes*: No, it is not May.
> G.: Is it a path to somewhere?
> O.: No, it is not way.
> G.: Is it the opposite to night?
> O.: No, it is not day.

And so on until the word is discovered or the company fall asleep.

London Society for 1864 provides this description of Dumb Crambo:

The actors retire and settle on a word, that has to be guessed by the former, who are merely informed of the sound of the final syllable. They again retire, and think over it. When agreed as to what they consider is the word, they come on the stage and act in dumb that which they have fixed on. For instance, they are told the word ends in 'igh', and as the spelling is unknown, they act shy. . . . Should the company see the right word has been acted, they say so, and applaud: if not, the actors are hissed out, and have to try again.

While forms of acted charades gained popularity during the nineteenth century, written charades persisted. Sydney Smith hated them. He wrote:

I shall say nothing of charades, and such sorts of unpardonable trumpery: if charades are made at all, they should be made without benefit of clergy, the offender should instantly be hurried off to execution, and be cut off in the middle of his dullness, without being allowed to explain to the executioner why his first is like his second, or what is the resemblance between his fourth and his ninth.   (*Wit and Wisdom*, 1882)

Perhaps he was thinking of the rather vulgar type of charade written by the irrepressible R. H. Barham in his *Ingoldsby Legends*:

> From Lady Snooks: 'Dear Sir, you know
> You promised me last week a Rebus;
> A something smart and *apropos*,
> For my new Album?'—Aid me, Phoebus.

'My first is follow'd by my second;
Yet should my first my second see,
A dire mishap it would be reckon'd,
And sadly shock'd my first would be.

'Were I but what my whole implies,
And pass'd by chance across your portal,
You'd cry, 'Can I believe my eyes?
I never saw so queer a mortal!'

'For then my head would not be on,
My arms their shoulders must abandon;
My very body would be gone,
I should not have a leg to stand on.'

The answer is *al(l)-bum.*

Lewis Carroll, of course, loved charades, and composed several for his child-friends and others. In 1875 he sent this to Mrs G. MacDonald:

My first lends his aid when I plunge into trade;
My second in jollifications:
My whole, laid on thinnish, imparts a neat finish
To pictorial representations.

The solution is *copal*—the name of a hard resin used to make varnish. But in a later letter to Gaynor Simpson, Carroll humorously suggests that the answer is:

Gain. Who would go into trade if there were no gain in it?
Or (the French for 'gold'). Your jollifications would be *very* limited if you had no money.
Gaynor. Because she will be an ornament to the Shakespeare Charades—only she must be 'laid on thinnish', that is, *there mustn't be too much of her.*

In his next letter, Carroll wrote:

Forgive me for having sent you a sham answer to begin with.
My first—*Sea.* It carries the ships of the merchants.
My second—*Weed.* That is, a cigar, an article much used in jollifications.
My whole—*Seaweed.* Take a newly painted oil-picture; lay it on its back on the floor, and spread over it, 'thinnish', some wet seaweed. You will find that you have 'finished' that picture.

By the beginning of the twentieth century, however, written charades were dying out, surviving only in the simplified form of RIDDLE-ME-REES: charades based on letters rather than syllables.

A Posy of Puzzles, presented with the January 1904 issue of *Little Folks* magazine, includes several Riddle-Me-Rees sent in by children, such as this:

> My first is in mouse, but not in rat;
> My second is in bonnet, but not in hat;
> My third is in store, and also in rock;
> My fourth is in hen, but not in cock;
> My fifth is in rye, but not in rice;
> My whole is a wood for furniture.
> —Aristides A. Messinesi, Patras, Greece (Aged 11½).

The answer is *e-b-o-n-y*.

As written charades went out of fashion, acted charades became perhaps the best-known of all party games, developing several variations such as Adverbs, Proverbs, and The Game. In ADVERBS, the players have to answer questions or perform actions 'in the manner of the word'. Thus, if the chosen adverb is *sulkily*, the players have to answer in a sulky manner, or perform a suggested action in a sulky way.

A memorable game of Adverbs occurs in Noël Coward's play *Hay Fever*, in which the chosen adverb is *winsomely*. Several of the people present try to explain how the game is played:

JUDITH: Choose an adverb, and then—

SIMON: Someone goes out, you see, and comes in, and you've chosen a word among yourselves, and she or he, whoever it is, asks you some sort of question, and you have to—

SOREL (*moves up to Simon*): Not an ordinary question, Simon; they have to ask them to do something in the manner of the word, and then—

SIMON: Then, you see, you act whatever it is—

SOREL: The answer to the question, you see?

RICHARD (*apprehensively*): What sort of thing is one expected to do?

JUDITH: Quite usual things, like reciting 'If', or playing the piano—

RICHARD: I can't play the piano.

SIMON: Never mind; you can fake it, as long as it conveys an idea of the word.

JACKIE: The word we've all thought of?

SOREL (*impatient*): Yes, the word we've chosen when whoever it is is out of the room.

PROVERBS is not normally an acting game, although E. M. Baker in *Indoor Games* (1912) describes an acted form of it. One team acts out a proverb for the other team to guess:

Thus one of the players might come into the room, holding a large jar, in such a way that the audience cannot fail to see that it is empty. This jar he must repeatedly rap with his knuckles, a hollow sound being produced, thus in dumb show illustrating the proverb, 'The empty vessel makes the greatest sound.'

Baker describes this game as Acting Proverbs and distinguishes it from the more familiar Proverbs, in which one person is sent out of the room while the others agree on a proverb. When the outsider returns, he or she asks each person a question. The first person's answer must include the first word of the proverb, the second person's answer must contain the second word of the proverb, and so on until the outsider guesses it. Proverbs must be chosen carefully, as some, like 'Procrastination is the thief of time', would almost inevitably give themselves away.

The poet Wilfred Owen played the game in 1910, and A. A. Milne described an embarrassing round of Proverbs in *Not That it Matters* (1919):

I remember, too, another evening when we were playing 'proverbs'. William, who had gone outside, was noted for his skill at the game, and we were determined to give him something difficult; something which hadn't a camel or a glass house or a stable door in it. After some discussion a member of the company suggested a proverb from the Persian, as he alleged. It went something like this: 'A wise man is kind to his dog, but a poor man riseth early in the morning.' We took his word for it, and, feeling certain that William would never guess, called him to come in. Unfortunately William, who is a trifle absent-minded, had gone to bed.

In his *Drawing-Room Amusements* (1879), 'Professor Hoffmann' says:

There is another, and we think rather stupid form of this game, known as 'Simultaneous Proverbs'. A proverb having been chosen, and a word assigned to each player, all at a given signal shout simultaneously each his or her own word, and from the Babel of sound thus created the proverb must be guessed.

THE GAME is a form of charades that returns to the miming tradition of Dumb Crambo. Players have to act out to their team-mates a word or phrase, often the title of a book, film, play, or television programme. The mimer can indicate that it is a play by miming the opening of curtains, or that it is a television programme by drawing a rectangle in the air with his fingers to represent a television screen.

It is well known not only because it has found its way on to television (under the title of 'Give Us a Clue') but also because it is said to be the Queen's favourite game. Robert Lacey describes the way it has been played in the Royal household:

In less formal moods the Queen liked most of all to play with her guests 'The Game'. Two teams would sit at opposite ends of the room with a referee in the middle holding a list of names which they must mime—*Forever Amber*, perhaps, or even 'Elle trouvait dans l'adultère toutes les platitudes de mariage'. Players raced up to be given their assignment, and once they had mimed it successfully one of their team mates could go up for the next task.

Eleanor Roosevelt remembered that The Game was not appreciated by at least one of the Queen's guests:

One evening during my visit at Windsor Castle, when Mr Churchill was there, we played The Game—a form of charades which is also popular in America. Queen Elizabeth acted as a kind of master of ceremonies and chose the words that the rest of us were called upon to act out in such a way that they could be guessed. She puzzled for some time over various words and occasionally turned to Mr Churchill for assistance, but without success. The former Prime Minister, with a decoration on the bosom of his stiff white shirt and a cigar in his hand, sat glumly aside and would have nothing to do with The Game, which he obviously regarded as inane and a waste of time for adults.

Winston Churchill was not the only person to dislike The Game, as is shown in this poem by Ogden Nash:

> I do not know its name.
> Mostly it's called The Game.
>
> Or sometimes Indications,
> Or other variations.
>
> But whatever be its name
> I was happy ere it came.
>
> But now that it has come,
> I'm a bum.
>
> Figure of fun and shame
> I do not like The Game.
>
> To be honest, to be candid,
> I do not understandid;

I amn't very good at it,
I'm never understood at it.

I am seized by mental gout
When acting phrases out.

I am lost in foggy mazes
When guessing others' phrases.

I'm a gabbling babbling moron
At quotations from The Koran.

Yea, even Mother Goose's
Leave me stammering excuses.

Be mine, be mine the blame,
But I do not like The Game . . .

Many enjoy it vastly,
I find it ghastly.

Acrostics

An ACROSTIC is a poem or puzzle in which the first letters of each line spell out a word, phrase, or name. Occasionally the last letters of each line spell out the word, in which case it is sometimes called a TELESTICH. A double acrostic has the first and last letters of each line forming words, while a triple acrostic uses letters in the middle of lines as well.

The name 'acrostic' is an English form of the Latin word *acrostichis*, which derives from the Greek *akron* meaning 'end' and *stikhos* meaning 'line of verse'.

Acrostics date from before the time of Christ. Cicero says in his *De Divinatione* that the Roman poet Quintus Ennius, who died in 169 BC, wrote a poem with the initial letters forming the words 'Quae Q. Ennius fecit'—'Q. Ennius wrote this'. Cicero also points out that the Sibylline prophecies were acrostics—which made him think that they were written by humans rather than divinely inspired. The Roman playwright Plautus prefixed acrostics to his comedies to summarize the plots.

A particularly interesting example of a Roman acrostic was found during excavations at Pompeii and (in 1868) at the old Roman city of Cirencester. It is a word square (q.v.) which can be read from left to right or from right to left (or even upwards and downwards): a mixture of an acrostic, a word square, and a palindrome (q.v.):

S A T O R		R O T A S
A R E P O		O P E R A
T E N E T	or	T E N E T
O P E R A		A R E P O
R O T A S		S A T O R

This may be translated as 'The sower, Arepo, guides the wheels with care.' It seems ordinary enough but it may have a mystical significance, like the Greek word for 'fish'—*ichthys*—which consists of the first letters of the Greek words for 'Jesus Christ, the Son of God, the Saviour'. The SATOR acrostic may have been used as a charm or as a way for persecuted Christians to recognize one another.

The word *tenet*, at the centre of the acrostic, forms a cross and the acrostic's letters can be rearranged in that shape:

```
                  P
                  A
                  T
                  E
                  R
  P A T E R N O S T E R
                  O
                  S
                  T
                  E
                  R
```

while the remaining letters (two A's and two O's) can be placed at the ends of the cross to represent alpha and omega—the beginning and the end. The letters can also be arranged to make a prayer: 'Oro Te, Pater; oro Te, Pater; sanas'—'I pray to Thee, Father; I pray to Thee, Father; Thou healest'.

Several of the Psalms in the Bible are acrostics. In Psalm 119, for example, each group of eight verses is preceded by 'Aleph', 'Beth', 'Gimel', etc. These are the letters of the Hebrew alphabet in order, and the stanzas each begin with that particular letter. Such acrostics were probably used as a form of mnemonic: to help people remember the sequence of verses.

Commodianus, a Christian poet who wrote in Latin in the fourth century AD, composed eighty short poems in acrostic form; Aldhelm or Ealdhelm, who was made the first Bishop of Sherborne in AD 705, wrote several acrostics. His treatise 'On Virginity' is prefaced by an acrostic starting with the line 'Metrica tirones nunc promant carmina castos' ('Now we have finished the prose version, let us write in verse of these examples of chastity'). The acrostic consists of thirty-eight lines corresponding to the thirty-eight letters of this line. The second line begins with E and ends with O, the third begins with T and ends with T, and so on. The last line is the first line written backwards, another example of an acrostic mingling with a palindrome.

The English poet Sir John Davies established the practice of prais ing somebody by writing an acrostic using their name. In 1599 he wrote twenty-six 'Hymns to Astroea' in honour of Queen Elizabeth.

Every poem is an acrostic using the name Elisabetha Regina; Hymn VIII, for example, describes the Queen with extreme flattery:

To All the Princes of Europe

Europe, the Earth's sweet Paradise,
Let all thy Kings that would be wise,
In politic devotion,
Sail hither to observe her eyes,
And mark her heavenly motion.
Brave Princes of this civil age,
Enter into this pilgrimage.
This saint's tongue is an oracle,
Her eye hath made a Prince a page,
And works each day a miracle.

Raise but your looks to her, and see
Even the true beams of majesty,
Great Princes, mark her duly;
If all the world you do survey,
No forehead spreads so bright a ray,
And notes a Prince so truly.

Such verses were criticized by better poets. In his 'Mac Flecknoe' (1682), Dryden advises a weak playwright to 'Leave writing plays, and choose for thy command Some peaceful province in Acrostick Land'. In *The Spectator* No. 60, Joseph Addison says: 'The acrostic was probably invented about the same time with the anagram, tho' it is impossible to decide whether the inventor of the one or the other were the greater blockhead.' Addison testifies to the existence of triple acrostics, saying: 'I have seen some of them where the verses have not only been edged by a name at each extremity, but have had the same name running down like a seam through the middle of the poem.'

While Addison was condemning acrostics in England, they remained popular in France. The poet Grosnet wrote the following acrostic praising his own city:

Paisible domaine,
Amoureux vergier,
Repons sans dangier,
Iustice certaine,
Science haultaine,
    c'est Paris entier.

(H. B. Wheatley, *Of Anagrams*, 1862)

And he eulogized the French King, Louis XIV:

> Louis est un héros sans peur et sans reproche;
> On desire le voie, aussitôt qu'on l'approche,
> Un sentiment d'amour enflamme tous les coeurs;
> Il ne trouve chez nous que des adorateurs;
> Son image est partout, excepté dans ma poche. (Ibid.)

However much the purists might frown on them, acrostics proved remarkably resilient. This acrostic puzzle from the *London Magazine* for November 1762 continues the tradition of praising a lady:

> A place of confinement, as dark as the night;
> What's us'd as a token when persons unite;
> That part of the day, when the sun disappears,
> And leaves us surrounded with numerous fears;
> What the heart ne'er enjoys when the mind's void of rest;
> A word often us'd to deny a request.
> These initials, when properly placed, you'll find,
> The name of a damsel, that's constant and kind;
> With modesty grac'd and with beauty adorn'd;
> With wisdom endu'd, and to virtue conform'd.

The solutions to the riddling lines form an acrostic which spells the name of Miss Green:

> G R A V E
> R I N G
> E V E N I N G
> E A S E
> N O

Enigmas, Historical and Geographical, written in 1834 by 'A Clergyman's Daughter', attempts to educate children in history and geography by means of similar puzzles:

> What river's that, and where's it found,
> Which Pope says does with eels abound?
> What Scottish lake, by high hills bounded,
> Is too with birch and oak surrounded?
> What stream in Devon's said to run
> Into the sea near Otterton?

And tell what bay, on Cuba's coast,
Is justly deem'd its pride and boast?
These sev'ral names will bring to view,
A Scotch reformer bold and true,
Who died in fifteen seventy two.

The answer is:

K E N N E T
N E S S
O T T E R
X A G U A

In 1846 Edgar Allan Poe wrote a 'Valentine' poem which spelt out the name of Frances Sargent Osgood in the first letter of the first line, the second letter of the second line, and so on.

A flood of acrostics books appeared during the middle of the nineteenth century. One, containing a hundred acrostics, bore the title *A Century of Acrostics on the most eminent names in Literature, Science, and Art, down to the present time: chronologically arranged* (1855). Typical of its contents is this ode to the Prince Consort:

Accomplish'd Prince! from whose aesthetic mind,
Like Hamlet's, philosophic and refin'd,
Burst the bright vision of that Palace fair,
Enchanting wondering nations gather'd there:
Rare favourite of fortune! well, I ween,
Thou art fit consort, worthy of our Queen.

Queen Victoria may have contributed to the immense appeal of the acrostic during her reign. She was believed to be very fond of the double acrostic, which had developed from a verse-form into a type of puzzle. Here is one that she is said to have constructed herself, 'for the royal children'. As in most such puzzles, clues are given to words whose first and last letters spell out the answer. In this case, the initial letters spell the name of a British town, and the final letters say what it is famous for—in reverse order.

A city in Italy	N a p l e S
A river in Germany	E l b E
A town in the United States	WashingtoN
A town in North America	CincinnatI

A town in Holland	AmsterdaM
The Turkish name of Constantinople	StambouL
A town in Bothnia	T o r n e A
A city in Greece	L e p a n t O
A circle on the globe	E c l i p t i C

(C. E. Capel, *Victorian Enigmas*, 1861)

The lines in an acrostic like this are called the 'lights' and the words at the end are 'uprights' or 'pillars'. These double acrostic puzzles were probably invented early in the 1850s. Writing in 1856, Cuthbert Bede (pseudonym of the Revd Edward Bradley) called them 'Acrostic Charades' and described them as 'agreeable novelties, lately introduced'. The rhyming preface to *Acrostics by the Hitchin Acrostic Club* (1868) says: 'Just now Acrostics—double ones—With some are quite a passion, And may be until double heads Of hair go out of fashion.'

The craze continued into the twentieth century, often reflecting the social history of the times. Just as Queen Victoria's use of ' A town in Bothnia' dates her puzzle, so this 1935 acrostic from *The Strand Problems Book* is typical of the film-mad Thirties:

> Here you may see, despite the veil of haze,
> A heavenly body with most moving ways.
> 1. A bustle that surrounds both you and me.
> 2. This is not lawful; still may sometimes be.
> 3. A priest (or beast—if an odd spelling's found).
> 4. The dregs of vinegar maternal sound.

The solution is:

> F u s S
> I l l i c i T
> L a m A
> Mothe R

The triple acrostic (a comparative rarity) is found as late as 1944 in *The Second Penguin Problems Book*:

> Left, middle and right
> Give us choice of a light.
>
> 1. The kind of glance which he who's lost his heart
>   Bestows on her who wears the latter part.

2. Here is one
   With a gun.
3. This is bound
   To go round.
4. Simplify taste
   And eliminate waste.
5. My meaning is made plain
   By my saying it again.

The answer to this puzzle is:

A d o R i n G
Musk E t e e R
B a n D a g E
E c o n O m i z E
R eite R atic N

   In this century, the rise of crosswords has meant the decline of acrostics, although they have not disappeared entirely, and there is at least one modern puzzle-magazine devoted entirely to acrostic puzzles. Perhaps the master of acrostics was Lewis Carroll, the inventor and ardent player of so many word games. Carroll wrote acrostic puzzles as well as acrostics to his child-friends, as in the poem prefixed to *Sylvie and Bruno*, or the dedication to 'The Hunting of the Snark':

INSCRIBED TO A DEAR CHILD:
IN MEMORY OF GOLDEN SUMMER HOURS
AND WHISPERS OF A SUMMER SEA

Girt with a boyish garb for boyish task,
Eager she wields her spade; yet loves as well
Rest on a friendly knee, intent to ask
The tale he loves to tell.

Rude spirits of the seething outer strife,
Unmeet to read her pure and simple spright,
Deem, if you list, such hours a waste of life,
Empty of all delight!

Chat on, sweet Maid, and rescue from annoy
Hearts that by wiser talk are unbeguiled.
Ah, happy he who owns that tenderest joy,
The heart-love of a child!

Away, fond thoughts, and vex my soul no more!
Work claims my wakeful nights, my busy days—
Albeit bright memories of that sunlit shore
Yet haunt my dreaming gaze!

With typical Carrollian ingenuity, this acrostic not only spells out the name 'Gertrude Chataway' but also echoes the sounds of that name in the first words of each stanza.

But Lewis Carroll's best acrostic poem is the one at the end of *Through the Looking-Glass*, in which he remembers the day (4 July 1862) when he started telling the 'Alice' story to the three Liddell girls, notably Alice Pleasance Liddell who was the inspiration for *Alice in Wonderland*. This is not only a clever example of an acrostic but a fine poem in its own right:

A boat, beneath a summer sky
Lingering onward dreamily
In an evening of July—

Children three that nestle near,
Eager eye and willing ear,
Pleased a simple tale to hear—

Long has paled that sunny sky:
Echoes fade and memories die:
Autumn frosts have slain July.

Still she haunts me, phantomwise,
Alice moving under skies
Never seen by waking eyes.

Children yet, the tale to hear,
Eager eye and willing ear,
Lovingly shall nestle near.

In a Wonderland they lie,
Dreaming as the days go by,
Dreaming as the summers die:

Ever drifting down the stream—
Lingering in the golden gleam—
Life, what is it but a dream?

Word Squares

A WORD SQUARE is made up of words of equal length that read both horizontally and vertically. In most word squares the words are the same in both directions, but in some (sometimes called 'double word squares') the horizontal words differ from the vertical ones.

Typical word squares look like this:

```
S A D        O F T        L A N E
A L E        F O E        A R E A
D E N        T E N        N E A R
                          E A R S


S T U N G        E S T A T E
T E N O R        S H A V E N
U N T I E        T A L E N T
N O I S E        A V E R S E
G R E E T        T E N S E R
                 E N T E R S
```

Here are some examples of the rarer 'double word square':

```
O R A L        S L I N K
M A R E        W O M A N
E V E N        O V A T E
N E A T        R E G A L
               D R O L L
```

The earliest word square is probably the SATOR acrostic which is described elsewhere (see p. 32). Double acrostics often look like word squares, although they are not always composed of the same number of letters in both directions. The SATOR acrostic dates from the first century AD but it may have been anticipated by the 'stocheidon' type of inscription which was used in ancient Greece from the sixth century BC. In the 'stocheidon' style, a series of letters was arranged in horizontal lines which could only be read horizontally, not vertically. The lines were generally of equal length and finished when the line was full, even where this occurred in the middle of a word. The resulting chequered pattern was for aesthetic effect: it showed the Greeks' feeling for order in setting out the letters. This style was used for inscriptions on the bases of statues and other works of art. By the first half of the fifth century BC, engravers were adding straight horizontal and vertical lines to help them place the letters evenly. The result often looked like a modern crossword.

This is the pattern of the stele of Moschion, which dates from the end of the second or the beginning of the third century AD. It consists of letters arranged in a square in such a way that, starting at the centre, the inscription can be read innumerable times by moving in various directions (in the same way as a modern 'word search' puzzle, q.v.).

The inscription on the stele was *'Οσίριδι Μοσχίων ὑγιασθεὶς τὸν πόδα ἰατρείαις*—that is, 'Moschion to Osiris, for the treatment which cured his foot'. It is obviously the work of a man called Moschion, who was grateful to the god Osiris for a miraculous cure.

Probably as a development of the acrostic, word squares became popular in Britain in the nineteenth century. In *Notes and Queries* for 2 July 1859, 'W.W.' writes:

Of course you and many of your readers are acquainted with the game of 'squaring' a given word, which has of late been current in society. I do not know whether any notice of this ingenious amusement falls within your field. If so, you will perhaps put upon record the 'squaring of the circle' which I send to you. It is as follows:

```
C I R C L E
I C A R U S
R A R E S T
C R E A T E
L U S T R E
E S T E E M
```

Later correspondents add the following examples of word squares:

```
A I S L E     M I G H T     C R E W     C R E S T
I D I O M     I D L E R     R A V E     R E A C H
S I E V E     G L I D E     E V E R     E A G E R
L O V E R     H E D G E     W E R E     S C E N E
E M E R Y     T R E E S               T H R E E
```

```
Q U E E N      C R I M E A
U S A G E      R E M A N D
E A S E S      I M A G E D
E G E S T      M A G P I E
N E S T S      E N E I D S
               A D D E S T
```

The last two presumably resulted from attempts to make word squares on words which were of particular interest to Victorians.

These early word squares seem to have been simply exercises in making a square out of a given word. Word squares soon became a game in which clues had to be solved in order to build up the square. In this respect, the word square was the direct forerunner of the crossword.

F. Planche's *Guess Me* (1872) includes forty such word squares, mostly of four or five words, such as these:

1. To watch over	G U A R D
2. Below there	U N D E R
3. A fair lady's name	A D E L A
4. A memorial of the feast	R E L I C
5. A severe lawgiver	D R A C O

The name of an insect my *first*;	G N A T
My *second* no doubt you possess;	N A M E
My *third* is my second transposed;	A M E N
And my *fourth* is a shelter, I guess.	T E N T

Excursions into Puzzledom (1879) by 'Tom Hood and his Sister' contains several word squares of this type, which the authors call 'a square of every word'. They distinguish these from word squares like the following, in which the vertical letters do not actually make words:

The initial and top lines give one feature,
The final and bottom lines give two organs.
Without the one you could not smell,
Nor hear without the others well.

1. A feature	N O S E
2. A mountain in Greece	O S S A
3. What some grapes are	S O U R
4. Organs of sense	E A R S

This book also includes picture word squares, such as the one illustrated above, to which the answer is:

```
P  E  T
E  V  E
T  E  A
```

Little Folks for January 1890 includes a 'geographical word square' set by 'Winifred Sandys (Aged 14¾)':

1. A town in Tuscany	P	I	S	A
2. A river in Germany	I	S	A	R
3. A lake in the north of Scotland	S	A	I	N
4. A river of Italy	A	R	N	O

A. B. Gomme's *Games for Parlour and Playground* (1898) makes word squares a competitive game:

Square words is another good game with letters. For this the player chooses a word, say *Man*, consisting of three letters, which he hands to his neighbour, telling him or her to form a square word from it by the addition of two more words of three letters each. . . . Of course a player should be aware, before he gives a word to his neighbour, that a square word can be made from it.

Among the examples given by Gomme are these squares:

```
M A N        D A R E        M E A D
A T E        A M E N        E C H O
N E T        R E A D        A H E M
             E N D S        D O M E
```

Following the word square, other shapes became popular: the diamond, the octagon, the pyramid, the half-square, and more. The November 1875 issue of *St Nicholas* (an American magazine 'for girls and boys') contains this 'diamond puzzle':

1. A consonant	L
2. To place anything	S E T
3. An account	S C O R E
4. A wild animal	L E O P A R D
5. To mark out	T R A C E
6. Before	E R E
7. A consonant	D

The July 1876 issue of this magazine has this 'half word square':

1. A peculiar bird	P A R R O T
2. Apart	A L O O F
3. Part of a plant	R O O T
4. To decay	R O T
5. A preposition	O F
6. A consonant	T

Excursions into Puzzledom also includes several word diamonds, with complicated sets of clues:

1. A consonant here view—
   A vegetable too!
2. As big as a fly's drink
   On honeysuckle's brink.
3. What little people do
   When holidays accrue.
4. If you get this, you may
   Catch cold—so don't, I pray.
5. A consonant, but found
   In maps too, I'll be bound.

The answer horizontal you will meet
In sauce provided for a certain meat.
The answer perpendicular displays
Musical instruments of ancient days.
Beside this perpendicular there stand
Two others, one, of course, upon each hand.

The first with carpenters a common tool,—
Dog, cat, or bird, the second as a rule.

The answer to all this is:

```
        P
    S   I   P
C   A   P   E   R
    W   E   T
        S
```

Cassell's Book of Indoor Amusements (1881) has what it calls 'a diagonal puzzle', producing a word square in which the diagonals also make words:

My first is a ticket	L a b e L
My second is a voice in music	t E n O r
My third is a water-bird	d i V e r
My fourth is an expensive ornament	j E w E l
My last is a sharp instrument, useless to boys, but often longed for by boys.	R a z o R

Read from left to right, diagonally, and vice versa, as shown by the capital letters, and discover the names of two Irish writers of rollicking humour—Lever and Lover.

H. E. Dudeney, the puzzle expert who died in 1930, claimed to have been the first person to write word squares with versified clues, such as the following, in which the line numbers replace the answers to be found in those positions:

The Abbey

'Twas spring. The abbey woods were decked with *second*.
The abbot, with his *fifth*, no trouble reckoned;
But shared the meats and *seventh* which every man
Who loves to feast has *first* since time began.
Then comes a stealthy *sixth* across the wall,
Who *fourths* the plate and jewels, cash and all,
And ere the abbot and the monks have dined,
He *thirds*, and leaves no trace or clue behind.

The answer is:

```
P A L A T E D
A N E M O N E
L E V A N T S
A M A S S E S
T O N S U R E
E N T E R E R
D E S S E R T
```

Dudeney explains some of the answers:

The verb 'palate': to perceive by the taste, to relish, has the authority of Shakespeare: 'Not palating the taste of her dishonour' (*Troilus and Cressida*, Act IV, sc. 1; also *Antony and Cleopatra*, Act V, sc. 2). To 'levant' is, of course, to abscond dishonourably. (*World's Best Word Puzzles*, 1925)

Dudeney says that 'Very few seven-letter Word Squares have been made and we have never seen a good one of eight letters.' As can be seen from the examples so far given, most word squares consist of words of four, five, or six letters. Obviously the smallest type of word square uses two letters:

M A
A M

Three-letter words are used in the simplest puzzles for children:

T O T   S P Y
O U R   P I E
T R Y   Y E T

A correspondent in *Notes and Queries* for 3 September 1859 summed up the comparative difficulty of creating larger word squares:

The conclusion to be drawn about exercises of this kind is that four letters are nothing at all; that five letters are so easy that nothing is worth notice unless the combination have meaning; that six letters, done in any way, are respectable; and that seven letters would be a triumph.

Yet seven-word squares have been made quite often. For example, there is Dudeney's 'The Abbey', and he also created this:

N E S T L E S
E N T R A N T
S T R A N G E
T R A I T O R
L A N T E R N
E N G O R G E
S T E R N E R

Dmitri Borgmann cites several other such squares, including these:

```
M E R G E R S      P R E P A R E
E T E R N A L      R E M O D E L
R E G A T T A      E M U L A T E
G R A V I T Y      P O L E M I C
E N T I T L E      A D A M A N T
R A T T L E R      R E T I N U E
S L A Y E R S      E L E C T E D
```

The formation of eight-word squares usually necessitates the use of rare and unusual words. In the following square, *rosetter* is a word for a person who ties bows on chocolate boxes, and *tritical* means 'commonplace':

```
R O S E T T E R
O V E R R U L E
S E Q U I N E D
E R U P T I V E
T R I T I C A L
T U N I C A T E
E L E V A T E S
R E D E L E S S
```

In the following eight-word squares, *recenter* is the American spelling of 'recentre', *Aneityum* is one of the New Hebrides Islands in the south Pacific, and *remissed* is a rare word for 'remitted':

```
A G A R I C U S      C A P I T A T E
G E N E R A N T      A N E M O N E S
A N A C O N D A      P E P P I E S T
R E C E N T E R      I M P O L I T E
I R O N W O R T      T O I L E T T E
C A N T O N A L      A N E I T Y U M
U N D E R A G E      T E S T T U B E
S T A R T L E D      E S T E E M E D
```

```
R E M I S S E D
E V E N T I M E
M E T H A N E S
I N H A L E R S
S T A L L A G E
S I N E A T E R
E M E R G E N T
D E S S E R T S
```

Dmitri Borgmann claims that about 900 squares of nine words have been constructed. These delve even more deeply into obscure vocabulary and proper names. Here are four examples, in which the reader is left to work out the meanings of the difficult words with the help of a large dictionary and a gazetteer:

```
F R A T E R I E S        Q U A R E L E S T
R E G I M E N A L        U P P E R E S T E
A G I T A T I V E        A P P O I N T E R
T I T A N I T E S        R E O M E T E R S
E M A N A T I S T        E R I E V I L L E
R E T I T R A T E        L E N T I L L I N
I N I T I A T O R        E S T E L L I N E
E A V E S T O N E        S T E R L I N G S
S L E S T E R E D        T E R S E N E S S


A N G E L S H I P        I S O S C E L A R
N O O N E T I D E        S A R T O R I T E
G O L D V I L L E        O R G A N E T T E
E N D W E L L E R        S T A M A C H E D
L E V E L L I N E        C O N A C T O R S
S T I L L E N E S        E R E C T A B L E
H I L L I N E S S        L I T H O B I I D
I D L E N E S S E        A T T E R L I N G
P E E R E S S E S        R E E D S E D G E
```

It might be thought that a computer should be able to construct larger word squares with comparative ease, but when Frank Rubin of New York instructed a computer to find a ten-word square, it could find words for only eight of the ten lines:

```
A C C O M P L I S H
C O O P E R A N C Y
C O P A T E N T E E
O P A L E S C E N T
M E T E N T E R O N
P R E S T A T I O N
L A N C E T O O T H
I N T E R I O R L Y
S C E N O O T L
H Y E T N N H Y
```

Dmitri Borgmann and Darryl Francis constructed some ten-word squares by using tautonyms—words that consist of two words repeated:

```
O R A N G U T A N G
R A N G A R A N G A
A N D O L A N D O L
N G O T A N G O T A
G A L A N G A L A N
U R A N G U T A N G
T A N G A T A N G A
A N D O L A N D O L
N G O T A N G O T A
G A L A N G A L A N
```

Even using tautonyms, the difficulty of making a ten-word square is shown by the fact that this word square repeats several of its words. The field is still wide open for someone (or some computer) to construct a really acceptable ten-word square.

Word squares can be used as a game for children. Two players each draw a square of five by five. The first player calls out a letter and each player places the letter in one of the twenty-five boxes. The players call out letters alternately and try to make words across or down. Points are scored for words made—for example, five points for a five-letter word, four for a four-letter word, and so on. The player with the highest number of points is the winner.

This game has some of the appeal of Scrabble (q.v.), since one can not only use easy letters to make one's own words, but also difficult letters like Q and Z to make the game hard for one's opponent.

Word squares and crosswords (q.v.) are connected with several other games in which words are presented or entered on a grid-like pattern. In the scores of game magazines that are on sale nowadays in newsagents, the most popular game—rivalling even crosswords—appears to be WORD SEARCH. Readers are presented with a grid containing letters, from which words have to be made by moving from one square to the other, in the same way as a king moves in chess: horizontally, vertically, or diagonally.

An early ancestor of Word Search was what 'Professor Hoffmann' called 'Knight's Tour Letter Puzzles' in his *Puzzles Old and New* (1893). The player has to move in the same way as the knight moves in chess: two squares in one direction, then one at a 90–degree angle; or one square forward and then two at a 90-degree angle. This example by Hoffmann includes a well-known proverb.

```
R L T E Y L R O
Y H L T O B T A
T A A A   H T I
E L   E I N E O
D H W   Y E S Y
R T E S D   B W
Y N E S N D A E
H A A A W I D E
```

(*Early to bed, and early to rise,*
is the way to be healthy, and wealthy, and wise.)

In RAGAMAN (an anagram of 'anagram'), a grid of blank squares is drawn: usually 5 by 5, 7 by 7, or 9 by 9. The first player enters a letter in the centre square. The second player has to add a letter in one of the adjacent squares, to make a word or anagram with the letter that is already there. Thus, if the first player writes A, the second player can write M, and score two points for the word AM. The players continue alternately adding letters which make words or anagrams either horizontally, vertically, or diagonally. A player scores for each of the new words made by his one letter; it is possible to make four words with one move, with two diagonals as well as a vertical and a horizontal.

Sid Sackson's game called LAST WORD follows the same system but starts by filling the nine central squares with letters chosen at random from a book. So, if one opens a book and finds the sentence: 'They crept stealthily through the jungle', the nine central squares are filled in thus:

```
T H E
Y C R
E P T
```

The first player could then add E above E R T to make TREE and (diagonally) an anagram of HEY. The grid for Last Word is usually at least 9 by 9 squares. The game ends when a letter has been put in at least one square along each of the four sides of the grid. Players can only add letters if they can make at least two words with them. Scores are calculated by multiplying the numbers of letters in each of the words made with one move.

In the game of PI, players alternately add letters anywhere in a grid. A player scores if his opponent breaks one of two rules: (1)

three or more adjacent letters must form a word, and (2) no letter may be added if it prevents another word of two or more letters from being formed.

BLACK SQUARES is a more complicated game, invented by Harry Woollerton. The grid is usually about 12 by 12 squares in size. Players can insert any number of letters into the grid, as long as any sequence of letters, read vertically or horizontally, is either a word or can be made into a word by adding more letters. The players attempt to find 'black squares' which cannot be filled by any letter that makes a word with adjoining letters. Each player scores a point for each black square that he finds, and two points every time he challenges his opponent's choice of a black square by finding a suitable letter to put inside it.

While Black Squares is a game for two people, WORDSWORTH can be played by any number. Each player has his own grid, into which he enters letters called out by the players in turn. The player who makes the most words is the winner.

In SINKO, two players play with one 5 by 5 grid. The first player writes a five-letter word anywhere in the grid. The second player writes another five-letter word or adds letters to the first word to make another word. The winner is the last player who can add a word to the grid.

6

Crosswords

The CROSSWORD is the most popular and widespread word game in the world, yet it has had only a short history. It developed from the acrostic and the word square but gained its popularity by combining elements of these games with cryptic clues which are similar to riddles.

Crosswords usually consist of chequered diagrams (normally rectangular) in which the solver has to write words guessed from clues. The words are separated by black squares or by thick bars between squares. The spaces to be filled by words are called 'lights'. Crossword diagrams are now usually designed so that they look the same when they are turned upside down. But many early crosswords lacked this kind of pattern or were designed symmetrically, so that the left side was the mirror-image of the right side.

The man generally credited with inventing the crossword puzzle was a journalist named Arthur Wynne, who emigrated to New York from Liverpool. His first crossword appeared in a Sunday newspaper, the *New York World*, on 21 December 1913. Wynne called it a 'word-cross'. The puzzle had the word 'FUN' near the top because it appeared on the 'Fun' page of the newspaper. The shape resembled a word diamond, but the across words differed from the down words.

Readers expressed their approval of the experiment, so Wynne devised further puzzles for the paper. By the middle of January, the name had changed from 'word-cross' to 'cross-word'. Readers began to contribute their own crosswords.

In 1921 Margaret Petherbridge (who later became Mrs Margaret Farrar) took over the editing of the *World*'s crosswords. Among her innovations was the single-number clue, replacing the awkward '2-3' type of clue in 1923. During her time, the puzzles became regular in pattern, with the words interlocking instead of in several separate blocks.

Up to this time, crosswords had been a minority interest. But suddenly they became a craze, as the American publishers Simon and Schuster were to discover in 1924 when they published a book

2-3. What bargain hunters enjoy.
4-5. A written acknowledgment.
18-19. What this puzzle is.
22-23. An animal of prey.
26-27. The close of a day.
28-29. To elude.
30-31. The plural of is.
8-9. To cultivate.
12-13. A bar of wood or iron.
16-17. What artists learn to do.
20-21. Fastened.
24-25. Found on the seashore.
10-18. The fiber of the gomuti palm.
6-22. What we all should be.

6-7. Such and nothing more.
10-11. A bird.
14-15. Opposed to less.
4-26. A day dream.
2-11. A talon.
19-28. A pigeon.
F-7. Part of your head.
23-30. A river in Russia.
1-32. To govern.
33-34. An aromatic plant.
N-8. A fist.
24-31. To agree with.
3-12. Part of a ship.
20-29. One.
5-27. Exchanging.
9-25. To sink in mud.
13-21. A boy.

Arthur Wynne's first 'word-cross' puzzle

containing fifty crosswords, compiled by Margaret Petherbridge, Prosper Buranelli, and F. Gregory Hartswick. Simon and Schuster were uncertain whether the book would bring them fame or blame, so they published it under the imprint of 'The Plaza Publishing Company' ('Plaza' was the name of their telephone exchange). The book came with a free Venus pencil and Venus eraser.

Simon and Schuster's book became a best-seller. The crossword craze had begun, and crosswords replaced mah-jong as the most popular American game. D. St P. Barnard says: 'Two New York magistrates even went so far as to ration addicts who had neglected to support their families, to a maximum of two puzzles a day.' Doctors warned that crosswords could harm the eyesight and cause insomnia or neurosis. An American railway company put dictionaries in some carriages to help crossword-solvers. Libraries found that their dictionaries were getting excessive wear and tear from addicts of the new craze. The 1925 Broadway revue *Puzzles of 1925* included a scene in a 'Crossword Puzzle Sanatorium' for people who had been driven insane by their obsession.

Crosswords are often said to have started in Britain with the publication in the *Sunday Express* on 2 November 1924 of one of Arthur Wynne's puzzles, with certain changes to eliminate a word with an American spelling. However, *Pearson's Magazine* for February 1922 contains a crossword, which is referred to as 'a new form of puzzle in the shape of a Word Square'. The magazine adds: 'These new word squares are having a tremendous vogue in America just now.' *Pearson's Magazine* continued to publish 'Word Squares' regularly.

As in America, the height of the crossword craze in Britain came in 1924, when several British books of crosswords were published. *The Word Square Puzzle Book* (1924) comments that 'Word Squares are the very latest form of puzzle. They already have a big vogue in this country, and an even bigger one in America.' Some of the crosswords in this book have black squares which make the shape of a dog, a railway engine, and a Christmas tree.

The Cross Word Pocket Puzzle Book, published in the same year, gives these instructions for solving the puzzles:

Every white square must be filled by a letter. Begin your word in a numbered square and continue to the right, or straight down, until a black square or the edge of the puzzle is reached. The number against the clue indicates the square upon which the suggested word must start, and the group under which the clue is classified shows the direction the word must take.

Another 1924 publication, *The Cross Word Puzzle Book*, has this prefatory note:

THIS IS NOT A TOY!

To Fathers and Mothers, Uncles and Aunts

It is just possible you may pick this book up thinking of it as a present for the younger children. Will you please do us this one favour—in the name of humanity? Just solve half a dozen of the puzzles, taken at random, *yourself*, before you pass it on. It's a small thing to ask—you'll be able to go back to your work in about a week.

The *Sunday Times* published its first crossword on 11 January 1925, with a note that 'The *Sunday Times*, which has always made a feature of such popular pastimes and skilled games as Acrostics, Chess, and Auction Bridge, has fallen a victim to the universal craze of Cross-Word puzzles.' This was a prize crossword with patterns that were not always regular, and simple clues like 'quadruped' (Answer: *ass*) and 'adverb' (Answer: *up*). The *Daily Telegraph* followed suit on 30 July 1925 and has published a daily crossword ever since, even though its crossword was originally introduced as merely the first of a six-week series. The first puzzle contained several two-letter words ('adverb', Answer: *so*; 'pronoun', Answer: *it*) but these soon became unacceptable in most crosswords because they were considered to be too elementary.

The crossword craze was now well established in Britain. Both Queen Mary and Stanley Baldwin were reported to have tried solving crosswords. In *Punch* for 1 July 1925, 'the Sage' asks:

'What would you say has been the dominant feature of our social life in these last six months?'

'Unquestionably the Cross-word Puzzle,' replied the Cynic. 'I am not forgetting that among our young barbarians and Philistines we have of late seen an outburst of the cult of assertive ugliness. But the allure of Epstein and Oxford trouserings has been for the few; the Cross-word Puzzle captivated the general. Coming, like most of our enthusiasms, with the *cachet* of a foreign derivation, its appeal to the British bosom has been universal. It touched all classes, because it made demands upon a modicum of intelligence common to them all. But its vogue, which has been marked by an exceptional vitality, is now moribund.'

To which Mr Punch replies:

I lament its decline. It has been an educational force. I myself acknowledge that its operations have made me familiar with words, largely of three letters, which had previously been outside the range of my vocabulary. It has also extended, however slightly, my knowledge of geography.

The British crossword became a more difficult puzzle than the American version, which tended to have more straightforward clues and a larger diagram.

In Britain the cryptic clue was developed by such pioneers as Edward Powys Mathers who, under the name of 'Torquemada' (the first Grand Inquisitor of the Spanish Inquisition), composed puzzles for *The Saturday Westminster* in 1925 and then for the *Observer* from 1926 to 1939.

The Saturday Westminster puzzles (reprinted in 1925 as *Cross-words in Rhyme for those of Riper Years*) had clues in the form of rhyming couplets—for example, 'Nimbus of a Cockney saint, Please correct me if I ain't (Answer: *'alo*). Torquemada's first crossword in the *Observer* appeared on 14 March 1926, alongside the 207th puzzle in that newspaper's long-running series of double acrostics, which crosswords were soon to replace altogether.

Torquemada is credited with being the first to use bars instead of black squares to divide up the words. He also popularized the 'theme' puzzle and—most importantly—the cryptic clue.

Cryptic clues are deliberately mysterious and usually ambiguous. They often take one of the following forms: an anagram ('Lost Arabs shaken to see bird.' Answer: *albatross*); a word hidden in a phrase ('Material used in many long dresses.' Answer: *nylon*) or in another word ('An important city in Czechoslovakia.' Answer: *Oslo*); an ambiguous definition ('He makes father late.' Answer: *patricide*); a charade (q.v.) ('Mental exercise which hardly puts you in mind of Henry VIII.' Answer: *thin-king*); a reversal ('Ward (8).' Answer: *drawback*); a 'container and contained' clue ('City that suits Ron in toto.' Answer: *Toronto*); a rebus (q.v.) ('Only a hundred left? It must be divided in two, then.' Answer: *c-left*); a misspelling to indicate an unusual pronunciation ('What makes dat guy's appearance no longer dat guy's?' Answer: *disguise*); or a pun (q.v.) ('The fireplace is enormous, we hear.' Answer: *grate*, i.e. great).

When Torquemada died in 1939, his place was taken by 'Ximenes' (Derrick Somerset Macnutt) who took his pseudonym from Torquemada's successor in the Inquisition. Ximenes introduced several new types of crossword including 'Misprints' in which misprints occur in either the clues or the answers; he also started competitions for clue-setting which became very popular among solvers.

Ximenes was followed at the *Observer* in 1972 by 'Azed' (alias Jonathan Crowther), whose pseudonym was a reversal of the name of another Grand Inquisitor, Don Diego de Deza. Azed has continued—and perhaps intensified—his predecessors' reputation for difficult crosswords. A typical Azed crossword might include words like *paneity* (the state of being bread) or *nunatakkeri* (points of rock appearing above the surface of land-ice). As Jonathan Crowther has said: 'The Azed series caters deliberately and unashamedly for those who like their puzzles on the tough side.' So that, when you see 'number' in an Azed clue, you must be prepared for it to mean *more numb*, 'a wicked thing' may be a *candle*, and 'butter' can signify *ram* or *goat*.

Ximenes' favourite kind of clue was the '& lit.' type, in which the whole clue is a literal definition of the answer while its parts provide a cryptic reference to that answer. For example, 'They adorn many Scotsmen's heads' leads to the word *tams* not only because tams are Scottish hats but also because the first letters ('heads') of the first four words spell 'tams'.

Ximenes was the first compiler to formulate strict rules for devising crosswords. He insisted that compilers need not mean what they say but must say what they mean. Thus he would disapprove of the clue 'I am in the plot, that's clear' for the word *plain* because he felt it should read: 'I *is* in the plot' (i.e. I in plan).

Another area of dispute for compilers is the number of 'unchecked' letters. Unchecked letters are those which contribute to one word only and do not belong to interlocking words as well. The fewer unchecked letters there are in a word, the more difficult it is to guess them by solving interlocking words. British puzzles have as many as sixty or seventy per cent of the letters in the diagram unchecked, whereas American crosswords generally have few if any unchecked letters.

The crossword craze which started in the early 1920s continued for the rest of the decade. By 1927, when A. P. Herbert published his *Misleading Cases in the Common Law*, only a learned judge could still be ignorant of what a crossword was:

Sir Antony Dewlap: The action is unusual . . . by reason of the channel which the defendant has selected for his abuse. Melud, that channel is no other than the innocent and familiar 'Cross-word'—

Mr Justice Snubb: What is that?

Sir Antony Dewlap: Forgive me, melud. Melud, with great respect, melud, a cross-word puzzle is a form of puzzle, melud, in which a number of numbered squares in a chequered arrangement of—er—squares, melud, have to be filled in with letters, melud, these letters forming words, melud, which words are read both horizontally and vertically, melud—that is, both across and down, if your lordship follows me—and which words may be deduced from certain descriptions or clues, which are provided with the puzzle, melud, these descriptions having numbers, melud, which are to be filled in with the correct letters and words according to the descriptions which have the corresponding numbers, melud, whether horizontally or vertically, as the case may be. Does your lordship follow me?

Mr Justice Snubb: No.

Crosswords again appeared in a legal case in 1928 when four defendants at Bow Street Police Court were accused of publishing 'a scheme for the sale of chances in a lottery entitled the "New Blind Crossword" '. In this competition, the entry fee was one shilling, out of which prizes were distributed and £20 was given each week to charities for the blind. As a report said:

The question at issue was whether or not it could be said that skill entered into the contest. Sir Chartres Biron, who heard the case, himself spent some little time in trying to solve one of the puzzles, and admitted that he found considerable difficulty in discovering some of the words. He did not think he could say that no element of skill was involved. . . . He dismissed all the summonses under the Lottery Act. (*Competitor's Annual*, 1930)

By this time, prize crosswords had become very popular. Newspapers like the *People* and *News of the World* contained crosswords which could have several alternative answers, from which contestants had to choose the most appropriate. Torquemada said of this type of puzzle that 'It is not a puzzle at all: it is, with its toss-up of possible alternatives and its half-filled-in diagram, merely a little flagrant roulette wheel—good luck to it!—spun beneath the noses of the police' (*Torquemada Puzzle Book*, 1934).

Meanwhile the more respectable newspapers bowed to the demand for crosswords. The *Manchester Guardian* published its first puzzle in 1929. The *Listener* started its crosswords on 2 April 1930 and soon built up a reputation for having the very hardest ones, notably those composed by 'Afrit', Prebendary A. F. Ritchie of Wells Cathedral, whose pseudonym came from an evil demon in Arabian mythology.

The *Listener*'s first crossword had a musical theme and most of its successors were based on a particular subject. The diagram of the *Listener*'s first puzzle was divided up by bars and it was not symmetrical. The clues were fairly straightforward: e.g. 'Last three letters of Christian name of a great composer' (Answer: *ian*!). This first *Listener* crossword carried a note that: 'No prizes will be offered, but any reader who sends to us . . . the correct solution of any of our crosswords, will be entitled to an invitation to visit the BBC Studios on certain afternoons.'

It was also in 1930 that *The Times* finally succumbed to publishing a daily crossword. Many authorities say that the first *Times* crossword appeared on 1 February 1930 but the issues of 23 and 30 January reprinted the crossword from the *Times Weekly Edition*, which had been publishing them since 2 January that year. The puzzle of 1 February was, therefore, the *Times*'s first original crossword. Its clues were simple by modern standards, including quotations from Shakespeare and Rupert Brooke, and anagram clues like 'Retunes (anag.)' (Answer: *tureens*) and 'There's a lot in this voice' (Answer: *alto*). The New York *Evening Post* of 14 February reprinted this puzzle, saying that 'The Thunderer, like everything else, has changed with time.' A 'veteran American solver of crossword puzzles' took more than an hour and a quarter to finish it.

After 1 February 1930 *The Times* published a daily puzzle, despite opposition from some readers. One correspondent wrote: 'Let me entreat you to keep *The Times* from puzzles of all sorts. Space there is precious and prestige also.' Another reader wrote to say: 'I hate to see a great newspaper pandering to the modern craze for passing the time in all kinds of stupid ways.' Perhaps to answer such complaints, *The Times* printed a crossword in Latin, saying: 'It is possible that the Latin crossword may interest others who, from motives of the highest respectability, have hitherto shunned the English.' A Greek crossword followed about a month later.

The Times's crossword eventually attained the height of respectability. In 1970 the newspaper held its first 'National Crossword Competition', sponsored by the Cutty Sark whisky company. This competition drew 33,000 entries and became an annual event. For several years it was won by Dr John Sykes, the Editor of the *Concise Oxford Dictionary*. In 1972 he took an average of seven and a quarter minutes to solve each of the puzzles in the competition. A typically difficult clue from the 1975 contest was 'Raise your —— Bishop

Mousefare': the answer was *Hatto*, the name of a bishop who (according to legend) was eaten by rats.

The Times's contest was not the first such competition. Similar contests were held in the United States as early as 1925, and the *Daily Telegraph* organized one in 1942 to see who could solve their crossword most quickly. The quickest person took six minutes, three and a half seconds but accidentally misspelt one word, so the prize went to the next fastest solver, who took nearly eight minutes.

The *Daily Telegraph* crossword was again in the news in 1944, when one of its compilers, L. S. Dawe, was questioned by representatives of MI5 because he had used the words *Mulberry*, *Pluto*, *Neptune*, and *Overlord* in puzzles and each was a secret code-word associated with forthcoming war operations. Dawe managed to convince the MI5 people that it was pure coincidence.

In his biography of Queen Elizabeth II, *Majesty* (1977), Robert Lacey describes the Queen's morning routine thus: 'Beside her on the bed would be laid out all the newspapers, and she might turn to the back page of the *Daily Telegraph* to start on the more difficult of its two crosswords.' Robert Lacey also tells us that the Queen's sister, Princess Margaret, prefers the puzzle in *Country Life*, and has more than once won a prize in its crossword competition.

Crosswords from the *Daily Telegraph* and *The Times* were used on television in 1967 in a BBC2 programme called 'Crossword on Two'. Two teams, each of three people, were given half an hour to solve the puzzles.

Crosswords had a rather more serious function for Anthony Grey when he was kept in solitary confinement in China for two years during the late 1960s. They helped him to keep his sanity:

After studying the construction of crosswords I decided that I would compile them myself. I had never been very interested in these word-games before although one of my faults had always been punning. . . . As I walked back and forth in the yard later in the day I occupied my mind working out clues for them in the groan-provoking humorous style of crossword compilers down the ages! It allowed me to forget the watching eyes of the guards, occupied my empty mind, eased the tension in me as I walked. I would compile clues like 1 across in one of my early puzzles. 'What an irritated deep-sea diver must do to make the grade?' (4, 2, 2, 7). And the abysmally unfunny answer would be 'Come up to scratch'.

The crossword puzzle is now firmly established, not only in Britain and the United States but also in many other countries, from Yugoslavia to South Africa, from Jamaica to Israel. In an article in *Collier's* magazine in 1925, Prosper Buranelli and Margaret Petherbridge gave three reasons for its phenomenal success: 'the fascination of words common to an articulate race; self-education; and time-killing'. Another factor must be the challenge of solving the clues, each of which may be a miniature puzzle or riddle.

Edmund Akenhead, crossword editor of *The Times*, said that one of his favourite clues was a completely blank space (7 letters); the answer was *missing*. The journalist Philip Howard remembers a clue that was simply a capital letter O (8, 6); solution: *circular letter*.

The clues and answers to crosswords often reflect the interests and the social climate of the period. A 1927 *Daily Telegraph* clue was 'M. Poincaré's medical adviser' for *médecin*. Forty years later, the *Daily Telegraph*'s clue 'Mutual aid organisation to put to sea' leads to *SEATO*. A typically topical clue from a 1979 puzzle refers to John Travolta, a popular film-star: 'What does Travolta do on the beach?' —Answer: *John Brown's Body*.

The crossword creates a world of its own, as David Bolster suggested when he wrote to *The Times* in 1959, saying:

I have amused myself recently by visualizing 'Crossword Country'. It consists largely of tors covered with heather (ling) and the predominating fauna are ernes, hens, lions, asps, and she-cats. They feed, as appropriate, on grubs, sole, bass, ants, bees, and each other. There are, unfortunately, also humans, all dastards, renegades or rips, except for some dons, doctors, Royal Engineers and tars (ABs). Their names are Mac, Ian or Eli. . . .

Later correspondents added to the fauna emu, dodo, gnu, and kiwi, and to human names they added biblical ones like Elihu, Agag, and Noah. Apparently the inhabitants of Crossword Country are much plagued by a little devil (imp).

It may seem that crossword-solving is a very trivial pursuit, yet it has been claimed that crosswords extend one's vocabulary, stimulate the mind, and even encourage a healthy scepticism towards accepting things at their face value. They are predominantly a solitary pastime, although lone solvers are likely to find that bystanders want to help, even if no help is wanted.

The computer age has inevitably led to attempts to construct crosswords by computer. Experts have devised programs that fill in words on an empty diagram. The trouble is that, for British puzzles at least, constructing the puzzle is only half the task—and many compilers would say that it is one of the less difficult parts of the job.

Writing the clues demands more ingenuity and it is unlikely that computers can be programmed to construct cryptic clues of the type found in the more difficult British puzzles.

Many people are afraid of cryptic crosswords, believing that they demand special skills. But experts approach them according to orderly principles which make the process less daunting. Some solvers start by looking for a straightforward clue, since many cryptic puzzles contain one or two of these, such as quotations from famous authors, with one word omitted. If you know the quotation, this can be an easy way of getting the first word.

Another trick in solving cryptics is to look for the special words that 'signal' a particular type of clue. Thus an anagram is often signalled by the words 'jumbled', 'twisted', 'in a way', 'unruly', 'gone to pieces', etc. A pun can be signalled by a question mark, an exclamation mark, or the word 'perhaps'. The words 'in' and 'around' may indicate one word hidden within another, while 'back' or 'returning' may suggest reversal of some sort. 'We hear', 'they say', or 'by the sound of it' can signal a word that sounds like another word. Other cryptic conventions include 'love' or 'duck' to signify the letter O (*nought*); chronograms like 'thousand' (*M*) and 'ten' (*X*); points of the compass (North: *N*; Eastern: *E*; often suggested by a word like 'point' or 'direction'); and many other abbreviations such as 'left' (*L*), 'right' (*R*), and 'doctor' (*DR*).

Yet another type of crossword is the double-crostic, invented by an American, Elizabeth Kingsley. The first double-crostic was published in the *Saturday Review* for 31 March 1934. Each square was numbered, and the letters for these squares had to be taken from another diagram in which words were clued in the usual way. Thus the first clue: '1–14–23–50–95 A perfume of roses' led to *Attar*, the letters of which, when written in those numbered spaces, made part of a quotation from Tennyson's *Ulysses*. The literary quotation was an essential part of Elizabeth Kingsley's invention, for she had devised double-crostics to 'heighten an appreciation of fine literature'.

Ogden Nash, who was so critical of some word games (see pp. 30–1), said that 'Double-Crostics have saved my sanity in the grim loneliness of hotel rooms when I lecture my way around the country.'

7

Scrabble

'If there hadn't been any Depression in the Thirties there wouldn't be any Scrabble.' This authoritative statement comes from the man who invented the game, Alfred Butts.

Butts was an unemployed architect, living in New York, who experimented during the 1930s with a game in which words were made from individual letters printed on squares of cardboard. Butts called the game 'Lexiko'. To start with, it had no board, but that came later and the name was changed to 'It' and then to 'Criss-Cross'.

Alfred Butts made sets of the game to sell to his acquaintances but it remained unnoticed until 1948, when James Brunot, a friend of Butts, became interested in its commercial possibilities. Brunot and his wife started making the game in the living-room of their home in Newtown, Connecticut, obtaining parts for the game from various manufacturers.

In an attempt to find a better name for it, the Brunots sent a list of possibilities to a patent-research lawyer in Washington, asking him which names were not already copyrighted. 'Scrabble' was chosen because it sounded the best of the names that were not already protected.

During their first year, the Brunots sold only about 2,000 sets. Sales continued to be sluggish until 1952, when the game suddenly took off, thanks to the owner of Macy's store. He played the game while on holiday and, when he returned to work, he ordered a set from the toy department only to be told that they did not stock it. He told them to order it, and other toy shops followed suit.

The New York firm of Selchow and Righter was already making the boards for the Brunots, and in 1953 they bought the rights to the whole game. (In Britain, the rights are owned by J. W. Spear and Sons, Ltd.) James Brunot licensed the Cadaco-Ellis Company of Chicago to manufacture a cheaper type of Scrabble called 'Skip-a-Cross', costing $2, with cardboard letters and a board that was part of the box. In the standard set (costing $3) the letters (usually known as 'tiles') were made of wood but Brunot also devised a de luxe version priced at $10, with white plastic tiles which eventually became the norm. The wooden tiles, made of maple in Bavaria, had a grain in the wood which players learnt to memorize so that they could pick out the letters they required.

By the end of 1953, *Life* magazine reported:

The game . . . has in the past few months become as Mah Jong, miniature golf or Monopoly were in their respective primes (1923, 1930, 1937), and seems likely to surpass them all. At a modest estimate there are about 1.1 million Scrabble sets in the U.S. today and there are perhaps 10 million players. . . . In intellectual circles the game is played in French or Latin; in Hollywood games of dirty-word Scrabble are in constant progress; in New York the Guys-and-Dolls set has converted Scrabble into the hottest gambling game since gin rummy.

Scrabble became one of the most successful word games of the twentieth century. When the Queen Mother visited New York in 1954, she said that she was fond of Scrabble. Later, President Nixon admitted that Scrabble was his favourite form of relaxation. In 1975, readers of *Games and Puzzles* voted it 'Game of the Year'. And when mountaineer Chris Bonington and his colleagues ascended the south face of Annapurna, they spent their free evenings playing 'liar dice or Scrabble, with our tape-recorder blasting out music in the background'.

With its interlocking words and its use of juggled letters, Scrabble mingles the attractions of crosswords and anagrams (q.v.). When Alfred Butts invented the game, the first word had to be placed at the top left-hand corner of the board but nowadays the opening word is put in the middle of the board.

The board itself has 225 squares—15 by 15—of which some are 'premium squares', giving double or triple scores for individual letters or for whole words. The game is played by two, three, or four players each using up to seven tiles at a time to make words on the board. As each player uses some or all of his tiles, he makes up the number to seven again from the tile pool, ready for the next move. Instead of making a move, a player may exchange some or all of his tiles for fresh ones.

There are one hundred tiles altogether, each bearing a letter of the alphabet and a number indicating the value of that letter (its score when played). The set includes two blank tiles, which have no value but are very useful because they can represent any letter that the player chooses. The game's inventor included many I's to help make words in *-ing*, *-ion*, etc., but few S's, as he wished to prevent players from making a lot of plural words.

The letters with the highest value are those that are most difficult to use. For example, Q has a high value because it can normally only be used before the letter U, unless one employs such rare words as *cinq*. This word occurs in the Shorter Oxford English Dictionary but not in many others, so it depends which dictionary the players have chosen as a source for acceptable words.

The *Shorter OED* was used until 1980 as the arbiter in the British National Scrabble Championships, after which *Chambers's Twentieth Century Dictionary* took its place, perhaps because the latter contains many recondite words useful to Scrabble players: words like *dso, dsobo, dsomo, dzo, dzobo, jomo, zho, zhomo, zo, zobo,* and *zobu,* which all mean a Himalayan animal that is a cross between a cow and a yak. Yet the *Shorter Oxford English Dictionary* includes such words as *ai, ort, oyers,* and *ria,* which were all used by the winner of the 1973 Scrabble Championship, Mrs Anne Bradford of Barnet. Scrabble experts build up a knowledge of unusual words like *aalii, heaume, jaboty, xylyl,* and *zemstvo* which help them to dispose of unwanted letters.

Besides an extensive vocabulary, Scrabble champions require skill in the strategy of the game: placing high-scoring letters on the premium squares but not giving your opponent a chance to do the same; making more than one word with one move; making words to which you can later add extra letters.

The skills of the Scrabble expert are summed up in the following elegy by Clement Wood:

Death of a Scrabble Master

This was the greatest of the game's great players:
If you played BRAS, he'd make it HUDIBRASTIC.
He ruled a world 15 by 15 squares,
Peopled by 100 letters, wood or plastic.

He unearthed XEBEC, HAJI, useful QAID,
Found QUOS (see pl. of QUID PRO QUO) and QUOTHA,
Discovered AU, DE, DA all unitalicized
(AU JUS, DA CAPO, ALMANACH DE GOTHA).

> Two-letter words went marching through his brain,
> Spondaic-footed, singing their slow litany:
> AL (Indian Mulberry), AI (a sloth), EM, EN,
> BY, MY, AX, EX, OX, LO, IT, AN, HE . . .

> PE (Hebrew letter), LI (a Chinese mile), KA, RE,
> SH (like NTH, spectacularly vowelless),
> AY, OY (a cry of grief, pain or dismay);
> HAI, HI, HO— leaving opponents powerless.

> He, if the tiles before him said DOC TIME,
> Would promptly play the elegant DEMOTIC,
> And none but he fulfilled the scrabbler's dream,
> When, through two triple words, he hung QUIXOTIC.

> The day his adversary put down GNASHED,
> He laid—a virtuoso feat—beneath it GOUTIER,
> So placed, that six more tiny words were hatched:
> GO, NU, AT, SI, then (as you've seen, no doubt) HE, ER.

An expert player can regularly score more than four hundred points in every game. The values of all the tiles add up to 187, but it is possible to make much higher scores in a game by using the premium squares and by joining extra letters to words that are already on the board.

High scores are possible if one places a word that joins two 'triple word score' squares (thus multiplying one's score by nine) but this is difficult because these squares are eight spaces apart. As each player has only seven letters at a time, this necessitates the use of a letter that is already lying between the 'triple word score' squares. Alfred Butts's wife Nina did this when she put the word *quixotic* down the right-hand side of the board, using the X in *fox* which was already there, and thus scored 284 points in one move. The player who uses all his tiles in one move, scores a bonus of fifty points.

The seven-letter words which make the highest scores on their own are *bezique* (27 points), and *squeeze* (25 points), although some dictionaries include higher-scoring words like *zyxomma* (a kind of dragonfly—30 points), *popquiz* (29 points), *squeezy* (28 points) and *quartzy* (28 points). The highest theoretical score with a single word would be forty-nine points, but there seems to be no seven-letter word that includes the letters J, K, Q, X, and Z. To all these scores should be added the fifty-point bonus for using a seven-letter word.

The highest score possible in one move is achieved by inserting letters along the edge of the board to complete a fifteen-letter word. Scores of around 2,000 have been made by this method with such words as *benzoxycamphors*, *sesquioxidizing*, *jackpuddinghood*, *diazohydroxides*, and *oxyphenbutazone*.

As for the highest score in one game, it has been calculated that one person could theoretically score as many as 4,153 points in a game. When *Life* magazine wrote about Mr and Mrs Brunot in 1953, the highest total score they had made in a two-handed game was 809. The largest single score made in a competitive game is recorded as 744, made by an Englishman, Allan Simmons, in 1981. When Ron Jerome of Bracknell scored 3,881 points in thirty-two moves in 1974, he was not playing in a championship and he had to use strange words like *alexipharmakons*.

As well as the normal method of playing Scrabble, there are many variations, such as 'solitaire Scrabble' for one player; the 'double bag' game in which the vowels and consonants are kept in two separate bags; theme games in which the words have to refer to a particular subject; and 'unScrabble' or 'Scrabble in reverse'—in which players have to remove letters from the board.

The game is now available in several different forms: as well as the de luxe version which has a turntable attached to the board, there is Scrabble for Juniors, Travel Scrabble (in which the tiles lock into holes in the board), and magnetic Pocket Scrabble (in which the letters cling to the board). There are versions of the game in French, Dutch, Italian, Spanish, Russian, and Arabic, each with its particular set of letters. In the French form of the game, there are fifteen E's and some letters have different scores from those in the British version, because of the differing frequency with which they appear in the French language. The Dutch game has eighteen E's, two J's, and ten N's. The Spanish set includes tiles for CH, LL, and RR, while the German version has 119 tiles (including A, O, and U with umlauts) and German players use eight letters on their racks instead of seven.

The universal appeal of Scrabble is suggested by the game's appearance in novels. Vladimir Nabokov in *Ada* (1969) describes a Russian game called 'Flavita' which he says 'was fashionable throughout Estoty and Canady around 1790' and which closely resembles Scrabble. In Mickey Spillane's *The Erection Set* (1972), the hero visits a lady called Lucy Longstreet:

She was still there playing Scrabble on the porch with Beth, the coloured towel girl, both of them old and tired with screechy voices, armed with huge, dog-eared dictionaries.

When the hero revisits Lucy later on, he finds her alone:

She was sitting by herself at a card table with a Scrabble game half-finished. . . . When she picked four tiles out of the holder and laid them down it made a lousy job of Scrabble but a good piece of information. The word didn't fit, but it was clear enough. It spelled out *trap*.

In Marvin Kaye's *A Lively Game of Death* (1972), a dead man is found clutching three Scrabble tiles in his hand: a Z, a blank, and an H, 'evidently a desperate final message'. The amateur detective realizes that the message is not in the letters but in the numbers on each of the tiles: 10, blank, and 4—'Goetz was trying to tell us to look for his killer in the showroom next door, ten-zero-four.'

A game resembling Scrabble features in another detective novel. In David Whitelaw's *Lexicon Murders* (1945), cards from the game called LEXICON are used for a secret code, and a murderer leaves one card on each of the corpses. David Whitelaw was actually the inventor of Lexicon, a game in which players have to make words from letters printed on cards like playing cards. Each player has ten cards and can either make a word, add a letter or letters to a word already on the table, or exchange a card for another card on the table or in the heap of spare cards.

The game was patented in 1925, and by 1933 it was so popular that people were holding 'Lexicon drives', modelled on whist drives, for several tables of four players. David Whitelaw wrote more than fifty novels but he earned much more from Lexicon, which took him one morning to invent. The game was adapted into many languages and there was even a version in Braille.

Several other games based on the word-building principle have failed to achieve the popularity of Scrabble and Lexicon. Memoirs of Victorian and Edwardian life refer to a game of the period called 'WORD-MAKING AND WORD-TAKING', which had capital letters printed on pieces of cardboard. Lesley Lewes recalls her mother in about 1912 using the letters to teach her children to read. Gwen Raverat remembers:

Our chief intellectual exercise was the Letter Game: word-making and word-taking. . . . We gradually developed a regular word-game technique, and the rules were perfected to cover all exigencies. Any dictionary word was allowed, but no proper names, and a word could be stolen by adding a letter and changing the meaning. Many words known only to dictionaries were of great value: such as ZAX (a slate-cutter's tool); and other words such as PIX or WAX which were held to be practically unstealable.

SPELLING BEE was the name of a card game made in about 1900. The players divided the lettered cards among themselves and turned their cards face upwards one at a time, so that each player had two sets of cards—one with faces upwards and the other with faces concealed. When a player could form a word with his own top card and that of another player, he called out the word and received those cards and all the cards beneath them. The rules stated: 'All English words allowable, but no proper names or slang words.'

MY WORD is a card game in which players form four-letter words from cards bearing pairs of letters. KEYWORD was a board game similar to Scrabble, with bonuses scored for placing letters on one's own coloured squares or for making a three-letter word to match a pack of cards showing different three-letter words one at a time.

KAN-U-GO is a 'crossword card game' for two to seven players. It has a pack of fifty-eight lettered cards and two 'Kan-U-Go' cards which can be thrown in by a player who is playing his last letter card. As in Scrabble, players make words from the letters.

Four other games—AD LIB, ADDICTION, PERQUACKEY, and SHAKE WORDS—use lettered dice from which the players make words. Ad Lib uses thirteen dice with letters on each face. When the dice are shaken, words have to be made (within a time-limit) from the letters on the tops of the dice. Addiction similarly uses thirteen lettered dice which are tumbled one at a time down stairs on to a tray and then have to be inserted in a five-by-five frame.

BOGGLE is a comparatively new game, introduced by Palitoy Parker in 1977. Sixteen lettered dice are shaken on to a tray and players then have to make words from the exposed letters by moving from one letter to another in a straight or diagonal line—rather like the popular modern 'word search' games. Assisted by a computer, two Americans, Alan Frank and Steve Root, made no fewer than 2,047 words from the 'Boggle' sequence of letters:

```
G N I S
E T R P
S E A C
D B L S
```

Games like Boggle and Scrabble may seem comparatively new but they were anticipated in the nineteenth century by Lewis Carroll. As early as 1880 he noted in his diary that 'A game might be made of letters, to be moved about on a chess-board till they form words.' And in a letter on New Year's Day, 1895, he wrote to Winifred Hawke:

If ever you want a *light* mental recreation, try the '30 letter' puzzle. I tried it for the first time, the other day, with one of my sisters: and I think it very interesting. . . . Here is our rule. Take 4 or 5 complete alphabets. Put the vowels into one bag, the consonants into another. Shake up. Draw 9 vowels and 21 consonants. With these you must make 6 real words (excluding proper names) so as to use up *all* the letters. If *two* people want to do it, then after drawing a set of 30, pick out a set of duplicates for the other player. Sit where you cannot see one another's work, and make it a *race*. It seems to take from 5 to 10 minutes. It makes a shorter, but very good, puzzle, to draw 6 vowels and 14 consonants, and make 4 words; and yet a shorter one to draw 3 vowels and 7 consonants and make 2 words.

8

Anagrams

The thirteenth-century Jewish mystics known as the Cabbalists believed that there were magical properties in the Hebrew alphabet and that the letters used in sacred Jewish writings could be rearranged to work miracles and reveal truth. It was even believed that Jeremiah and other prophets created human beings ('golems') out of dust by reciting letters in a particular order: one order of letters created a male, another created a female; and by reversing the order you could turn the golem back into dust.

This belief in the power of shuffling letters of the alphabet continued from the Middle Ages into the Renaissance. It was thought that character or fate could be discovered by rearranging the letters of a person's name—making an ANAGRAM.

In the late sixteenth-century work, *The Art of English Poetry*, the anonymous author wrote of anagrams: 'They that use it for pleasure is to breed one word out of another not altering any letter nor the number of them, but only transposing of the same, whereupon many times is produced some grateful news or matter to them for whose pleasure and service it was intended.' The author himself found a promising omen for the future of Queen Elizabeth by rearranging her Latin name *Elissabet Anglorum Regina* into *Multa regnabis sene gloria* — 'Aged and in much glory shall ye reign.'

The ancient Greek writer Lycophron used the same method to flatter royalty, as C. C. Bombaugh recounts:

Lycophron, a Greek writer who lived three centuries before the Christian era, records two anagrams in his poem on the siege of Troy entitled *Cassandra*. One is the name of Ptolemy Philadelphus, in whose reign Lycophron lived:

ΠΤΟΛΕΜΑΙΣ = ΑΠΟ ΜΕΛΙΤΟΣ—made of honey.

The other is on Ptolemy's queen, Arsinoë:

ΑΡΣΙΝΟΗ = ΗΡΑΣ ΙΟΝ—Juno's violet.

Eustachius informs us that this practice was common among the Greeks, and gives numerous examples; such, for instance, as the transposition of the word Αρετη, virtue, into Ερατη, lovely. (*Gleanings for the Curious*, 1890)

Bombaugh also mentions how Josuah Sylvester, in dedicating his translation of Du Bartas's 'La Semaine' to James I, changed the King's name, James Stuart, into *A just master*.

John Taylor, known as the Water Poet, who was very fond of anagrams, turned James Stuart into *Muses tari at* and explained this strange phrase in verse:

> Great Sovereign, as thy sacred royal breast
> Is by the Muses whole and sole possessed:
> So do I know, rich, precious, peerless gem,
> In writing unto thee, I write to them.
> The Muses tarry at thy name: why so?
> Because they have no further for to go.

He also turned the name of the Queen, Marie Stuart, into *I am a true star* and that of the Countess of Southampton, Rachel Wriothesley, into *Holy liver, chast ever*. As these anagrams show, writers of the period allowed themselves considerable freedom in their treatment of letters, using *w* to represent two *u*'s or an *i* to stand for a *j* or *y*, or ignoring some letters altogether.

A similar liberty was taken by Lady Eleanor Davies, the wife of the poet Sir John Davies, to support her belief in her own prophetic powers. She thought these powers were proved by turning her maiden name, Eleanor Audeley, into *Reveale O Daniel*—an anagram only made possible by using *u* as *v* and *y* as *i*. J. A. Morgan tells how the wind was taken out of her sails:

The court attempted to expel the spirit from the lady; and the bishops argued the point with her out of Holy Writ; but to no purpose. She returned text for text, until one of the deans of the arches, says Heylin, 'shot her through and through with an arrow borrowed from her own quiver'. Taking up a pen, he wrote:—Dame Eleanor Davies—Never so mad a ladie! (*Macaronic Poetry*, 1872)

This effectively silenced Dame Eleanor.

People persisted in believing that anagrams could foretell the future. The Frenchman André Pujom carried this belief to extremes when he discovered that his name could be turned into *pendu à Riom* (i.e. 'hanged at Riom'), and committed a murder so that he would be hanged at Riom, the centre of criminal justice in Auvergne.

When Alexander the Great was intending to raise the siege of Tyre, he dreamt he saw a satyr dancing round him. His adviser Aristander realized that this was a good omen, since the Greek word Σατυρος, meaning satyr, could be turned into Σα Tυρος ('Tyre is yours'). Next day, the prediction was fulfilled.

Louis XIII, King of France from 1610 to 1643, appointed a man from Provence to be his Royal Anagrammatist, with a salary of £1,200 a year.

The seventeenth century was the high point of faith in the efficacy of anagrams. The poet George Herbert succumbed to the fashion by making an anagram of the Virgin Mary:

MARY
Ana- {   } gram
ARMY

How well her name an Army doth present,
In whom the Lord of Hosts did pitch his tent!

Such explanatory poems were sometimes very far-fetched, like this epitaph on a monument erected in Duloe, Cornwall, to Marya Arundell, who died in 1629:

Marya Arundell — Man a dry laurel
Man to the marigold compared may be,
Men may be liken'd to the laurel tree!
Both feed the eye—both please the optic sense;
Both soon decay—both suddenly fleet hence;
What, then, infer you from her name but this,
Man fades away—man a dry laurel is.

(*Notes and Queries*, 20 November 1875)

Mary Fage's *Fame's Roll* (1637) contains more than 400 poems praising various members of the royalty or nobility, each prefixed by an anagram. Anna Stuarte becomes *A nu neat star*; Charles, King of England, becomes *O cheef king, enlarg lands*; and William Fielding (the Earl of Denbigh) becomes *Lively man, gvid life*.

Mary Fage prefixed her collection with a poem that explains or excuses her methods of making anagrams:

Tush say they, what! a woman this work frame?
Her wit will not attain an anagram;
There many may be false within her book.
Yet Monsieur Critic, notwithstanding look

I pray thee on these following rules, and than
Anagrams here according to them scan.
E may most what concludes an English word,
And so a letter at a need afford.
H is an aspiration, and no letter;
It may be had or left, which we think better.
I may be I, or Y, as need require.
Q, ever after doth a V desire.
Two V's may be a double V, and then
A double V may be two V's again.
X may divided be, and S and C,
May by that letter comprehended be.
Z, a double S may comprehend.
And lastly, an apostrophe may ease
Sometimes a letter, where it doth not please.
Try th'anagrams hereby, and then you'll say
Whether I've used all the helps I may.

Such latitude would not be acceptable today, when anagrams must follow the basic rule laid down by William Drummond in his *Character of a Perfect Anagram* (1711): 'In an anagram there must not be fewer nor more nor other letters, but the same, and as many as in the name.' Yet Drummond adds: 'When the same letters occur many times in the name, then the omission of one or more is pardonable.'

John Dryden scoffed at anagrammatists who 'torture one poor word ten thousand ways', and Jonathan Swift made fun of anagrams in *Gulliver's Travels* (1726):

In the kingdom of Tribnia [i.e. Britain], by the natives called Langdon [i.e. London] . . . plots are discovered by 'the anagrammatic method'—by transposing the letters of the alphabet in any suspected paper, they can lay open the deepest designs of a discontented party. So, for example, if I should say, in a letter to a friend, 'Our brother Tom has just got the piles,' a skilful decipherer would discover that the same letters which compose that sentence, may be analysed into the following words, 'Resist, —— a plot is brought home, —— the tour.'

Anagrams had a practical purpose for some people, as a method of concealing their real name. *Voltaire*, whose real name was Arouet, formed his pseudonym by making an anagram of Arouet L. J. (*le jeune*, the younger) using the *u* as a *v* and the *j* as an *i*. Casanova gave the reason he suspected for this name-change in his *History of my Life*: 'Voltaire would never have attained immortality with the name of Arouet. . . . He would have lost all self-respect if he had constantly heard himself called *à rouer* ("whipping boy").'

Pseudonyms made in this way date back at least to 1539, when Calvin published his *Institutions* under the pen name *Alcuinus*, an anagram of 'Calvinus', the Latin form of his name. François Rabelais used the pseudonym *Alcofribas Nasier*, and Pietro Aretino, a seventeenth-century Venetian writer, called himself *Partenio Etiro*. Jean Tabouret published his *Orchésographie* under the name of *Thoinot Arbeau*. Sydney Dobell the poet gave himself the pseudonym of *Sydney Yendys*, made by reversing his Christian name, and when Honoré de Balzac collaborated on two novels in 1822, he made an anagram of his first name, calling himself Lord *Rhoone*.

Charles I and John Bunyan both found anagrams in their own names. Charles is said to have carved on a window of King's Newton Hall in Derbyshire *Cras ero lux*, turning the Latin version of his title Carolus Rex into 'tomorrow I shall be light'. John Bunyan wrote in *The Holy War* (1682),

> Witness my name, if anagramm'd to thee,
> The letters make, *Nu hony in a B.*

Charles Lutwidge Dodgson considered several pseudonyms before he chose the name Lewis Carroll, which came from Lutwidge-Ludovic-Louis-Lewis, and Charles-Carolus-Carroll. Other names he considered were anagrams of Charles Lutwidge: *Edgar Cuthwellis* and *Edgar U. C. Westhill.*

Lewis Carroll was naturally fond of anagrams. In his diary for 25 November 1868, he recorded:

Wrote a letter to the *Standard*, commenting on a wonderful sentence in *The Times* leader on Gladstone's defeat in Lancashire yesterday: 'The failure of the Liberal policy in one populous district only gives greater weight to the general decision of the country.' I also sent them an anagram which I thought out lying awake the other night: 'William Ewart Gladstone: Wilt tear down *all* images?' I heard of another afterwards, made on the same name: 'I, wise Mr. G., want to lead all'—which is well answered by 'Disraeli: I lead, Sir!'

Carroll later invented two more anagrams of Gladstone's full name: *A wild man will go at trees* and *Wild agitator! Means well.* Other people have devised: *We want a mild legislator; A man to wield great wills; Will mislead a great town; Wit so great will lead man; At will, great wise old man*; and *Go, administrate law well.* Someone even transposed 'Right Honourable William Ewart Gladstone' into *I'm a Whig who'll be a traitor to England's rule.*

In a letter to Maud Standen dated 18 December 1877, Carroll included an 'anagrammatic sonnet' in which each line has four feet and each foot is an anagram: a total of twenty-four anagrams to be solved:

> As to the war, try elm. I tried.
> The wig cast in, I went to ride.
> 'Ring? Yes.' We rang. 'Let's rap.' We don't.
> 'O shew her wit!' As yet she won't.
> Saw eel in Rome. Dry one: he's wet.
> I am dry. O forge! Th'rogue! Why a net?

There have been several suggested solutions to this puzzle, including this one:

> oats. wreath. myrtle. tidier.
> weight. antics. twine. editor (or rioted).
> syringe. gnawer. plaster. wonted.
> whose. wither. yeast. new-shot (or snoweth).
> weasel. merino. yonder. thewes (or seweth).
> myriad. forego. tougher. yawneth.

Roger Lancelyn Green suggested the following poetic solution:

> So at the raw myrtle it ride.
> Weight I scant—twine, or tied.
> In Grey's new rag. Plaster! End tow,
> Whose whiter at—yes, the snow!
> We seal no mire, or deny hew set.
> My raid forego? Hot urge—nay whet!

Other anagrams devised by Lewis Carroll were *Ah! We dread an ugly knave* for Edward Vaughan Kenealy, the defence lawyer for the Tichborne claimant in the famous trial of 1872, and *Flit on, cheering angel* for Florence Nightingale. In the Florence Nightingale anagram, Lewis Carroll was following the model which became prevalent in the nineteenth century: the anagram should be an appropriate description of the person or thing being anagrammed; the more appropriate the description, the better the anagram. Thus, as early as 1605, in *Remains*, William Camden found an appropriate anagram for Charles James Stuart—*Claims Arthur's seat* (referring to King Arthur). Of John Abernethy, a man who stated his views bluntly, Robert Southey said: 'Has any one who knows *Johnny the Bear* heard his name thus anagrammatized without a smile?' (*Doctor*, 1862).

The Masquerade (1797-8) included many of these appropriate anagrams, such as the following:

> revolution—*to love ruin*
> telegraph—*great help*
> misanthrope—*spare him not*
> presbyterian—*best in prayer*
> sweetheart—*there we sat*
> hysterics—*his set cry*
> enigmatical—*in magic tale*

Some of *The Masquerade*'s anagrams created phrases which were the opposite of the anagrammed word. These are sometimes called ANTIGRAMS:

> astronomers—*no more stars*
> festival—*evil fast*
> funeral—*real fun*

while others were sheer nonsense:

> apothecaries—*sheep at Cairo*
> harpsichord—*Richard hops*
> transposition—*no stop it rains*
> machine—*nice ham*

The Boy's Own Book (1828) contained several appropriate anagrams:

> Christianity—*it's in charity*
> Horatio Nelson—*honor est a Nilo* (i.e. his honour comes from the Nile)
> Parishioners—*I hire parsons*
> Penitentiary—*nay, I repent it*
> Radical reform—*rare mad frolic*
> Old England—*golden land*

Macmillan's Magazine for 1862 includes more of this type of anagram (often using *i* for *j*), explaining the less obvious ones in the improbable style of the modern game My Word (q.v.):

James Watt—*a steam wit*
Alfred Tennyson—*ferny land-notes*
James Boswell—*see, Sam, I'll bow*
Edward Gibbon—*Od! big braw Ned* (a complimentary exclamation by an enthusiastic Scotch admirer)
Oliver Cromwell—*more clover, Will* (an anagram beautifully representing Oliver's life when he was a quiet farmer, and had a servant-lad named Will).

It is impossible to list all the appropriate (and inappropriate) anagrams which have been devised. Here is a sample of some of the best, in alphabetical order:

Abandon hope, all ye who enter here—*Hear Dante! Oh, beware yon open hell*
Absence makes the heart grow fonder—*he wants back dearest gone from here*
angered—*enraged*
animosity—*is no amity*
the aristocracy—*a rich Tory caste*
astronomers—*moon-starers*
Beverly Sills—*silvery bells*
boardroom—*Broadmoor*
circumstantial evidence—*actual crime isn't evinced; can ruin a selected victim*
Cleopatra's Needle, London—*an old lone stone replaced*
Clint Eastwood—*Old West action*
conversation—*voices rant on*
Dante Gabriel Rossetti—*greatest born idealist*
desperation—*a rope ends it*
diplomacy—*mad policy*
disappointment—*made in pint pots*
endearments—*tender names*
evangelists—*evil's agents*
the eyes—*they see*
halitosis—*Lois has it*
Hamlet—*Thelma*
Henry Wadsworth Longfellow—*won half the New World's glory*
HMS Pinafore—*name for ship*
interrogatives—*tergiversation*
intoxicate—*excitation*

Ireland—*Erin lad*

ladies—*ideals*

Margaret Thatcher—*that great charmer*; *great charm threat*; *Meg, the arch-tartar*

Marie Antoinette—*i.e. meet a Trianon*

marriage—*a grim era*

Mary Whitehouse—*I may rue the show*

medical consultations—*noted miscalculations*

medication—*decimation*

mother-in-law—*woman Hitler*; *the warm lion*

nameless—*salesmen*; *maleness*; *lameness*

nuclear—*unclear*

one + twelve—*two + eleven*

orchestra—*carthorse*

organ—*groan*

Paradise Lost—*reap sad toils*

Paradise Regained—*dead respire again*

parliament—*partial men*

Piet Mondrian—*I paint modern*

point—*on tip*

prenatal—*parental*; *paternal*

prosecutor—*court poser*

punishment—*nine thumps*

Rome was not built in a day—*any labour I do wants time*

Saint Elmo's fire—*is lit for seamen*

sauciness—*causes sin*

semolina—*is no meal*

soft-heartedness—*often sheds tears*

a stitch in time saves nine—*this is meant as incentive*

total abstainers—*sit not at ale bars*

train—*it ran*

unadorned—*and/or nude*

vanities—*vain ties*

Victoria, England's Queen—*governs a nice quiet land*

waitress—*a stew, sir?*

Western Union—*no wire unsent*

William Shakespeare—*We all make his praise*; *I ask me, has Will a peer?*; *a weakish speller, am I?*

One of the most famous anagrams is also one of the simplest. The Latin words of Pilate's question to Jesus: 'Quid est veritas?' ('What is truth?') can be turned into the answer: '*Est vir qui adest*' ('It is the man who is before you').

Anagrams can be very complex, leading people to great flights of ingenuity. The nineteenth-century scientist Augustus de Morgan said that a friend made about 800 anagrams on his name, including these:

> Gus! Gus! a mature don!
> August man! sure, god!
> And Gus must argue, O!
> Go! turn us! damage us!
> Grudge us! Moan at us!
>
> (*Budget of Paradoxes*, 1872)

The word *monastery* has enjoyed a particular fascination for anagrammatists. One Edinburgh newspaper printed a story which included fifty anagrams of it, and Bombaugh quotes the following, which contains fourteen examples:

How much there is in a word—*monastery*, says I: why, that makes *nasty Rome*; and when I looked at it again, it was evidently *more nasty*— a very vile place *or mean sty*. Ay, *monster*, says I, you are found out. What monster? said the Pope. What monster? said I. Why, your own image there, *stone Mary*. That, he replied, is *my one star*, my Stella Maris, my treasure, my guide! No, said I, you should rather say, *my treason. Yet no arms*, said he. No, quoth I, quiet may suit best, as long as you have *no mastery*, I mean, *money arts*. No, said he again, those are *Tory means*; and Dan, *my senator*, will baffle them. I don't know that, said I, but I think one might make no *mean story* out of this one word—*monastery*. (*Gleanings for the Curious*, 1890)

Similar ingenuity has been employed by those who claimed that Francis Bacon wrote the plays of Shakespeare. In *Notes and Queries* for 30 November 1901, a correspondent pointed out that the last two lines of the Epilogue to Shakespeare's *The Tempest*:

> As you for crimes would pardon'd be,
> Let your indulgence set me free

can be anagrammed (with the addition of one 'a') to:

> 'Tempest' of Francis Bacon, Lord Verulam.
> Do ye ne'er divulge me, ye words!

However, subsequent correspondents pointed out that Bacon was not created Lord Verulam until 1618, eight years after *The Tempest* was probably written!

Perhaps rather more constructively, some writers have tried to make appropriate anagrams from famous lines in Shakespeare's plays, such as 'My kingdom for a horse' ('*OHMS. Go for dinky mare*') and 'Frailty, thy name is woman' ('*It's a whim of male tyranny*'). Hubert Phillips created some nonsensical anagrams from the titles of Shakespeare's plays:

> *Not men to a fish* (Timon of Athens)
> *Our idol met Jean* (Romeo and Juliet)
> *Free women love not gnat* (Two Gentlemen of Verona).

Hubert Phillips also wrote anagram puzzle verses, in which spaces had to be filled in with words that make anagrams of each other:

> 'The - - - - - - are terribly small,'
> Say I to my wife in the hall.
> Her big - - - - - - eyes
> Open wide: she replies:
> 'It was - - - - - - I ordered: that's all!'

The answers are: *melons, solemn,* and *lemons.*

W. R. Espy is fond of this type of puzzle:

I Hope to Meet my Bartender Face to Face

> 'Twould much - - - - - - you to me if, when I
> Have - - - - - - my fatal moment, and must die,
> You'd share one well - - - - - - drink, and pray there are
> Some more to come across that final bar.

The blanks are filled by *endear, neared,* and *earned.* These are similar to logogriphs (q.v.). Godfrey Bullard and Anthony Creery-Hill carried such verses to extremes in their HUNTERGRAMS (named after Hunter Skinner, who was fond of such poetry). These are poems containing as many as thirty-six anagrammed words, left blank for the reader to solve. Thus, Creery-Hill's poem 'Lament for Time Passing' starts:

> While contemplating hour by hour
> The glass of - - - - - - - -
> In March's final, turbid days
> I pen this halting rhyme:
> Its - - - - - - - -'- always brings us news
> Particularly sinister
> But yet - - - - - - - - - see the choice
> Of Britain's next Prime Minister;

And, ere -'- - -- - --- older, nor
Much farther down Life's road,
How - - - - - - - - - political
May then have ebbed and flowed!
I'd build a wall against them; - - -
-'- - - - - them if I could;
But not in groynes nor - - - - - - - - -
Can oceans be withstood.

The words filling the gaps are: *sandy Time*; *Ides mayn't*; *its end may*; *I'm ten days*; *many tides*; *nay I'd stem*; *yet in dams*.

Another type of anagram puzzle gives clues to pairs of words that are anagrams of one another:

hidden promise—*latent talent*
sea-going craft—*ocean canoe*
drink fit for a king—*regal lager*
object in outer space—*remote meteor*
invent a card game—*create écarté*
bring back the visitor—*recall caller*
barefooted dogs—*unshod hounds*
brave foreigner on the Baltic—*valiant Latvian*
glorified hopelessness—*praised despair*
race-course cadet—*Aintree trainee*
undisturbed invaders—*unstirred intruders*
a drummer in Concorde—*supersonic percussion*
Marks and Spencers making gold—*St Michael's alchemists*

Many party games are based on anagrams. Participants can be given jumbled letters to turn into words, usually in a particular category (the names of birds, flowers, towns, etc.), or they can be asked to make a word by adding one letter to an anagram ('add a letter to *least* and get a pale colour'—*pastel*). Contestants can be asked to make anagrams by adding one letter at a time to a given word (e.g. *an-tan-neat-meant-anthem*).

Anagrams as a pursuit in themselves seem to have declined in popularity after the Victorian era. They became an essential part of cryptic crosswords and it is in crosswords that they are most commonly found today. However, there is still a dedicated minority that continues to juggle letters for entertainment. In 1981 Richard Stilgoe published a book of stories about imaginary people whose names were all anagrams of his own name. These included *Gerald I. Ostrich*,

Sir Eric Goldhat, Eric Roadlights, Giscard O'Hitler, Dr Gloria Ethics, and *Giles T. Haircord.*

The American magazine *Word Ways* published several articles on anagrams in 1982, including one about anagrams from the titles of Sherlock Holmes stories, and an 'Anagram Composing Contest' in which competitors had to write anagrams on such lines as 'The wages of sin is death' (*'He "swings", dies; a hot fate'*) and 'April is the cruellest month' (*'Poet, hurt, tells lies in March'*).

Finally, a letter in the *Guardian* for 29 October 1982 asked: 'Is there any significance in the fact that "I help the great lady" is an anagram of *The Daily Telegraph*?'

9

The Rebus

A REBUS uses pictures, numbers, and letters of the alphabet, to make words and sentences. Every schoolchild used to know this rebus:

> If the B mt put :
> If the B. putting :

This means:

> If the grate be empty, put coal on.
> If the grate be full, stop putting coal on.

Another well-known rebus is this rhyme:

> YY U R
> YY U B
> I C U R
> YY 4 me.

Which means:

> Too wise you are
> Too wise you be.
> I see you are
> Too wise for me.

A form of this verse is found as early as the 1740s in a book called *Delights for Young Men and Maids*, which had twenty sentences made from different sequences of the same symbols:

> I c u b 2 yy for me
>
> U b I c 2 yy for me

and so on.

Rebuses can be very simple:

$$\frac{B}{E} = \textit{bone} \text{ (b on e)}$$

$$\frac{J}{AH} = \textit{Jonah (J on ah)}$$

$$\frac{\text{arrest}}{\text{you're}} = \textit{you're under arrest}$$

They can also be very ingenious:

$$\frac{\textit{I have to}}{\text{work}} \quad \text{because} \quad \frac{\textit{paid}}{\text{I am}} = \textit{I have to overwork because I am underpaid}$$

timing tim ing = *split second timing*

$$\begin{array}{l} \text{UR 2 GOOD} \\ \phantom{\text{UR }}2 \text{ ME} \\ \phantom{\text{UR }}2 \text{ BE} \\ \phantom{\text{UR }}4 \text{ GOT} \\ \hline 10 = \textit{You are too good to me to be forgotten} \\ = \end{array}$$

The word 'rebus' (pronounced *ree*-buss) comes from the Latin *res*, a thing. It may mean 'by things', because the rebus uses things, not words, to represent a phrase. A more complex explanation is given by 'a Cantab' in his *Charades, Enigmas, and Riddles* (1862):

Menage says the name is derived from certain tracts issued annually by the priests of Picardy, about Carnival time, for the purpose of exposing misdemeanours which had been committed in their neighbourhood. These pamphlets were entitled, *De Rebus quae geruntur* ('about things which are going on'), and the breakings and joinings of the words were filled in with pictures. Were not similar emblematic warnings employed by the Scythians? When Darius had invaded their country, and was in great straits, they sent him a bird, a frog, a mouse, and five arrows. The Persian monarch considered this as a surrender of their land, their streams, and their forces; but Gobryas, a looker-on, interpreted these objects as follows,—'Unless, O Persians, ye become birds and fly in the air, or become mice and hide yourselves beneath the earth, or become frogs and leap into the lakes, ye shall never return home, but be stricken by these arrows!'

The idea of the rebus first took shape in ancient Egypt about 3,000 BC in the form of hieroglyphics, which used pictures and other symbols as letters of the alphabet. Hieroglyphics were also used by the Hittites, Minoans, Mayas, and Incas. Egyptian hieroglyphics, like rebuses, were mainly phonetic signs—that is to say, they represented not the object pictured but some other thing that had a name with a similar sound. When Egypt was converted to Christianity in the second and third centuries AD, hieroglyphics were replaced by the Greek alphabet.

Arthur Watson noted that:

The ancient Greeks make frequent use of the rebus on the coins of their cities and islands. Thus the Greek colony of Selinus, in Sicily, which derived its name from the wild parsley growing there in profusion, was represented on its coins by an image of this plant. In the same way the coins of Rhodes bore a rose, those of Melos a pomegranate, those of Phocaea a seal, and the city of Ancona was represented by a bent arm, the word *angkon* meaning a bend. (*The Antiquary*, 1898)

Joseph Addison commented on the use of a rebus by Julius Caesar:

When Caesar was one of the masters of the Roman Mint, he placed the figure of an elephant upon the reverse of the public money; the word *Caesar* signifying an elephant in the Punic language. This was artificially contrived by Caesar, because it was not lawful for a private man to stamp his own figure upon the coin of the Commonwealth. . . . This kind of wit was very much in vogue among our own countrymen about an age or two ago, who did not practise it for any oblique reason, as the ancients abovementioned, but purely for the sake of being witty. . . . Mr Newberry, to represent his name by a picture, hung up at his door the sign of a yew-tree, that had several berries upon it, and in the midst of them a great golden *N* hung upon a bough of the tree, which by the help of a little false spelling made up the word *N-ew-berry*. (*The Spectator*, 1711)

Rebuses became popular in England for this kind of heraldic device about the time of Edward III. The Abbot of Ramsey's heraldic seal portrayed a ram in the sea. William Camden mentioned in his *Remains* (1605) 'a hare by a sheaf of rye in the sun for Harrison; Med written on a calf for Medcalfe; Chester, a chest with a star over it'.

The Revd Charles Boutell described a gravestone at Bowes in Yorkshire 'to mark the grave of some members of the De Bowes family. The rebus of this surname, two bows, is sculptured on the slab on one side of the stem of the cross.' (*Christian Monuments in England and Wales*, 1854.) As there were two bows, could it perhaps be a half-French pun on 'deux bows'?

In Ben Jonson's *The Alchemist* (1610), the swindling alchemist Subtle devises a sign for the shop of Abel Drugger:

> He first shall have a bell, that's *Abel*;
> And, by it, standing one, whose name is *Dee*,
> In a rug gown; there's D and *rug*, that's *Drug*:

> And right anenst him, a dog snarling *Er*;
> There's *Drugger*, *Abel Drugger*. That's his sign.

Such rebuses were very useful in the days when many people could not read. In his *English Surnames* (1842), Mark Antony Lower gave some more notable examples:

The parsonage-house at Great Snoring, in Norfolk, is only known to have been built by one of the family of *Shelton* by the device upon it representing a *shell* upon a *tun* (i.e. a barrel).

Quaint was the conceit of Robert Langton, who gave new windows to Queen's College, Oxford (where he received his education), and placed in each of them the letters TON drawn out to a most extraordinary length, or rather breadth, for *Lang-* (that is, *Long-*)*ton*.

The rebus of Ralph Hoge or Hogge . . . at the village of Buxted, in Sussex, was a *hog*. On the front of his residence this device remains carved on stone, with the date 1591; from which circumstance the dwelling is called the 'Hog-house'.

George Herbert used the rebus for less secular purposes in his poem 'Jesu' (1633):

> Jesu is in my heart, his sacred name
> Is deeply carved there: but th'other week
> A great affliction broke the little frame,
> Ev'n all to pieces, which I went to seek;
> And first I found the corner, where was *J*,
> After, where *ES*, and next where *U* was graved.
> When I had got these parcels, instantly
> I sat me down to spell them, and perceived
> That to my broken heart he was *I ease you*,
> And to my whole is *JESU*.

Another religious use for the rebus was discovered in the eighteenth century, when 'Hieroglyphic Bibles' were published. Pictures took the place of some of the words, to help children read the Bible with interest (see p. 88). In the same century the rebus developed into a kind of puzzle. *A New Collection of Enigmas* (1810) includes this:

> Three fourths of a cross and a circle complete,
> Two semicircles and a perpendicular meet,
> A triangle standing on two feet;
> Two semicircles and a circle complete.

The answer is TOBACCO.

THE FALL.

ONE day Eve saw a ⸻ which spoke to her, telling her to stretch forth her ✋ and pluck the 🍎 of the forbidden 🌳 and this she did, giving some of it also to 🧍. Their 👁 👁 were opened, and they knew they had sinned. They felt afraid, and hid themselves among the 🌳. But God found them out, and drove them from Eden, placing an 👼 with a flaming 🗡 at the 🏰.

to prevent their return. After this the ⸻ brought forth 🌾 s and 🌿 s and Adam had to 🔨 the ground and work hard to get things to grow.

CAIN AND ABEL.

THERE were two sons of Adam and Eve. Cain, the elder, was a 🧑‍🌾 and Abel, the younger, was a 🐑. Each of them brought . an 🏛 to God because of their sin. Cain brought the 🌾 .

1893 Hieroglyphic Bible 2524. g. 1 + 2

Thomas Owen's *Puzzles for Leisure Hours* (1876) contained rebuses as simple as the one mentioned at the start of this chapter ('If the grate be empty . . .') and puzzles of much greater complexity:

rebellion		rebellion
	In 1789	
FRA NCE		laws
monarchy thrown		religion
rebellion		rebellion

This means: 'In 1789 France was divided, monarchy overthrown, laws set aside, religion turned upside down, and rebellion at every corner.'

Pictures representing words were interspersed into the text of puzzles and of letters such as that from Lewis Carroll to Georgina Watson picture on page 89. As time went on, the complexity of such rebuses increased, until they looked like that pictured on page 90, reproduced from the *Competitor's Annual* of 1930. Rebuses

The ○◉◐○◉

My 🦌 Ina,

Though 👁 don't give birthday presents, still ···*April* write a birthday ✉. *June* 👁 came 2 your 🚪 2 wish U many happy returns of the day, 🛢 the 🐱 met me, ✋ took me for a 〰, ✋ hunted me👉 and👉 till 👣 could hardly 🏚 However somehow 👁 got into the 🏠, ✋ there a 🐱 met me, ✋ took me for a 🐿, and pelted me

1975 JOHN FISHER *Magic of Lewis Carroll* (from *Letters* (1979) I. 142–3)

consisting of letters and numbers meanwhile continued to thrive, and *Foulsham's Fun Book* of 1933 has this verse:

> 2 U, O! 2 U
> I vow 2 B true;
> 2 C U Y I
> In XTC HI!
> I H8 LN G.,
> Always following me;
> 4 U, O! U R
> NICR-looking by far!
> So when I   C L N,
> My head I shall toss;
> & U, if U chance 2,
> B sure 2 look X.

Foulsham also has simpler forms of rebus:

EGNC (*Aegean Sea*)
FEG (*effigy*)

XLNC (*excellency*)
AYZ (*a wise head*)
DK (*decay*)
OICURMT (*Oh, I see you are empty*)
XQQ (*excuse*)
DDEE (*disease*)

A few years ago, Double Diamond beer was advertised with such phrases as 'DD 4 U'. In February 1983, the music journal *New Musical Express* advertised a forthcoming appearance by a band called U2 with the words 'U2 4U 2C'. But rebuses seem to have gone out of fashion and they are seldom found except in the pages of children's comics or adult word-game magazines. One of the latter, as recently as 1982, included the following:

CRe = vanishing cream

FECpoxTION = smallpox infection

A ^{I} C = archaic

CRED IBILITY = credibility gap

Let us leave the last word to the Irish humorist Myles na Gopaleen, from his *Literary Criticism*:

> My grasp of what he wrote and meant
> Was only five or six %
> The rest was only words and sound
> My reference is to Ezra £.

10

Chronograms

Writing in *The Spectator* of 9 May 1711, Joseph Addison described a strange way of using words to indicate a date:

There is another near relation of the anagrams and acrostics, which is commonly called a chronogram. This kind of wit appears very often on many modern medals, especially those of Germany, when they represent in the inscription the year in which they were coined. Thus we see on a medal of Gustavus Adolphus the following words, ChrIstVs DuX ergo trIVMphVs. If you take the pains to pick the figures out of the several words, and range them in their proper order, you will find they amount to MDCXVVVII, or 1627, the year in which the medal was stamped: for as some of the letters distinguish themselves from the rest, and overtop their fellows, they are to be considered in a double capacity, both as letters and as figures. Your laborious German wits will turn over a whole dictionary for one of these ingenious devices. A man would think they were searching for an apt classical term, but instead of that they are looking out a word that has an L, and M, or a D in it. When therefore we meet with any of these inscriptions, we are not so much to look in 'em for the thought, as for the year of the Lord.

The CHRONOGRAM has some fairly obvious limitations, for it can only employ words containing the letters used as Roman numerals: C (100), D (500), I (1), L (50), M(1000), V (5) and X(10). I is sometimes used for J, and V can be used instead of U, while the letter W can be obtained by printing two V's.

As Addison suggested, the letters which make up such a date are usually shown larger than the surrounding letters. An eighteenth-century satirist, Richard Cambridge, visualized chronograms drawn up in ranks like undisciplined soldiers:

> Not thus the looser chronograms prepare,
> Careless their troops, undisciplin'd to war,
> With ranks irregular, confus'd, they stand,
> The chieftains mingling with the vulgar band.

(*Scribleriad*, 1752)

Such strange uneven rows of letters can be found on old medals, bells, church windows, tombstones, and the title-pages of books. On medals the chronogram commemorates the date of an event; on bells it indicates when the bell was made; and in epitaphs it shows when a particular person died.

Inevitably, chronograms are found most often in Latin inscriptions. Indeed, some Latin words are complete chronograms: *cui*, *illi*, *lux*, *vix*, etc. In the *Epigrammata* of Bernard Bauhusius (or Bauhuis) SJ, printed at Antwerp in 1616, one verse ends:

> Scripsimus anno haec
> Quo cunctis licuit scribere JVDICIVM.

thus expressing the date of 1613 in a single Latin word. The word LILICIDIVM ('the slaughter of the lily') is inscribed on a medal commemorating the Battle of Tasniers in Flanders (1709), when the Duke of Marlborough defeated the French.

Most chronograms, however, use several words, like this inscription on the treble bell at the church of Clifton-on-Teme:

> henrICVs Ieffrey keneLMo DeVoVIt

which commemorates the year when the bell was cast. Such inscriptions are found on bells as late as 1887 (at Repton) and 1903 (at Overbury in Worcestershire). Other chronograms have been found in Britain on a monument in Westminster Abbey, on the ceiling of Winchester Cathedral, and over the door of Sherborne School. British chronograms most often occur in Latin sentences but R. Tisdale's *Pax Vobis* (1623) includes chronograms both in Latin and English. This book celebrates the twenty-first year of King James's reign, with chronograms such as this:

IaMes by the graCe of goD, Is a kIng, noVV neVer Vnhappy (MDCVVVVIII or 1623).

The tower of St Edmund's Church in Salisbury was rebuilt in 1653, and the event was marked by the inscription: 'praIse hIM o yee ChILDren'.

Chronograms—like the related rebus (q.v.)—were very popular in Britain at this time. In 1647, Sir John Birkenhead said of the Westminster divines that 'Of late they are much in love with chronograms, because, if possible, they are duller than anagrams. Oh how they have torn the poor bishops' names, to pick out the number six-hundred sixty-six!' ('Assembly-Man', *Harleian Miscellany*, 1745).

The 1652 publication-date of a book printed in London was expressed by a chronogram in the editor's name on the title-page:

Hugo Grotius, his Sophompaneas, or Joseph, a tragedy, with annotations by franCIs goLDsMIth.

In the same book, the epitaph of Thomas Walters, a schoolmaster who died in 1651, concludes with lines giving the full date of his death:

> the Last nIght of DeCeMber
> he resteD froM aLL hIs Labors.

When the Dutch fleet threatened the Thames in the year of the Fire of London, George Wither devised the following prayer: 'LorD haVe MerCIe Vpon Vs.'

Perhaps surprisingly, chronograms were not used by the ancient Romans, but they are found written in Hebrew as early as 1208, in Latin from 1210, and in Arabic from 1380. James Hilton, the nineteenth-century authority on chronograms, credits the sixteenth-century German writer Joseph à Pinu with popularizing the chronogram: 'he seems to have been the first to have published pamphlets and books wholly devoted to the subject'.

Chronograms had a particular attraction for religious men, sometimes leading them to make fools of themselves. H. B. Wheatley recounted the following sad tale:

A passage of Scripture, arranged chronogrammatically, was made the vehicle for a prophecy by Michael Stifelius, a Lutheran minister at Wirtemberg, who foretold that on the 3rd of October 1533, at ten o'clock in the morning, the world would come to an end. The passage from which he elicited this wonderful, and as it proved inaccurate, prediction, is in John xix. 37— 'They shall look on him whom they pierced', VIDebVnt In qVem transfiXerVnt, making MDXVVVVVIII or 1533; but the month, the day and the hour seem only to have existed in the excited imagination of Stifelius himself. . . . On the day that Stifelius predicted the end of the world, a very violent storm arose while he was preaching to his congregation, who believed his prophecy was coming to pass, when lo! suddenly the clouds disappeared, the sky became clear, and all was calm except the people, whose indignation was aroused, and they dragged the prophet from his pulpit and beat him sorely for thus disappointing them. (*Of Anagrams*, 1862)

The Jesuits took a particular delight in creating chronograms, or in making them from passages in Virgil, Horace, Ovid, and even the Bible. A Jesuit translated Thomas à Kempis's *Imitation of Christ* into chronograms, with each line making the date of publication: 1658. A Latin book published at Salzburg in 1663 praised the Virgin Mary with 2,727 chronograms. Its author was a parish priest named Mauritius Nagengast but he calls himself 'Alter Idiota'—'another idiot'.

The craze for chronograms spread from Germany to England towards the end of the sixteenth century. Shakespeare alluded to the kind of letter-play used in chronograms when he made the pedantic Holofernes in *Love's Labour's Lost* say:

> If sore be sore, then L to sore makes fifty sores; O sore L!
> Of one sore I an hundred make, by adding but one more L.

An epitaph on Queen Elizabeth signifies the year she died, 1603: 'My Day Closed Is In Immortality.' And in the parish church of Warminster, an epitaph on Hester Potticary gives the year and her age when she died:

> pVre VesseLs of MerCy enIoy happIness VVIth goD   (1673)
> VertVe In her Is not VVItherIng   (24)

The chronogram habit persisted in Britain right into Victorian times. The bad weather of 1879 led 'some ladies at a pleasant country house in Essex' to write, 'thIs year VVe haVe a LIVing reCoLLeCtIon of MVD!' And in 1880, the following epitaph was written for a naughty dog named 'Floss' which was punished for its conduct somewhere in Bedfordshire: 'In thIs year CaCo CanIne fLoss Met a VVatery enD, ah! grIeVoVs eVent. heIgho!'

James Hilton compiled three books about chronograms between 1882 and 1895. He claimed to have collected no fewer than 38,411 chronograms. The title-page describes his first book as: 'an eX-CeLLent neVV book of ChronograMs gathereD together and noVV set forth by I. hILton'. A reviewer wrote:

It is impossible to think of any more witless, pointless effort of literary ingenuity. . . . We confess to a feeling of dread lest the thing should spread and become common. Nothing can be more likely unless it is nipped in the bud. We have hardly yet got rid of 'double acrostics'. They linger still in the back pages of some of the 'society papers'. But chronograms are so much more foolish, so much more senseless, and so much easier to make and to guess, that there is every reason to fear an outbreak of them before long. (*Saturday Review*, 6 January 1883)

These fears were unjustified. Despite Hilton's massive research, chronograms remained a historical curiosity and they now seldom appear except as parts of puzzles or crossword clues. Here is a comparatively rare twentieth-century example:

> To five and five and forty-five
> The first of letters add,
> 'Twill give a thing
> That killed a king,
> And drove a wise man mad.
>
> (*Notes and Queries*, 11 May 1929)

Possible answers include *law* and *love*. Another explanation is *lava*, since Pyrrhus, the king, was killed by a tile made of lava, and Empedocles committed suicide by jumping into the crater of Etna.

When the *Observer*'s crossword-compiler, Azed, held a dinner to celebrate his 250th puzzle, the menu included CoCkaLeekie soup and ChiCken maryLand. These chronograms are imperfect because they contain the letters I and M which should have been taken into account.

The same fault afflicted some of Paul Hallweg's chronograms when he tried to revive the form in 1982. However, he introduced a new requirement: that the 'number' letters should make the first sound of each word. So he commemorates 1969, the year of the first landing on the moon, with: 'Men Can Make Lunar eXcursions In eXtravagance', and he marks 1903's first aeroplane flight with: 'Man's Creativity Manifested In Impossible Invention'.

11

Palindromes

The word PALINDROME comes from the Greek *palindromos* which means 'running back again'. A palindrome is a line, word, poem, or longer item which reads the same backwards as it does forwards.

It is unlikely that palindromes date back to the time of the Garden of Eden, even though one of the best-known examples is *Madam, I'm Adam*, which one might imagine Adam saying to Eve (whose name itself is a palindrome).

Palindromes were possibly invented about the third century BC by the Thracian poet Sotades, which accounts for their alternative name of 'Sotadics'. In his *Epigrams*, the Roman poet Martial says: 'I do not . . . read backwards in obscene Sotadics.' Sotades' poetry was noted for its 'coarseness and scurrility', and H. B. Wheatley tells us that 'an end was put to his existence by Ptolemy Philadelphus, who, irritated at his satires, had him thrown into the sea'. Quintilian quotes these palindromic lines from Sotades:

> *Roma, tibi subito motibus ibit amor,*
> *Si bene te tua laus taxat, sua laute tenebis,*
> *Sole medere pede, ede, perede melos.*

Sidonius Apollinaris, a Gallo-Roman of the fourth century AD, was responsible for the earliest surviving example of another kind of palindrome, in which the order of the words (not the letters) is reversed:

> *Sacrificabo macrum nec dabo pingue sacrum.*

When these words are read in the right direction, they could be the words of Cain ('I will sacrifice the lean and will not sacrifice the fat'); read backwards they could be spoken by Abel ('I will sacrifice the fat and will not sacrifice the lean'), referring to Genesis 4: 3, 4: 'Cain brought of the fruit of the ground, an offering unto the Lord. And Abel, he also brought of the firstlings of his flock, and of the fat thereof.'

Another palindrome attributed to Sidonius is:

> *Signa te signa; temere me tangis et angis;*
> *Roma tibi subito motibus ibit amor.*

Note that it borrows one of the lines quoted previously from Sotades. C. C. Bombaugh in his *Gleanings for the Curious from the Harvest-fields of Literature* (1890) says that these lines were supposedly spoken by the Devil to St Martin when the latter was travelling to Rome to visit the Pope. St Martin met Satan and made him carry him on his back towards the Holy City, urging him on by making the sign of the Cross. Satan's words mean: 'Cross, cross yourself; you annoy and vex me unnecessarily for, owing to my exertions, Rome—the object of your wishes—will soon be near.'

Bombaugh also quotes the lawyer's palindromic motto—*Si nummi immunis*—which William Camden translated as 'Give me my fee, and I warrant you free'. And Bombaugh mentions a lady who was banished from the court of Queen Elizabeth, 'on suspicion of too great familiarity with a nobleman then high in favour'. This lady adopted the emblem of the moon covered by a cloud, with the palindromic motto *Ablata at alba*, that is 'Banished but blameless'.

Palindromes were certainly popular in England in the late sixteenth and early seventeenth centuries, but most of them were in Latin. William Camden in his *Remains* (1605) quotes several, including one that alludes to 'Odo, holding Master Doctor's mule, and Anne with her tablecloth':

> *Odo tenet mulum, madidam mappam tenet Anna.*

Camden also says: 'A scholar and a gentleman, living in a rude country town where he had no respect, wrote this with a coal in the Town Hall: "*Subi dura a rudibus*".' It means 'Endure rough treatment from uncultured brutes'.

The earliest traceable palindrome in English was devised by John Taylor. In his *Nipping or Snipping of Abuses* (1614), he wrote:

This line is the same backward, as it is forward, and I will give any man five shillings apiece for as many as they can make in English.
> *Lewd did I live, & evil I did dwel.*

This palindrome depends on an ampersand in the middle and an old spelling of 'dwell'. Nowadays, it would be better written as 'Evil I did dwell; lewd did I live.'

In the same book, John Taylor has these lines:

> *To Anna Queen of Great Britain*
> These backward and these forward lines I send,
> To your right royal high majestic hand . . .
> > *Deer Maddam reed:*
> > *Deem if I meed.*

The Victorians loved palindromes. During the nineteenth century the pages of *Notes and Queries* were full of discussion about a famous Greek example, ΝΙΨΟΝ ΑΝΟΜΗΜΑΤΑ ΜΗ ΜΟΝΑΝ ΟΨΙΝ. This means 'Cleanse your sins and not only your face' and it echoes the second verse of Psalm 51: 'Wash me throughly from mine iniquity, and cleanse me from my sin.' It has been inscribed in ancient churches throughout the world, chiefly on fonts and containers for holy water. It has been found, for example, around the recess of the holy-water stoup in St Sophia at Constantinople; in the churches of Notre Dame and St Stephen's in Paris; on the rim of a large silver dish used to hold rose-water on feast days at Trinity College, Cambridge; and on fonts in many British churches, such as St Mary's at Nottingham, Longley Castle Chapel in Norfolk, Dedham and Harlow in Essex, and Sandbach in Cheshire.

Edgar Allan Poe has been credited with the authorship of a puzzle published in the *Saturday Evening Post* in 1827. The solution is an acrostic (q.v.) consisting of palindromic words:

> First find out a word that doth silence proclaim,
> And backwards and forwards is always the same;
> Then next you must find a feminine name
> That backwards and forwards is always the same;
> An act or a writing or parchment whose name
> Both backwards and forwards is always the same;
> A fruit that is rare whose botanical name
> Read backwards and forwards is always the same;
> A note used in music which time doth proclaim,
> And backwards and forwards is always the same;
> Their initials connected a title will frame
> That is justly the due of the fair married dame,
> Which backwards and forwards is always the same.

The answer is:

$$M \quad U \quad M$$
$$A \quad N \quad N \quad A$$
$$D \quad E \quad E \quad D$$
$$A \quad N \quad A \quad N \quad A$$
$$M \quad I \quad N \quad I \quad M$$

This poem echoes one written 116 years earlier by Jonathan Swift in *The Windsor Prophecy*:

> Root out these carrots, O thou, whose name
> Is backwards and forwards always the same;
> And keep close to thee always that name,
> Which backwards and forwards is almost the same.

This is a warning to the Queen (Anna) against the Duchess of Somerset (carrots) who had red hair, and in favour of Lady Masham who was a friend of Swift and bedchamber woman to Queen Anne.

As might be expected, Lewis Carroll was interested in palindromes as in all other forms of word play. In *Sylvie and Bruno Concluded* we find this:

Sylvie was arranging some letters on a board—E-V-I-L. 'Now Bruno,' she said, 'what does *that spell?*'

Bruno looked at it, in solemn silence, for a minute. 'I know what it *doesn't* spell!' he said at last.

'That's no good,' said Sylvie. 'What *does* it spell?' Bruno took another look at the mysterious letters, 'Why, it's "LIVE", backwards!' he exclaimed. (I thought it was, indeed,)

'How *did* you manage to see that?' said Sylvie.

'I just twiddled my eyes,' said Bruno, 'and then I saw it directly.'

In his diary for 30 June 1892, Carroll wrote: 'Invented what I think is a new kind of riddle: "A Russian had three sons. The first, named Rab, became a lawyer; the second, Ymra, became a soldier. The third became a sailor: what was his name?"' The answer is *Yvan*, as the three spell *Bar*, *Army*, and *Navy* backwards. These words are not perfect palindromes, since they cannot read the same in both directions, yet they illustrate the fascination of seeing what happens when you turn words around.

This was the kind of fascination felt by Hazel Shade in Vladimir Nabokov's novel *Pale Fire* (1962). She liked reversing words, making *pot* into *top* and *spider* into *redips*. Even in the world of pop music one can find this interest. The American singer Stevie Wonder made a record album in 1968 under the name of *Eivets Rednow*. The title of an LP by Black Sabbath in 1983 was *Live Evil*. And the Swedish vocal quartet Abba regularly spells its palindromic name as ABᙠA. Their hit record 'SOS' had the distinction of having palindromes both for the song-title and for the name of the group.

Palindromes are not easy to invent. A writer in 1867 described both the agony and the ecstasy of trying to create a perfect palindromic sentence:

Those only who have amused their leisure with such trifles know how difficult it is to construct a palindromic verse which can assert its claims to sense and grammar. In fact, the consonantal collocations peculiar to every language offer, when reversed, the greatest possible difficulty. The common English *th* (for instance), when reversed into *ht*, will illustrate my meaning sufficiently. You may make ridiculous lines, like the following, addressed (if you please) to a costermonger's dying cur—'Go droop—stop—onward draw no pots poor dog'—or you may make a dozen Latin ones . . . but I never yet saw any, in any language, which deserved to be called *good*. (*Notes and Queries*, 22 June 1867)

There are, in fact, many good English palindromes, although the best ones tend to be short. Most people know a few familiar ones, such as the words attributed to Napoleon, '*Able was I ere I saw Elba*', or those written to honour the man who devised the Panama Canal: '*A man, a plan, a canal— Panama*' (attributed to Leigh Mercer).

The composer Henry Purcell is said to have written: '*Egad! A base tone denotes a bad age.*' There are many other palindromes that make acceptable sense, such as the dramatic:

> *God! a dog!*
> *Ooh, a yahoo!*
> *Draw, O coward!*
> *Niagara, O roar again!*
> *Nurse, I spy gypsies, run!*

Some palindromes tell a short story:

> *Sad? I'm Midas.*
> *Dennis and Edna sinned.*
> *Now, Ned, I am a maiden nun; Ned, I am a maiden won.*
> *Snug & raw was I ere I saw war & guns.*

Others sound almost proverbial:

> *Sums are not set as a test on Erasmus.*
> *Sex at noon taxes.*
> *Live not on evil.*

The world of palindromes is populated with people called *Ada*, *Anna*, *Bob*, and similarly useful names:

> *Adam, I'm Ada.*
> *Bob: 'Did Anna peep?' Anna: 'Did Bob?'*
> *Sir, I demand— I am a maid named Iris.*
> *'Tis Ivan, on a visit.*
> *I moan, Naomi.*

As palindromes get longer, sense tends to be left behind, although some examples use unexpectedly long words:

> *No, it is opposition.*
> *Harass sensuousness, Sarah.*
> *Satan, oscillate my metallic sonatas.*
> *Kay, a red nude, peeped under a yak.*
> *A new order began, a more Roman age bred Rowena.*
> *Straw? No, too stupid a fad. I put soot on warts.*
> *Doc, note. I dissent. A fast never prevents a fatness. I diet on cod.*
> *Degas, are we not drawn onward, we freer few, drawn onward to new eras aged?*

Much longer palindromes than these have been devised but they seldom make good sense. This never stops the dedicated palindrome-writer from trying. Alastair Reid says:

The dream which preoccupies the tortuous mind of every palindromist is that somewhere within the confines of the language lurks the Great Palindrome, a nutshell which not only fulfils the intricate demands of the art, flowing sweetly in both directions, but which also contains the Final Truth of Things.

However, Reid's own longest creation is hardly profound:

T. Eliot, top bard, notes putrid tang emanating, is sad. I'd assign it a name: 'Gnat dirt upset on drab pot toilet'.

In his book *Passwords* (1959), Reid quotes palindromes in French ('*Eh, ça va, la vache?*') and Spanish ('*Dabale arroz a la zorra el abad*') as well as one attributed to James Thurber: '*Peel's lager on red rum did murder no regal sleep*' (which is explained as an advertisement disguised as a line from *Macbeth*!).

Experts like Graham Reynolds, Leigh Mercer, and J. A. Lindon have written some extremely long palindromes, and Giles Selig Hales claimed in 1980 to have written 'the world's longest palindrome' of 58,795 letters.

One of the best long palindromes was written by Joyce Johnson for a *New Statesman* competition in 1967. It has 126 words, 467 letters:

HEADMASTER'S PALINDROMIC LIST ON HIS MEMO PAD

Test on Erasmus

Deliver slap

Royal: phone no.?

Ref. Football.

Is sofa sitable on?

XI—Staff over

Sub-edit Nurse's order

Caning is on test (snub slip-up)

Birch (Sid) to help Miss Eve

Repaper den

Use it

Put inkspot on stopper

Prof.—no space

Caretaker (wall, etc.)

Too many d— pots

Wal for duo? (I'd name Dr O)

See few owe fees (or demand IOU?)

Dr of Law

Stop dynamo (OTC)

Tel: Law re Kate Race

Caps on for prep

Pots—no tops

Knit up ties ('U')

Ned (re paper)

Eve's simple hot dish (crib)

Pupil's buns

T-set: no sign in a/c

Red roses

Run Tide Bus?

Rev off at six

Noel Bat is a fossil

Lab to offer one 'Noh' play—or 'Pals Reviled'?

Sums are not set.

Perhaps more sense can be found in palindromes based on re-ordering words rather than letters. J. A. Lindon is an expert at this, creating such sentences as:

So patient a doctor to doctor a patient so.
Girl, bathing on Bikini, eyeing boy, finds boy eyeing bikini on bathing girl.

An epitaph in the churchyard of St Winwalloe's Church at Gunwalloe in Cornwall reads:

Shall we all die?
We shall die all;
All die shall we—
Die all we shall.

And in Roger Scruton's *Fortnight's Anger* (1981), occurs the following palindromic poem:

Night, whispering to Morning, said:
'Have we death? Is life
Unlimited by prolonged persistence?'
'Birds have nests, as absurdity
Made new for long life,'
Said Morning. Morning said:
'Life longs for new-made
Absurdity, as nests have birds—
Persistence prolonged by
Unlimited life is death;' we have said
Morning to whispering Night.

There is a slight cheat in this poem in the change from *long* to *longs* in ll. 5 and 7. Most such palindromic poems tend to be abstract and allusive.

Another form of palindrome consists of words made from symmetrical letters, so that they look the same when read upside down or in a mirror. Such words include NOON and SWIMS, the tradename OXO, and the phrase NO X IN NIXON. By placing symmetrical letters in a vertical line, several words can be made which look the same in a mirror, such as HOW, AWAY, TOOTHY, TOMATO, AUTOMATA, and HOITY-TOITY.

What is the longest palindromic word in English? There are several seven-letter palindromes, such as *deified*, *repaper*, *reviver*, and *rotator*. Nine-letter palindromes include *evitative*, *redivider*, the trade-name *Rotavator*, and *Malayalam* (a language of Southern India that has given English the words 'copra' and 'teak').

There are even some palindromic words of eleven letters. *Detartrated* may not qualify, as there is doubt if it is really used in science, but the third edition of *Webster's Dictionary* (1961) lists *kinnikinnik*, a kind of tobacco used by American Indians, while C. F. and F. M. Voegelin's *Classification and Index of the World's Languages* (1977) gives *Ooloopooloo* as the name of a dialect spoken in Queensland, Australia.

The last word in palindromic ingenuity goes to the inhabitants of a town in California called Yreka. This town once had a shop called *Yreka Bakery*. The palindromic name seemed lost when the shop had to close down, but it reopened as the *Yrella Gallery*.

Pangrams

Like the search for the perfect palindrome, the pursuit of the perfect PANGRAM has obsessed many people. It is an attractive problem because it has a simple, set goal: to compose a sentence that contains each letter of the alphabet, preferably including each letter only once.

The most familiar pangrams include all the letters of the alphabet but give some of them more than once. The phrase often used in learning to type—*The quick brown fox jumps over the lazy dog*—uses three *e*'s, two *h*'s, four *o*'s, two *r*'s, two *t*'s, and two *u*'s. These duplications can be slightly reduced by changing one 'the' into 'a', but this pangram still totals thirty-three letters.

Another well-known pangram—*Pack my box with five dozen liquor jugs*—has one letter less, but it still duplicates several letters. *Waltz, bad nymph, for quick jigs vex* is even better but it repeats the *a* and the *i*.

Here are some other attempts, with their respective letter-totals:

John P. Brady, give me a black walnut box of quite a small size.	48
Six plump boys guzzled cheap raw vodka quite joyfully.	46
Quixotic knights' wives are found on jumpy old zebras.	44
Jim just quit and packed extra heavy bags for Liz Owen.	44
Sexy zebras just prowl and vie for quick, hot matings.	43
By Jove, my quick study of lexicography won a prize.	41
Sympathizing would fix Quaker objectives.	36
Many-wived Jack laughs at probe of sex quiz.	35
Xylophone wizard begets quick jive form.	34
The five boxing wizards jump quickly.	31
Jackdaws love my big sphinx of quartz.	31
Quick waxy bugs jump the frozen veldt.	31
Judges vomit ; few quiz pharynx block.	30
How quickly daft jumping zebras vex.	30
Quick wafting zephyrs vex bold Jim.	29
Foxy nymphs grab quick-jived waltz.	29
Waltz, nymph, for quick jigs vex Bud.	28

Blowzy frights vex, and jump quick.   28
Brick quiz whangs jumpy veldt fox.   27

The sense of pangrams grows less as the pangrammatist tries to improve them. Sometimes the writer is tempted to cheat, but even *Baby knows all his letters except d, f, g, j, m, q, u, v, and z* contains forty letters—well above the target of twenty-six.

Pangrams are difficult to make in all languages, and particularly hard in English because the language has many more consonants than vowels, and most words need at least one vowel. Dmitri Borgmann found five words which together comprise the whole alphabet—*phlegms, fyrd, wuz, qvint,* and *jackbox*—but could not make a sensible sentence out of them. OULIPO'S *Atlas de Litterature Potentielle* gives the shortest French pangram as *Whisky vert: jugez cinq fox d'aplomb.* This has twenty-nine letters, fewer than *Zoe, grande fille, veut que je boive ce whisky, mais je ne veux pas* and *Monsieur Jack, vous dactylographiez bien mieux que votre ami Wholf.*

Ingenious searchers have often discovered pangrams in pieces of literature. These lines from Shakespeare's *Coriolanus* are almost a pangram, except for the missing letter *z*:

> O ! a kiss
> Long as my exile, sweet as my revenge!
> Now, by the jealous queen of heaven, that kiss
> I carried from thee, dear, and my true lip
> Hath virgin'd it ever since.   (v. iii. 44–8)

Milton's *Paradise Lost* contains a pangrammatic sequence from the *z* in *grazed* to the *b* in *both*:

> Likening his Maker to the grazed ox,
> Jehovah, who, in one night, when he passed
> From Egypt marching, equalled with one stroke
> Both her first-born and all her bleating gods.   (i. 486)

The Beth Book (1897) by Sarah Grand (a pseudonym of Frances Elizabeth Clarke McFall) includes the following seventy-six letter sentence which contains all the letters of the alphabet in the sixty-five letters from the *x* of *exquisite* to the *z* of *gauze*:

It was an exquisite deep blue just then, with filmy white clouds drawn up over it like gauze.

Pangrams have even been discovered in the Bible, as in this passage from Ezra 7: 21, which is an imperfect pangram because it lacks the letter *j*:

And I, even I Artaxerxes the king, do make a decree to all the treasurers which are beyond the river, that whatsoever Ezra the priest, the scribe of the law of the God of heaven, shall require of you, it be done speedily.

Some pangrammatists, like anagrammatists, allow themselves the licence of using *i* for *j*, and *u* for *v*, which was normal in old spelling. This enabled Augustus de Morgan to produce the pangram: *I, quartz pyx, who fling muck beds*. De Morgan said:

I long thought that no human being could say this under any circumstances. At last I happened to be reading a religious writer—as he thought himself—who threw aspersions on his opponents thick and threefold. Heyday! came into my head, this fellow flings muck beds; he must be a quartz pyx. And then I remembered that a pyx is a sacred vessel, and quartz is a hard stone, as hard as the heart of a religious foe-curser. So that the line is the motto of the ferocious sectarian, who turns his religious vessels into mud-holders, for the benefit of those who will not see what he sees. (*Budget of Paradoxes*, 1872)

Augustus de Morgan also cites the following:

> *Quiz my black whigs; export fund.*
> *Dumpy quiz, whirl back fogs next.*
> *Get nymph; quiz sad brow; fix luck.*

Pangrams of all twenty-six letters used once have been written but they tend to verge on the meaningless. They often depend on recondite words like *crwd* or *crwth* (a Welsh musical instrument), *cwm* (a Welsh valley), *qoph* (a Hebrew letter), and *qvint* (a Danish unit of weight). Here are some of them, with translations appended where necessary:

Cwm fjord-bank glyphs vext quiz
(an eccentric's annoyance at finding ancient inscriptions on the side of a fjord in a valley).

Vest cwm fly zing jabs Kurd qoph.
(an annoyed fly in a valley, humming shrilly, pokes at the nineteenth letter of the Hebrew alphabet drawn by a Kurd).

Nth black fjords vex Qum gyp wiz.
(an esteemed Iranian shyster was provoked when he himself was cheated:

an alleged seaside ski resort he purchased proved instead to be a glacier of countless oil-abundant fjords).

Quartz glyph job vex'd cwm finks
  (despicable vandals from the valley are thwarted by finding a block of quartz with carvings already on it).

J. Q. Schwartz flung V. D. Pike my box.

TV quiz drag-nymphs blew cox, J.F.K.

Blowzy night-frumps vex'd Jack Q.

And so the search continues for even better pangrams. The field is still wide open for someone to devise one that makes perfect sense but has only twenty-six letters. Perhaps the computer can help us to discover such a pangram, although Cashell Farrell's experiments with a computer only produced good pangrams of more than forty letters, such as *The qualmish Afghan Jew packed over sixty fez with bees*. The computer has much more work to do, especially as the twenty-six letters of the alphabet can be combined in 403,290,000,000,000,000,000,000,000 different ways.

Lipograms and Univocalics

Human ingenuity has sometimes found an outlet in composing writings which either omit a particular letter of the alphabet or include only one of the vowels. The former are called LIPOGRAMS, the latter, UNIVOCALICS.

The Greek poet Lasus (born in Achaia, 538 BC) wrote an ode on the Centaurs and a hymn to Ceres without once using the letter *s*. Addison in *The Spectator* (1711) described another Greek poet of the fifth century AD:

Tryphiodorus was a great master in this kind of writing. He composed an *Odyssey* or epic poem on the adventures of Ulysses, consisting of four and twenty books, having entirely banished the letter *A* from his first book, which was called *Alpha* (as *lucus a non lucendo*) because there was not an alpha in it. His second book was inscribed *Beta* for the same reason. In short, the poet excluded the whole four and twenty letters in their turns, and showed them, one after another, that he could do his business without them.

The Latin author Fulgentius wrote a similar work, with twenty-three chapters each omitting one letter of the Latin alphabet. Athenaeus mentions an ode by Pindar from which the letter *s* is absent. Such Latin writings inspired medieval authors to try their hands at lipograms. In his *History of Christian-Latin Poetry* (1927), F. J. E. Raby writes of Peter Riga, a canon of Notre Dame at Rheims who died about 1209 and who

earned a great reputation by his *Aurora*, a versification of Old Testament themes. . . . The most remarkable verses in this collection are those which summarize the two Testaments in twenty-three chapters. In the first chapter the letter *a* does not appear. . . . In the second chapter *b* is avoided, and so on throughout the alphabet. Misplaced ingenuity could go no farther.

The practice became popular in Spain. Lope de Vega wrote five stories each of which omitted one of the five vowels. An anonymous seventeenth-century Spanish novel, *Estebanillo González*, ends with a romance which manages without the letter *o*. And a Spaniard named Don Fernando Jacinto de Zurita y Haro is said to have written a 170-page discourse in which the letter *a* never appears. However, he allowed himself to use that letter when he reached the end of the work and expressed his gratitude that it was finished with the words 'Laus Deo' ('Praise the Lord!').

Isaac d'Israeli says that lipograms were also found in Persia:

The Orientalists are not without this literary folly. A Persian poet read to the celebrated Jami a gazel of his own composition, which Jami did not like: but the writer replied it was notwithstanding a very curious sonnet, for the letter *Aliff* was not to be found in any one of the words! Jami sarcastically replied, 'You can do a better thing yet; take away *all the letters* from every word you have written.' (*Curiosities of Literature*, 1824)

In 1816 a French playwright named Ronden wrote his *Pièce sans A* for the Théâtre des Variétés in Paris. W. S. Walsh described the opening night:

The curtain rose. Duval entered from one wing, Mengozzi from the opposite side of the stage. The first words the latter intoned were—

Ah, monsieur! vous voilà.

The whole audience roared with laughter at this curious beginning of a piece without A. The laughter gave the prompter time to set the actor right. He corrected himself with—

Eh, monsieur! vous voici.

So goes the story. To which there is only one objection, namely, that nothing like the sentence quoted is to be found in the published piece. To be sure, it contains others very like it. The author may have made an alteration in proof. He confesses, by the way, in his preface, that the performance was not suffered to proceed to the end. (*Handy-Book of Literary Curiosities*, 1892)

Walsh also gave some verses which combine a lipogram with a pangram (q.v.), as each stanza omits the letter *e* but includes all the other letters of the alphabet:

> A jovial swain should not complain
> Of any buxom fair,
> Who mocks his pain and thinks it gain
> To quiz his awkward air.

Quixotic boys who look for joys
Quixotic hazards run;
A lass annoys with trivial toys,
Opposing man for fun.

A jovial swain might rack his brain,
And tax his fancy's might;
To quiz is vain, for 'tis most plain
That what I say is right.   (Ibid.)

Thomas De Quincey scoffed at lipograms:

Some of us laughed as such a self-limitation as a wild bravado, recalling
that rope-dancing feat of some verse-writers who, through each several
stanza in its turn, had gloried in dispensing with some one separate consonant, some vowel, or some diphthong, and thus achieving a triumph such
as crowns with laurel that pedestrian athlete who wins a race by hopping
on one leg, or wins it under the inhuman condition of confining both legs
within a sack. (*Confessions of an English Opium-Eater*, 1856)

Nevertheless, the urge to write lipograms has continued into the
present century. In 1939 Ernest Vincent Wright published a
50,000-word novel which entirely omitted the letter *e*: the commonest letter in the English language. The Frenchman Georges Perec
achieved the same thing in his novel *La Disparition* (1969). A. Ross
Eckler rewrote the rhyme 'Mary Had a Little Lamb' in several ways,
each time omitting one of its commonest letters. This is his version
without the letter *s*:

Mary had a little lamb,
With fleece a pale white hue,
And everywhere that Mary went
The lamb kept her in view;
To academe he went with her,
Illegal, and quite rare;
It made the children laugh and play
To view a lamb in there.

In modern children's games, the lipogram occurs in a game called
TABOO. One player asks another a question, which must be answered
sensibly in words that do not contain a specified letter. Sometimes
the game is played with a particular word or part of speech—not a
letter—designated as 'taboo'. Patrick Beaver describes a Victorian
parlour game called Flour Merchant in which the answers must not
include the words *flour*, *I*, *yes*, and *no*. In his *Letters from Spain*

(1822), J. Blanco White mentions a game called THE SOLDIER in which 'the players being questioned by the leader about the clothing they mean to give a decayed veteran, must avoid the words *yes*, *no*, *white*, and *black*'.

In the nineteenth century, YES AND NO was another name for what we call Twenty Questions (q.v.) but nowadays it usually means a game in which players have to answer questions without using the words 'yes' and 'no'. This was popularized during the 1950s by Michael Miles in a television game called 'Take Your Pick', which included a 'yes–no' section during which the host asked contestants questions and they won prizes if they avoided saying 'yes' or 'no' for a specified time.

UNIVOCALICS are writings that use only one vowel, such as the following which uses only *e*:

> Persevere, ye perfect men,
> Ever keep the precepts ten.
> (W. T. Dobson, *Literary Frivolities*, 1880)

In 1824 Lord Holland wrote a piece entitled 'Eve's Legend' which confines itself to the same vowel. This extract is typical: 'Men were never perfect, yet the three brethren Veres were ever esteemed, respected, revered, even when the rest, whether the select few, whether the mere herd, were left neglected.' (W. T. Dobson, *Poetical Ingenuities*, 1882)

In his *Gleanings for the Curious* (1890), C. C. Bombaugh gives a univocalic poem for each vowel of the alphabet. Here are two of them:

The Approach of Evening

> Idling, I sit in this mild twilight dim,
> Whilst birds, in wild, swift vigils, circling skim.
> Light winds in sighing sink, till, rising bright,
> Night's Virgin Pilgrim swims in vivid light!

Incontrovertible Facts

> No monk too good to rob, or cog, or plot.
> No fool so gross to bolt Scotch collops hot.
> From Donjon tops no Oronoko rolls.
> Logwood, not Lotos, floods Oporto's bowls.
> Troops of old tosspots, oft, to sot, consort.
> Box tops, not bottoms, school-boys flog for sport.

No cool monsoons blow soft on Oxford dons,
Orthodox, jog-trot, book-worm Solomons!
Bold Ostrogoths, of ghosts no horror show.
On London shop-fronts no hop-blossoms grow.
To crocks of gold no dodo looks for food.
On soft cloth footstools no old fox doth brood.
Long storm-tost sloops forlorn, work on to no port.
Rooks do not roost on spoons, nor woodcocks snort,
Nor dog on snowdrop or on coltsfoot rolls,
Nor common frogs concoct long protocols.

For a *New Statesman* competition in 1967, George Marvill wrote a univocalic which is also a palindrome (q.v.) (its only vowel is *o* and it can be read backwards as well as forwards). It is a conversation between two owls (or is it three?):

'Too hot to hoot!'
'Too hot to woo!'
'Too wot?'
'Too hot to hoot!'
'To woo!'
'Too wot?'
'To hoot! Too hot to hoot!'

14

Letter Games

There are many games in which letters are removed from or added to words, or juggled about in various ways. These include Beheadments, Curtailments, Transpositions, and Ghosts.

BEHEADMENTS and CURTAILMENTS

In Beheadments, the first letter is removed from a word; in Curtailments, the last letter is removed. Sometimes this process happens again and again until you are left with a one-letter word. Thus the word *sheathed* can be beheaded or curtailed to make a series of shorter words: *sheathed–sheathe–sheath–heath–heat–eat–at–a*. Sometimes letters are taken from inside the word. Thus *startling* can be turned into at least eight other words by deleting various letters (*starling, starting, start, tart, art, tar, star, staring*).

A famous story about a beheadment concerns a university professor who put up a notice that he 'would meet his classes tomorrow'. Some joker beheaded 'classes' and made it into 'lasses', but the professor then got his own back by deleting the 'l'.

The seventeeth-century poet George Herbert beheaded several words in his poem 'Paradise':

> I bless thee, Lord, because I GROW
> Among thy trees, which in a ROW
> To thee both fruit and order OW.
>
> What open force, or hidden CHARM
> Can blast my fruit, or bring me HARM,
> While the enclosure is thine ARM?
>
> Enclose me still for fear I START.
> Be to me rather sharp and TART,
> Than let me want thy hand and ART.

When thou dost greater judgements SPARE,
And with thy knife but prune and PARE,
Ev'n fruitful trees more fruitful ARE.

Such sharpness shows the sweetest FREND:
Such cuttings rather heal than REND:
And such beginnings touch their END.

Beheadments became a popular game in the nineteenth century, as in these examples from *Frolics of the Sphynx* (1812):

Composed of only five letters am I,
And us'd to express a day that is dry,
Or bright and unclouded, not such as we find,
When the fogs of November enervate mankind;
One letter remove, and you've often read o'er,
This favourite play of a bard we adore,
And sympathiz'd much o'er the scenes of distress,
Which on his old hero so heavily press,
And have lent, with compassion, all that which remains
To the highly wrought grief of his magical strains,
When this little word three letters contains. (*clear*)

What word is that in the marriage ceremony, which if you change one letter of, many would marry who do not? (Change 'as long as ye both shall *live*' for *love*!)

In my entire state I serve to flatter the vanity of what remains when one letter is taken away; remove another and I am an animal rather useful than admired. (*glass*)

Another beheadment giving the word *glass* occurs in *Charades, Enigmas, and Riddles* (1862):

What is pretty and useful in various ways,
Though it tempts some poor mortals to shorten their days;
Take one letter from it, and then will appear
What youngsters admire every day in the year!
Take two letters from it, and then, without doubt,
You are what it is, if you don't find it out.

Lord Macaulay wrote the following puzzle, which includes both beheadments and curtailments. Such puzzles were sometimes called LOGOGRAMS although that word can also be a synonym for logogriph (q.v.).

> Cut off my head, and singular I act,
> Cut off my tail, and plural I appear;
> Cut off my head and tail, to nothing I contract,
> Nothing to wise men's sight or blind man's ear.
> What is my head cut off?—a sounding sea;
> What is my tail cut off?—a flowing river:
> And through their mingling depths I fearless play,
> Parent of sweetest sounds; yet mute for ever.   (*cod*)
>
> (*Charades, Enigmas, and Riddles, collected by a Cantab*, 1862)

Lewis Carroll composed this rhyming puzzle which also uses beheadment and curtailment:

> A monument—men all agree—
> Am I in all sincerity,
> Half cat, half hindrance made.
> If head and tail removed should be,
> Then most of all you strengthen me;
> Replace my head, the stand you see
> On which my tail is laid.   (*tablet*)
>
> (*Strand Magazine*, December 1898)

Beheadments and curtailments were often mixed with reversing or juggling the letters of a word—which were called respectively REVERSALS and TRANSPOSITIONS. For example, *The New Sphinx* (*c.* 1806) has this:

> Complete, you have a piece of leather;
> Revers'd, you've many parts together;
> Transpos'd, a fish is now your share:
> Curtail'd, you've got into a snare.
> Again curtail'd, and I bestow
> Upon your pate a hostile blow.   (*strap–parts–sprat–trap–tap*)

In what is called a TRANSDELETION, one letter is deleted from a word and the remaining letters are shuffled to give a new word. If we delete a *c* from *concentrations*, we can reshuffle the remaining letters to spell *consternation*. If we delete the *a* from *precariousness*, we can make *repercussions*.

Devotees of transdeletions love to remove letters from a word one by one until only one is left, as in this sequence: *reactivation-ratiocinate -recitation-intricate-interact -nitrate-attire -irate -rate - rat- at-a.* The opposite process is caled WORD-BUILDING. Letters are added to a word one at a time to create new words. In 1922, Elizabeth Wordsworth wrote a book entitled *Word Puzzles for Winter Evenings* containing twenty-six puzzles in which numbers represent words with one more letter than the previous word. Elizabeth Wordsworth says: 'I am indebted for the original suggestion of this idea to an entertaining paper on amusements, by the Dean of St Paul's.'

A Lodger

As in (1) lodging dark I fed
(2) breakfast, in a town,
'Where (3) thou?' to myself I said;
A (4) came trickling down.
My (5) was sad, and drear, and old,
I thought I'd have some tea!
Alas, the (6) had grown cold!
Small comfort there, for me.
'Thou art a (7), ' I exclaimed,
As, ugly, grey, and thin,
But not the very least ashamed,
My landlady came in.
'I wish I were in France, for there
In far (8) I think,*
They give you coffee made with care,
And always fit to drink.'
But soon one thought, a (9) stern
Smote on me, as I sat,
'In (10) your bread you earn,
So make the best of that.'

    * Name of French Department.

The missing words are *a*, *at*, *art*, *tear*, *heart*, *heater*, *cheater*, *Charente*, *chastener*, and *Manchester*.

GHOSTS

The game of word-building leads naturally to another game based on the same principle—the very well-known game called Ghosts or Donkey.

The first player thinks of a word of three or more letters, and calls out its first letter. The second player adds another letter, which continues but does not complete a word, and so on, until one player is forced to finish a word. Any player who adds a letter can be challenged by the next player to say what the word will be. Any player who loses such a challenge or completes a word becomes 'a third of a ghost'. When he loses again, he becomes 'two-thirds of a ghost' and the third time he is 'a whole ghost' and is out of the game.

Proper names, abbreviations, and foreign words are not usually allowed. Anyone who talks to a 'partial' ghost during the game loses one 'life', so 'partial' ghosts try to make other players talk to them.

As an example of the game, the first player might think of the word *mat* and call out *m*. The second player might think of *mile* and call out *i*. The third player might think of *middle* but he cannot call out *d* because *mid* is a complete word. So he might think of *mite* and call out *t*. The fourth player thinks of *mitre* and calls out *r*. The fifth player has to add the *e* because he cannot think of another word besides *mitre*. But a cleverer player might think of *mitral* or *mitrailleuse*, which are words in the *Concise Oxford Dictionary*.

SUPERGHOSTS is a variation of the game, in which letters can be added at the beginning as well as the end. James Thurber was an addict of Superghosts, and he described its agonies and ecstasies in an essay entitled 'Do You Want to Make Something Out of It?':

I sometimes keep on playing the game, all by myself, after it is over and I have gone to bed. On a recent night, tossing and spelling, I spent two hours hunting for another word besides 'phlox' that has 'hlo' in it. I finally found seven: 'matchlock', 'decathlon', 'pentathlon', 'hydrochloric', 'chlorine', 'chloroform', and 'monthlong'. There are more than a dozen others, beginning with 'phlo', but I had to look them up in the dictionary the next morning, and that doesn't count. . . .

Starting words in the middle and spelling them in both directions lifts the pallid pastime of Ghosts out of the realm of children's parties and ladies' sewing circles and makes it a game to test the mettle of the mature adult mind. As long ago as 1930, aficionados began to appear in New York parlours, and then the game waned, to be revived, in my circle, last year. The Superghost aficionado is a moody fellow, given to spelling to himself at table, not listening to his wife, and staring dully at his frightened children, wondering why he didn't detect, in yesterday's game, that 'cklu' is the guts of 'lacklustre', and priding himself on having stumped everybody with 'nehe', the middle of 'swineherd'.

LOGOGRIPHS

Logogriphs (sometimes called logograms, see p. 115) are puzzles in which clues are given to a word by referring to other words that can be made from some or all of its letters. The logogriph is therefore similar in some ways to Words Within Words and also to the game of Huntergrams described in the chapter on anagrams.

H. B. Wheatley described logogriphs in this way:

The mode adopted is to fix on some word—usually one with a sufficient number of vowels to allow of considerable transposition—and to find out all the words which can be formed from the whole, or from any portion, of its letters. Some verses are then to be constructed, in which synonymic expressions for those words must be used, and the puzzle or game will consist in the discovery of these concealed words, and through them of the principal or leading word in which all of them are included. If the opposing party has sufficient talent, he may throw his discovery of the words also into a poetic reply.

Wheatley's example is a verse that includes these lines:

> I dreamt, as sleeping on my bed I lay,
> In mazy folds rich *hangings* round me fell,
> *That*, like a mimic *drop*-scene at the play,
> Did *move* and *change*, as under magic spell.
>
> (*Of Anagrams*, 1862)

Wheatley gets fifty-four different words from the letters in *curtains*, which is the word clued as *hangings* in the second line above. The italicized words in the third and fourth lines are clues to it—*rain* and *stir—turn*. The reply also uses words made from the letters in *curtains*, beginning:

> *As* the *sun* sank to rest *in* the waves of the west,
> *I* too sought repose on my *satin* divan . . .

The Masquerade (1797) includes several logogriphs, of which one makes fifty-eight different words from the letters in *thread*, and the following gets thirteen words out of *large*:

What to the king alone pertains;	(*regal*)
And what respect in gen'ral gains;	(*age*)
A title English nobles bear;	(*earl*)
And what a farmer's horses wear;	(*gear*)
What fictitious ne'er can be;	(*real*)
With what betokens poverty;	(*rag*)
A word that has an angry cast;	(*rage*)
Another, that we use for last;	(*lag*)

> What in a dish of souse is good;   (*ear*)
> A limb, when lost, supply'd with wood;   (*leg*)
> A wind, of brisk yet gentle fame;   (*gale*)
> A Yorkshire river's ancient name;   (*Are*)
> And 'last, not least', the spacious whole
>   Will lead you to the wish'd-for goal.   (*large*)

Later logogriphs fell into a simpler pattern, like this one from *Excursions into Puzzledom* (1879) by 'Tom Hood and his Sister':

I am a word of eight letters, signifying a season very welcome to little people. My 8, 6, 5, is melancholy, and my 2, 4, 3, is not nice. My 3, 6, 5, is a youngster, who should make my 1, 6, 7, in fine weather . . .

In this way, many clues are given to the word, which is *holidays*.

London Society for 1867 described a similar kind of puzzle called a METAGRAM. In this example, it calls the letters of the hidden word 'feet':

> On six feet, I am a noxious drink,
> Of whose effects you shudder to think.
> Change only my second foot, and then
> You convert me into the horrible den
> Where the culprit, who gave the noxious drink,
> Awaits the fate of which you shudder to think.   (*poison— prison*)

WORDS WITHIN WORDS

The basic idea for Words Within Words is first found in logogriphs (q.v.). Words Within Words is a very simple but fascinating game. *Chambers's Journal* for 20 April 1872 called it simply 'Words' and said it was 'the best drawing-room game of all'.

It involves making as many words as possible from the letters of a chosen word. The winner is the person who makes the largest number of words that none of the other players has thought of. *Chambers's Journal* for 20 April 1872 gives as an example the word *Cambridge*, saying:

Would it be imagined that this comparatively short word breaks up into sixty-one others! Bridge, image, ream, ridge, badger, crag, bride, acre, admire, game, dear, brig, crib, acare, braid, ride, scard, dream, dame, mare, gird, raid, bard, bream, abide, bare, garb, mire, drab, amber, bier, bear, bird, grab, grace, gear, dare, rice, race, mead, crab, brace, bead, cram, grade, read, brim, cigar, dire, dram, cadi, rage, grim, cider, maid, cream, badge, crime, cage, drag, mirage.

The author of this article warns that 'when played among grown folks, only good-natured people that don't mind being laughed at should indulge in it, for the mistakes in spelling thus publicly disclosed are always numerous'. He adds that his children have found no fewer than 170 words in *handkerchief.*

Later writers called the game Word-Builder, Word-Hunt, Word-Making, Hidden Words, In-Words, Keyword, Multiwords, and Target. The magazine *Tit-Bits* for 12 December 1899 included a 'word-forming competition' in which competitors each had to make up to fifty words out of *undenominationalism*. The prize of 'a sovereign a word' went to the reader whose words collectively contained the greatest number of letters.

A. A. Milne disliked the game, saying in his essay 'For a Wet Afternoon':

The most common paper game of all, that of making small words out of a big one, has nothing to recommend it; for there can be no possible amusement in hearing somebody else read out 'but', 'bat', 'bet', 'bin', 'ben', and so forth, not even if you spend half an hour discussing whether 'ben' is really a word.

Nevertheless, Words Within Words has remained a firm favourite among children. Peter de Pravo noted that 'When I was a young shaver, the long word we were supposed to dissect and resynthesize was nearly always "Constantinople". (Why? Because there are nowhere near as many possibilities in "Byzantium" or "Istanbul", of course.)' It is true that long words—especially *Constantinople*— are usually chosen for this game but short words can yield a surprisingly high score. For example, the six-letter word *bridge* can make at least a dozen words: *bide, bier, bird, bred, bride, bring, dire, dirge, dreg, grid, ride,* and *ridge.* The eight-letter word *scramble* can yield more than fifty different words, but Alan Frank claims to have found 273 words in the seven-letter *psalter.*

Of course, as the words get longer, the possibilities tend to increase by a geometrical progression. Boris Randolph found 2,500 words in Webster's *Dictionary* that could be made from the letters in the name of its author, *Noah Webster.*

Geography

Geography is a simple game, made more complicated by the fact that it has all kinds of other names: Grab on Behind, Heads and Tails, Last and First, Trailing Cities, etc.

A category is decided upon—it is often 'towns'—and the first player calls out a name in that category. Each player calls out another word in succession, but each word must begin with the last letter of the preceding word. So the sequence might turn out as follows: *Oxford, Derby, Yeovil, Leicester, Ross-on-Wye*, and so on. If the category is 'trees', the sequence might be: *acacia, ash, hazel, larch, hornbeam, maple*, etc.

Hidden Words

In Hidden Words or Buried Words, you have to find words that are hidden within sentences. For instance, if you are told to look for a hidden animal in 'He came looking for trouble', you could find the word *camel* in *came* and *l—ooking*. The game is as popular among modern children as it was among the Victorians, who liked to conceal the names of animals, birds, towns, countries, and flowers.

Aunt Judy's Magazine for 1 December 1869 included such hidden-word puzzles as these:

In what town did Falstaff receive the most full and affectionate response to his enquiry for recruits?   *Llandaff.*
What town did Alexander the Great rob and pillage on his journey to the north?   *Oban.*
From what town may the African coast be espied most clearly on a sunny day?   *St Bees.*

The *Girl's Own Paper* of 1881 contained these 'hidden animals':

Impossible! O, pardon me, by no means.   (*leopard*)
The lamb is one of my pets.   (*bison*)
At last a girl moved.   (*stag*)
He made errors on purpose.   (*deer*)
I must give it up, I grieve to say.   (*pig*)
Well, I only got terrified out of my wits (2 animals).   (*lion* and *otter*)

Sometimes the words were hidden in a poem, such as this from John Edward Field's *Buried Cities* (1871) in which each line conceals the name of a city or town:

Come near, O men of wisdom, and search you through my ditty;   (*Rome*)
For buried in this rubbish cities fair are lying low: (*Ely*)
Search till on every line you see stand up a risen city,   (*Paris*)
Till walls and arches, terraces and turrets, upward grow.   (*Chester*)

To make the problem more difficult, F. Planche in *Guess Me* (1872) spells the names of a dozen birds *backwards* in this piece:

When Mary ran across our new orchard in such a hasty manner, we all wondered why she did so; but her cousin Victor rapped her knuckles, for which Dick cudgelled him soundly. 'Stop!' cried Jane. 'How can you? Of all ugly fellows, I declare you are the worst!' 'I call this a lark,' Ralph exclaimed, laughing heartily. 'You would not laugh if you had had such a blow or rap!' said Mary, with the tears in her eyes. 'Can't you see that I weep?' 'Never mind,' interrupted Ellen, archly. 'Let us all kiss and be friends.'

The hidden birds are: *canary, crow, wren, owl, parrot, duck, hen, gull, lark, sparrow, peewit,* and *crane.*

In his *World's Best Word Puzzles* (1925), H. E. Dudeney gave a series of sentences which each conceals words that together make up a proverb:

1. A naughty cat ran away. 2. They found a closely-written roll in gathering up the rubbish. 3. It is the best one I have ever seen. 4. The rug at her stairway is not a valuable one. 5. He is an old acquaintance of mine. 6. Amos soon saw through the stratagem.

The hidden proverb is *A rolling stone gathers no moss.*

Darwin Hindman reversed the process with a game that gives a proverb and asks you to find as many words as you can inside it. Thus *Appearances are often deceitful* will yield the words: *pear, ear, ran, an, of, oft, ten, tend, end, deceit,* and *it.* Another way of hiding words is to alter the spaces between them. In olden days, a post in a village street bore a sign which read:

TOTI EMU LESTO

It took some people a while before they realized that the post was designed to tie mules to. Lewis Carroll wrote a story called 'Novelty and Romancement' in which a poet is excited to see a sign reading: 'Simon Lubkin, Dealer in Romancement' but disappointed when he realizes that Mr Lubkin actually deals in Roman cement.

There is still a sign outside the Plough public house in the Oxford-shire village of East Hendred, inviting travellers to spend an hour there. The message (see next page), when decoded, reads: 'Here stop and spend a social hour in harmless mirth and fun. Let friendship reign. Be just and kind, and evil speak of none.'

NOTICE

HERESTO PANDS PEN D ASOCI
AL HOU R INHAR M (LES SMIRT)
HA   ND   FUNLET   FRIENDS
HIPRE   IGN   BE   JUSTAN   DK
INDAN DEVIL SPEAKOF NO NE

CRYPTARITHMS or ALPHAMETICS

A CRYPTARITHM or ALPHAMETIC is a puzzle in which letters are substituted for numbers in an arithmetical sum. A typical cryptarithm looks like this:

```
    S  E  N  D
    M  O  R  E
    G  O  L  D
  ─────────────
  M  O  N  E  Y
```

The answer to this is:

```
    5  4  7  8
    1  6  2  4
    9  6  3  8
  ─────────────
  1  6  7  4  0
```

The word *cryptarithm* was first used in 1931 following a suggestion by M. Vatriquant in *Sphinx* magazine. In 1955, J. A. H. Hunter suggested the word *alphametic* to describe a cryptarithm in which meaningful words are used instead of ordinary letters of the alphabet.

The *Strand Magazine* for July 1924 contained this problem:

$$T \ W \ O \ \times \ T \ W \ O \ = \ T \ H \ R \ E \ E$$

The solution is:

$$1 \ 3 \ 8 \ \times \ 1 \ 3 \ 8 \ = \ 1 \ 9 \ 0 \ 4 \ 4.$$

Cryptarithms include not only problems of addition and multiplication, but also subtraction and division, as in the following examples:

```
    V  E  N  U  S         5  4  7  3  9
  − E  A  R  T  H    =   − 4  6  1  2  0
  ─────────────────     ─────────────────
       M  A  R  S             8  6  1  9
```

```
                 E M U                        2 1 5
           _____            _____
  N I L ) M I N I M S         6 3 4 ) 1 3 6 3 1 0
           M E N D                     1 2 6 8
           _____            _____
               H U M                       9 5 1
               N I L                       6 3 4
           _____            _____
             I M P S                     3 1 7 0
             I M P S                     3 1 7 0
           _____            _____
```

SPELLING BEES

In the eighteenth and nineteenth centuries, when Americans got together for a social gathering where work was done, they called it a 'bee'—probably because the bee is a social insect. They held 'spinning bees', 'quilting bees' and even 'lynching bees'.

Then in the 1870s came a new kind of gathering—the 'spelling bee', a contest in spelling words. In *The Times* of 16 April 1875, a correspondent from Philadelphia reported that:

The American people have during the past few weeks been indulging in a new pastime, which is becoming as universal as it is popular. This is the 'Spelling Bee', a New England invention which has made rapid strides over the country. 'Spelling' for prizes is the prevailing infatuation, and every town and village is having its 'bee', attended by crowds who cheer the successful and laugh at those who are afflicted with a 'bad spell'.

This correspondent described a spelling bee at the Academy of Music in Philadelphia. The eighty contestants—forty women and forty men—were mostly schoolteachers. The words they had to spell included difference, dialogue, corrigible, chirography, and alibi. A young woman lost by spelling *musketeer* as *muscateer*. Other misspelt words included chloroform, duellist, gourmand, and peregrination. A lady schoolteacher won the competition.

The craze for spelling bees soon spread to Britain. *Leisure Hour* in 1876 reported that 'the walls are placarded with announcements of bees, the newspapers teem with reports of bees, and everybody is talking of bees'. The craze was such that a *Spelling Bee Guide* was published to help participants in such competitions, with lists of difficult words.

The *Annual Register* described an early British contest that took place in 1875:

Under the auspices of Sir Andrew Lusk, Bart., M.P., and Mr Samuel Waddy, Q.C., M.P., a Spelling Bee has been held at the Myddelton Hall, Islington. The American rules were observed:—these are that the spelling be oral; Webster's Dictionary is to decide cases of disputed orthography; the competitors are limited to fifty; one word misspelt rules the speller out; referees decide disputed points between the interrogator and the competitor. Thirty-two gentlemen and eighteen ladies essayed their skill before a crowded audience. In the end the sexes divided the prizes equally, though the first prize fell to a gentleman. The words that proved too much for the powers of all except the prize-takers were not very difficult. 'Rhododendron', 'apocryphal', 'philippic', 'hebdomadally', and 'camelopard' put a large number hopelessly out of the contest, and at last 'sesquipedalian' was only spelt correctly by Mr Jameson, the winner. Prizes to the amount of eight pounds rewarded the six successful spellers out of the fifty who entered.

When the craze subsided, the spelling bee took its place as a game of enduring interest, mainly among children. Several variations arose, such as the contest in which words have to be spelt backwards, or spelt by each person saying one letter in succession.

Lord Palmerston is said to have dictated a sentence to eleven Cabinet Ministers, none of whom could spell it correctly. The sentence was: 'It is disagreeable to witness the embarrassment of a harassed pedler gauging the symmetry of a peeled potato.'

15

Alphabet Games

The alphabet provides a natural basis for many types of games and word play. Poets from Chaucer to Edward Lear and beyond have written 'ABC's', starting each verse with a letter of the alphabet. One of the earliest children's alphabets dates from the seventeenth century or even earlier:

> A was an apple-pie;
> B bit it,
> C cut it,
> D dealt it,
> E eat it,
> F fought for it,
> G got it,
> H had it,
> I inspected it,
> J jumped for it,
> K kept it,
> L longed for it,
> M mourned for it,
> N nodded at it,
> O opened it,
> P peeped in it,
> Q quartered it,
> R ran for it,
> S stole it,
> T took it,
> U upset it,
> V viewed it,
> W wanted it,
> X, Y, Z, and ampersand
> All wished for a piece in hand.

Such alphabetic ingenuity was not restricted to children. In 1745, the Jacobite Lord Duff composed this toast:

ABC	A Blessed Change.
DEF	Down Every Foreigner.
GHJ	God Help James.
KLM	Keep Lord Mar.
NOP	Noble Ormond Preserve.
QRS	Quickly Resolve Stuart.
TUVW	Truss Up Vile Whigs.
XYZ	'Xert Your Zeal!

(W. T. Dobson, *Poetical Ingenuities*, 1882)

One of the most famous alphabetic poems is called 'The Siege of Belgrade' and was probably written by Alaric Watts:

An Austrian army awfully array'd,
Boldly by battery besieg'd Belgrade;
Cossack commanders cannonading come,
Dealing destruction's devastating doom.
Every endeavour engineers essay—
For fame, for fortune fighting—furious fray!
Generals 'gainst generals grapple—gracious God!
How honours Heav'n heroic hardihood—
Infuriate—indiscriminate in ill,
Kinsmen kill kindred, kindred kinsmen kill.
Labour low levels longest, loftiest lines—
Men march 'mid mounds, 'mid moles, 'mid murd'rous mines.
Now noisy noxious numbers notice naught,
Of outward obstacles opposing ought;
Poor patriots! partly purchas'd, partly press'd,
Quite quaking quickly, 'quarter, quarter,' quest.
Reason returns, religious right redounds,
Suwarrow stops such sanguinary sounds.
Truce to thee, Turkey, triumph to thy train,
Unjust, unwise, unmerciful Ukraine,
Vanish vain vict'ry, vanish vict'ry vain.—
Why wish we warfare? wherefore welcome were
Xerxes, Ximenes, Xanthus, Xaviere?
Yield, yield, ye youths, ye yeomen yield your yell;
Zeno's, Zorpater's, Zoroaster's, zeal
Attracting all, arms against acts appeal.

(*Trifler*, 7 May 1817)

A correspondent in *Notes and Queries* for 6 November 1886 asked if it was possible to make a sentence composed of the sounds of all the letters of the alphabet. J. H. Lundgren replied with the following:

O   LN   P   J   IV FEG   W   R   MT   SA   Y   U   C
Oh Ellen, pea jay, ivy effigy, double you are! empty essay! why? you see

H   DK   B   XQZ
age decay; be excused!

Lewis Carroll tried the same thing in a letter to Annie Rogers, but
he only covered the first five letters of the alphabet:

> My dear Annie,
>
> I send you
> A picture, which I hope will
> B one that you will like to
> C. If your Mamma should
> D sire one like it, I could
> E sily get her one.

Such attempts finally bore fruit in a complete comic alphabet
which was popularized by the comedians Clapham and Dwyer in the
late 1920s and analysed at inordinate length by Eric Partridge in
his book *Comic Alphabets* (1961). It was anticipated by a humorous
Greek alphabet devised by Jonathan Swift in the 1720s, which made
phrases by prefixing each Greek letter to the word *guinea*— *alpha
guinea* (i.e. half a guinea), *beta guinea* (bet a guinea), *gamma guinea*
(game a guinea), *delta guinea* (dealt a guinea), and so on.

The English comic alphabet is much better. Here is one form of it,
with some of the many variations:

A for 'orses (i.e. hay for horses)
B for mutton (i.e. beef or mutton)
C for thighlanders (or C for yourself, or C for miles)
D for dumb (or D for mation, or D for Mitty)
E for brick
F for vescence (or F for been had)
G for police
H for retirement
I for Novello (or I for lutin')
J for oranges
K for teria
L for leather
M for sis

N for a penny (or N for a dig, or N for lope)
O for the garden wall (or O for the rainbow, or O for a drink)
P for whistle (or P for a penny, or P for ming fleas, or P for idious Albion)
Q for buses (or Q for seats, or Q for a song)
R for mo (or R for Askey)
S for you (or S for Williams)
T for two
U for instance
V for La France (or V for la différence)
W for a bob (or W for quits)
X for breakfast
Y for husband (or Y for heaven's sake, or Y for mistress)
Z for breezes.

Some versions of this alphabet need updating from time to time, since they date themselves by referring to personalities who were well known at a particular time. S has been used to refer to Esther Williams, Esther Coleman, and Esther Rantzen, while E has been applied to Eva Bartok and Eva Peron, and A, B, and K were formerly used respectively for Ava Gardner, Lord Beaverbrook, and Kay Francis.

Another alphabetic amusement is to make a sentence from words beginning with the letters of the alphabet in their correct order. An advertisement in *The Times* in 1842 read as follows:

To widowers and single gentlemen.—*Wanted* by a lady, a *situation* to super-intend the household and preside at table. She is agreeable, becoming, careful, desirable, English, facetious, generous, honest, industrious, judi-cious, keen, lively, merry, natty, obedient, philosophic, quiet, regular, sociable, tasteful, useful, vivacious, womanish, xantippish, youthful, zealous, &c.

A party game can be made from the challenge to write a sentence of this kind, preferably one that tells a story. Here are some examples:

Able bodied conscientious dustmen emptying filthy garbage handle in-describable junk. Kitchen leftovers make noxious odours producing quite revolting stenches. This unwholesome vegetation won't exactly yield zeal.

A born coward, Darius eventually found great happiness in judicially kicking loud-mouthed nepotists openly picking quarrels, rightly saying that un-kindness vitiated warring Xerxes' youthful zeal.

The game of TELEGRAMS as described by A. A. Milne is based on the same idea:

A game is not really a game unless somebody can win it. For this reason I cannot wholly approve 'telegrams'. To concoct a telegram whose words begin with certain selected letters of the alphabet, say the first ten, is to amuse youself anyhow and possibly your friends; whether you say, 'Am bringing camel down early Friday. Got hump. Inform Jamrach'; or, 'Afraid better cancel dinner engagement. Fred got horrid indigestion.—Jane.' But it is impossible to declare yourself certainly the winner.

Telegrams can also be played by selecting a word and making the players write a telegram using the letters of that word as the initials of the words in the telegram. Ideally the telegram should have some connection with the chosen word. Thus, if the word is *Christmas*, the telegram might read: 'Come home, Richard. I'm serving turkey, mince, and sausages.'

A similar game is ACRONYMS, in which players take a word or phrase, and make an appropriate sentence from words beginning with its letters. Thus *shovel* could be described as 'sharp hand-operated vertical earth lifter', *snail* could be 'slimy nocturnal animal invading lettuces', and *brain* could be 'box retaining assorted interesting notions'. This game is a favourite theme for competitions in the *New Statesman*, from which are gathered these examples using the titles of films and plays:

Just a white shark.
Space, time, and relativity with a ridiculous script.
This has everything: syrupy outbursts, uplifting nannies, dancing over flowery mountains, unctuous songs involving children.
Clichés harvest awards! Runners in old-time shorts. Oxford flummery. Flabby idealism. Rotten ending.
Endless vivacity in the Argentine.
A nauseating nymphet ineffably embalmed.

Innumerable games depend on working through the alphabet. Perhaps the oldest is I LOVE MY LOVE, which is mentioned in Pepys's *Diary* for 4 March 1669 and Charles Dickens's *Christmas Carol* (1843). The first player has to describe his or her sweetheart, using words that begin with A. The next player uses words that begin with B, and so on. In *The Girl's Own Book* (1869), Lydia Child gives a typical response from someone who has been assigned the letter A:

I love my love with an A because he is Artless. I hate him with an A because he is Avaricious. He took me to the sign of the Anchor, and treated me to Apples and Almonds. His name is Abraham, and he comes from Alnwick.

Some players of this game omit the letters X, Y, and Z, but Lydia Child gives examples for each of these. This is her version for X:

I love my love with an X because he is a Xylographer. I hate him with an X because he is a Xerophagian. He took me to the sign of the Xebec, and treated me to Xiphias-fish and Xeres wine. His name is Xavier, and he comes from Xalapa.

The categories vary in different versions of this game. Sometimes the players only have to say why they love their loves. In other cases, they have to add what they gave their love as a present. *Cassell's Book of Indoor Amusements* (1881) notes that:

This simple game must be one of no recent invention if the tale be true told by Mr Foote, the celebrated wit. He narrates that one day the Ladies Cheere, Fielding, and Hill were amusing themselves by playing at the children's game of 'I Love My Love'. Lady Cheere began by saying, 'I love my love with an N, because he is a Night' (Knight); Lady Fielding followed with, 'I love my love with a G, because he is a Gustus' (Justice); and Lady Hill added, 'I love my love with an F, because he is a Fizishun' (Physician). So much for the spelling powers of the ladies in the olden times.

Another favourite Victorian game was THE MINISTER'S CAT, also known as THE PARSON'S CAT or THE VICAR'S CAT. It is described in A. B. Gomme's *Games for Parlour and Playground* (1898):

The first player begins by saying, 'The parson's cat is an ambitious cat', the next player 'an affable cat', the next 'an amiable cat', and so on, until they have all named an adjective beginning with A. The next time of going round the adjectives must begin with B, the next time C, and so on, until the whole of the alphabet, or as much of it as is possible, has been gone through. The game is made more difficult and more interesting by each player having to repeat what the previous players have said, and then adding his or her own contribution.

Sometimes the players have to name the cat as well as describing it, so they might say, 'The minister's cat is an agile cat and its name is Archibald.' The letter X is usually omitted, although the cat could be described as xenophobic and named Xerxes, Xavier, or Xenocrates.

In A WAS AN APPLE PIE, named after the children's alphabet quoted at the start of this chapter, participants have to think of verbs that start with successive letters of the alphabet. The first player might say: 'A was an apple pie. A *ate* it.' The second might say: 'B *baked* it.' The third might say: 'C *chose* it,' and so on.

TRAVELLER'S ALPHABET follows the same principle. A player names a country or town to which he is going. He is then asked 'What will you do there?' and has to reply using verbs, adjectives, and nouns that begin with the same letter as the place-name. So if someone says, 'I am going to Halifax' he might then say, 'I shall hum harmonious hymns' or 'I shall have harmful habits'. Usually the place-names have to start with successive letters of the alphabet, so the next player would have to think of a place beginning with I. *Foulsham's Fun Book* (1933) quotes the following exchange heard during the game:

Austere Lady— I hear you are going on a journey to Cambridge. What will you do there?

Nasty Little Boy— I shall catch caterpillars and let them crawl on my collar.

CATEGORIES or GUGGENHEIM presents the same sort of challenge. It is a pencil-and-paper game in which each person is given a list of categories to write down the left-hand side of their paper. The categories can be such things as animals, fishes, birds, towns, books, or composers. A word of five or six letters is chosen and the players write this along the top of their paper, and have to use each letter of it as the initial for a word under each category. Here is an example, where the chosen word is *pencil*:

	P	E	N	C	I	L
Flower:	pansy	edelweiss	narcissus	clarkia	iris	lupin
Animal:	pig	elephant	newt	cat	iguana	lion
City:	Portsmouth	Ely	Newport	Chester	Inverness	Leicester
Writer:	Pepys	Eliot	Noyes	Chaucer	Ibsen	Lamb
Composer:	Puccini	Elgar	Nielsen	Copland	Ireland	Liszt

A player scores a point for each word that no other player has written, or one point for each of the players who have not got the same word. In the latter case, if twenty people are playing and only one person has written 'Puccini' for the composer beginning with P, that person scores nineteen points. Categories sometimes differs from Guggenheim in using a single letter of the alphabet rather than a word of several letters.

Some authorities suggest that the game Guggenheim is so called because it was first played in the Guggenheim family. But Frank Scully gives another explanation in his book, *Fun in Bed* (1934). He says that Howard Dietz, Jerome Kern, and P. G. Wodehouse were playing a game of Categories. One category was 'printers' and Kern wrote down 'Gutenberg'. P. G. Wodehouse had never heard of Gutenberg and did not believe Kern's assertion that Gutenberg was the first printer. Some months later, when Dietz suggested another game of Categories, Wodehouse said: 'All right, but no more of your Guggenheims.'

(16)

Playing with Poetry

In the days when poetry was a favourite pastime of the leisured classes, it was natural for people to turn their attention to playing games and tricks with poems. Most of the games which follow have now died out or are found only rarely.

Poets generally have an idea for a poem and then sit down to find the right words to express that idea. However, a few writers have written poetry the other way round—starting with the words (or, more exactly, the words at the end of each line) and then writing the poem. They begin with a list of rhymed words—called *bouts-rimés* (or rhymed endings)—and try to make a poem out of them.

Isaac d'Israeli wrote:

I find the origin of *Bouts-rimés*, or 'Rhyming Ends', in Goujet's Bib. fr. xvi. p. 181. One Dulot, a foolish poet, when sonnets were in demand, had a singular custom of preparing the rhymes of these poems to be filled up at his leisure. Having been robbed of his papers, he was regretting most the loss of three hundred sonnets: his friends were astonished that he had written so many which they had never heard. 'They were *blank sonnets*,' he replied; and explained the mystery by describing his *Bouts-rimés*. The idea appeared ridiculously amusing; and it soon became fashionable to collect the most difficult rhymes, and fill up the lines. (*Curiosities of Literature*, 1824)

Bouts-rimés became a popular pastime in eighteenth-century Britain. People began to send each other sets of rhymes to turn into verse. Thus in 1727 Mary Granville sent Mrs Pendarves a letter containing six words for her to versify: *bless, less, find, mind, grove,* and *love*. Mrs Pendarves replied by sending back another six words for Mary Granville (*tender, render, joy, boy, fasting, lasting*) as well as this poem:

When friendship such as yours our hours *Bless*,
It soothes our cares and makes affliction *Less*.
Oppressed by woes, from you I'm sure to *Find*
A sovereign cure for my distempered *Mind*;
At court or play, in field or shady *Grove*,
No place can yield delight without your *Love*.

> (*Autobiography and Correspondence of Mary Granville*
> (*Mrs Delany*), 1861)

The most famous exponent of bouts-rimés in the eighteenth century was Lady Anna Miller, who held weekly literary gatherings in her house at Batheaston, near Bath. Lady Miller kept an antique Italian vase prominently displayed, into which her guests placed the verses they had written, employing a given set of rhymed words. The writers of the best poems were crowned by Lady Miller with a laurel wreath. When a collection of this poetry was published, Horace Walpole called it 'a bouquet of artificial flowers'. The best way to get your poem praised was, of course, to make it honour the hostess and her house, as in the following:

> From Bath to Easton haste your flight,
> Prepare for scenes of sweet delight:
> Miller, to please, exerts her power,
> And asks you to her charming bower,
> Where Nature joins, in concert meet,
> With Taste, to make the place complete:
> May joy and mirth there ever glow,
> As long as Avon's streams shall flow.

> (*Poetical Amusements at a Villa near Bath*, 1776)

Such bouts-rimés inevitably produced verse of poor quality. As Leigh Hunt remarked, a set pattern of rhymes usually suggested a very conventional type of poem:

How many 'poems' are there among all these nations, of which we require no more than the rhymes, to be acquainted with the whole of them? You know what the rogues have done, by the ends they come to. For instance, what more is necessary to inform us of all which the following gentleman has for sale, than the bell which he tinkles at the end of his cry? We are as sure of him, as of the muffin man.

Grove,	Heart,	Kiss,
Night,	Prove,	Blest,
Rove	Impart,	Bliss
Delight.	Love.	Rest.

(The Liberal, 1822)

It is even possible to make a poem out of rhymes alone:

Boy,	Gun
Gun;	Bust.
Joy,	Boy
Fun.	Dust.

In the nineteenth century, bouts-rimés became a parlour game, described by 'Professor Hoffmann' in *Drawing-Room Amusements* (1879) as follows:

A number of slips of paper are distributed, and each person is invited to write two words that rhyme. The slips are then collected and read aloud, and each player is then required to write a stanza introducing all the rhymes in question.

In *The Book of Indoor Games* (1933), Hubert Phillips and B. C. Westall have a different version of the game:

One player begins by reciting what purports to be a line of verse. . . . Thus he might say: 'I found a tack upon my chair.' The next player must follow with a line that rhymes with it (and conforms reasonably with its metre), e.g. 'I cannot think who placed it there.' The next one goes on: 'At any rate, it isn't fair.' The next one: 'My clothes are now the worse for wear,' and so on. The first player who fails drops out, loses a life, or pays a forfeit; and extra points may be awarded for the neatest and wittiest lines.

An amusing development of this game is to take a line from a well-known poem (preferably the first line), and add a rhyming line that deflates the seriousness. Here are some examples:

> I think that I shall never see—
> My contact lens fell in my tea.

> In a cowslip's bell I lie—
> I'm the tiniest little guy!

> I wandered lonely as a cloud—
> Someone should have said 'B.O.!' out loud.

> Was this the face that launched a thousand ships?
> No wonder there are keel-marks on her lips.

Full fathom five thy father lies.
I pushed him. I apologize.

When lovely woman stoops to folly,
I want to be around, by golly!

Tiger, tiger, burning bright,
How you save electric light!

CENTOS

Cento is the Latin word for a patchwork cloak, and it is applied to a
kind of poetry made up of separate lines taken from different poets.
Other names for centos are 'mosaics' and 'patchwork verses'.

The cento seems to have originated in ancient Greece. There are
examples in some of the plays of Aristophanes, in which the playwright concocts verses out of lines taken from Homer and Aeschylus.
Lucian, a Greek writer of the second century AD, mentions 'a very
funny song' made by patching together pieces from Anacreon,
Hesiod, and Pindar.

Roman poets were fond of making centos from lines by Virgil. In
the late second century, for example, Hosidius Geta wrote a piece
called *Medea* in which all the characters spoke in Virgilian lines.
Ausonius (born about 310 AD in Bordeaux) wrote a 'Nuptial Cento'
from pieces of Virgil, at the order of the Emperor Valentinian. Ausonius described a cento as: 'a task for memory only, which has to
gather up scattered tags and fit these mangled scraps together into
a whole, and so is more likely to provoke your laughter than your
praise'.

The Latin poetess Proba Falconia of the fourth century used lines
from Virgil to write the stories of Adam and Eve and the life of Christ.
Later religious writers like Columban (sixth century) and Waldram
(ninth century) followed her pattern, cannibalizing the works of such
poets as Virgil, Horace, and Ovid. The Scottish poet Alexander Ross
wrote a cento in Latin called 'Virgilius Evangelizans' (1634), again
plundering the writings of Virgil.

Perhaps the earliest English cento is included in Dodsley's *Collection of Poems by Several Hands* (1775). It celebrates Shakespeare's
birthday by stringing together lines from his plays. It begins:

Peace to this meeting,
Joy and fair time, health and good wishes.
Now, worthy friends, the cause why we are met,
Is in celebration of the day that gave
Immortal Shakespeare to this favoured isle,
The most replenished sweet work of Nature
Which from the prime creation e'er she framed.
O thou, divinest Nature! how thyself thou blazon'st
In this thy son! formed in thy prodigality
To hold thy mirror up, and give the time
Its very form and pressure!

The author of this cento changed some of Shakespeare's lines to fit the sense. At least it is a better poem than the piece quoted by the Duke in Mark Twain's *Huckleberry Finn*, which is how he remembers Hamlet's famous soliloquy:

To be, or not to be; that is the bare bodkin
That makes calamity of so long life;
For who would fardels bear, till Birnam wood do come to Dunsinane,
But that the fear of something after death
Murders the innocent sleep,
Great nature's second course,
And makes us rather sling the arrows of outrageous fortune
Than fly to others that we know not of. . . .

Centos usually have this kind of unsatisfactory ramshackle quality. Laman Blanchard was joking when he defended centos in this way:

That poem can be of no inferior order of merit, in which Milton would have been proud to have written one line, Pope would have been equally vain of the authorship of a second, Byron have rejoiced in a third, Campbell gloried in a fourth . . . and so on to the end of the Ode. (*George Cruikshank's Omnibus*, 1842)

Blanchard cites a typical cento by 'the late Sir Fretful Plagiary':

Blind Thamyris, and blind Maeonides,	(*Something like Milton*)
Pursue the triumph and partake the gale!	(*Rather like Pope*)
Drop tears as fast as the Arabian trees,	(*Why, this is Shakespeare*)
To point a moral or adorn a tale.	(*Oh! it's Dr Johnson*)

(Ibid.)

One of the best-known centos is the following, here abridged:

I only know she came and went,	*Powell*
Like troutlets in a pool;	*Hood*
She was a phantom of delight,	*Wordsworth*
And I was like a fool.	*Eastman*

One kiss, dear maid, I said, and sighed,	*Coleridge*
Out of those lips unshorn,	*Longfellow*
She shook her ringlets round her head,	*Stoddard*
And laughed in merry scorn. . . .	*Tennyson*

I clasped it on her sweet, cold hand,	*Browning*
The precious golden link!	*Smith*
I calmed her fears, and she was calm,	*Coleridge*
'Drink, pretty creature, drink.'	*Wordsworth*

(J. A. Morgan, *Macaronic Poetry*, 1872)

By 1857, 'Uncle George' was writing in *Parlour Pastime for the Young* that centos were 'scarcely ever used now, except as a pastime for young people'. He described them as a game in which each person has to contribute a line of verse, rather in the manner of bouts-rimés (q.v.). However, centos are occasionally found even today. The *Times Literary Supplement* of 25 December 1981 published a cento by Philip Drew, of which this is the first stanza:

Now sleeps the crimson petal: now the white
In summer's twilight weeps itself away:
Now fades the glimmering landscape on the sight—
Fields where soft sheep from cages pull the hay,
Green cowbind, and the moonlight-coloured may,
A formless grey confusion covers all.
Along the wide canals the zephyrs play:
The woods decay, the woods decay and fall.

This verse is made up respectively from lines by Tennyson, Byron, Gray, Arnold, Shelley, Thomson, Parnell, and Tennyson.

CHAIN VERSE

Chain verse—also known as 'concatenation verse'—is a minor form of versifying which had only a few adherents in the eighteenth and nineteenth centuries. In this type of poetry, the last word of one line is repeated at the start of the next line, or the last line of one stanza is used as the first line of the next stanza.

Isaac d'Israeli tells us that chain verse was invented by 'Capitaine Lasphrise, a French self-taught poet, whose work preceded Malherbe's'. Lasphrise wrote chain verse like this:

> Falloit-il que le ciel me rendit amoureux,
> Amoureux, jouissant d'une beauté craintive,
> Craintive à recevoir la douceur excessive,
> Excessive au plaisir qui rend l'amant heureux. . . .
>
> (*Curiosities of Literature*, 1824)

Here are two English examples. The first repeats the last word, or the last two words, of each line:

> *Truth*
>
> Nerve thy soul with doctrines noble,
> Noble in the walks of time,
> Time that leads to an eternal
> An eternal life sublime;
> Life sublime in moral beauty
> Beauty that shall ever be;
> Ever be to lure thee onward
> Onward to the fountain free;
> Free to every earnest seeker,
> Seeker for the Fount of Youth,
> Youth exultant in its beauty,
> Beauty of the living truth.
>
> (J. A. Morgan, *Macaronic Poetry*, 1872)

This eighteenth-century poem by John Byrom repeats the last line of each stanza at the beginning of the next. It became a hymn in the *Irish Church Hymnal*:

> *The Desponding Soul's Wish*
>
> My Spirit longeth for thee,
> Within my troubled breast;
> Although I be unworthy
> Of so divine a guest.
>
> Of so divine a guest,
> Unworthy though I be;
> Yet has my heart no rest,
> Unless it come from Thee.

Unless it come from Thee,
In vain I look around;
In all that I can see,
No rest is to be found.

No rest is to be found,
But in thy blessed love;
O! let my wish be crown'd,
And send it from above!

ECHO VERSE

Echo verse resembles chain verse in its use of repetition. It is verse in which the last word of a line is echoed, often making a completely new word. This creates a kind of dialogue in which the echo comments ironically on what the speaker says. For example, there is a short poem in the *Greek Anthology* which begins:

α. Ἀχὼ φίλα, μοι συγκαταίνεσόν τι.—β. τί ;

That is to say:

'Echo! I love: advise me somewhat.'—'What?'

An epigram by Martial shows that echo verses were familiar to the Romans. They became widespread in England after the sixteenth-century poet Sir Philip Sidney wrote a poem called 'Philisides', which starts thus:

	Echo
Fair rocks, goodly rivers, sweet woods, when shall I see peace?	Peace.
Peace? What bars me my tongue? Who is it that comes me so nigh?	I.
Oh! I do know what guest I have met; it is Echo.	'Tis Echo.
Well met Echo, approach: then tell me thy will too.	I will too.

George Herbert's 'Heaven' holds a similar conversation with Echo:

O who will show me those delights on high?
        Echo.   *I.*
Thou Echo, thou art mortal, all men know.
        Echo.   *No.*

Wert thou not born among the trees and leaves?
                    Echo.   *Leaves.*
And are there any leaves, that still abide?
                    Echo.   *Bide*
What leaves are they? impart the matter wholly.
                    Echo.   *Holy.*
Are holy leaves the Echo then of bliss?
                    Echo.   *Yes.*
Then tell me, what is that supreme delight?
                    Echo.   *Light*
Light to the mind: what shall the will enjoy?
                    Echo   *Joy*
But are there cares and business with the pleasure?
                    Echo.   *Leisure.*
Light, joy, and leisure; but shall they persever?
                    Echo.   *Ever.*

Although George Herbert used echo verses for a religious purpose, they were more often used in humour and satire. Here is the start of an echo verse written by Abraham Cowley in 1641 as part of the contest between Cavaliers and Roundheads:

Now Echo on what's religion grounded?
                    Round-head.
Whose its professor most considerable?
                    Rabble.
How do these prove themselves to be the godly?
                    Oddly.
But they in life are known to be the holy.
                    O lie.

Here is a humorous echo verse from about 1760:

If I address the Echo yonder,
What will its answer be, I wonder?
                    Echo— I wonder.
O wondrous Echo, tell me, *blessé,*
Am I for marriage or celibacy?
                    Echo— Silly Bessy.
If then to win the maid I try,
Shall I find her a property?
                    Echo— A proper tie.
If neither being grave nor funny
Will win the maid to matrimony?
                    Echo— Try money.

> If I should try to gain her heart,
> Shall I go plain, or rather smart?
>> *Echo*— Smart.
> She mayn't love dress, and I, again, then
> May come too plain, and she'll complain then?
>> *Echo*— Come plain, then.
> To please her most, perhaps 'tis best
> To come as I'm in common dressed?
>> *Echo*— Come undressed.
> Then, if to marry me I tease her,
> What will she say if that should please her?
>> *Echo*— Please, sir.
> When cross nor good words can appease her—
> What if such naughty whims should seize her?
>> *Echo*— You'd see, sir.
> When wed she'll change, for Love's no stickler,
> And love her husband less than liquor?
>> *Echo*— Then lick her.
> To leave me then I can't compel her,
> Though every woman else excel her.
>> *Echo*— Sell her.
> The doubting youth to Echo turned again, sir,
> To ask advice, but found it did not answer.
>> (W. T. Dobson, *Literary Frivolities*, 1880)

Echo verses went out of favour, and only occasional echoes of them were heard in the nineteenth and twentieth centuries, such as Geoffrey Hellman's 'I am the King of Siam, I am' and this couplet from the *Sunday Times* in 1831 'on the charge made for seats at the Opera House to see and hear the Orpheus of violinists':

> What are they who pay three guineas
> To hear a tune of Paganini's?
>> *Echo*. Pack o' ninnies!

EQUIVOQUES

Equivoques or 'equivocal verses' were probably a French invention. The fashion for them is said to have been started by a French poet appropriately called Crétin, who died in 1525. They are verses that can be read in two different ways, usually by taking the lines in two different orders.

In the following poem from *The Weekly Pacquet of Advice from Rome* (1679), the Protestant will read the lines straight across, while the Catholic would read down each column:

The Jesuit's Double-Faced Creed

I hold for sound faith	What England's church allows
What Rome's faith saith	My conscience disavows
Where the king's head	The flock can take no shame
The flock's misled	Who hold the Pope supreme
Where th'altar's dress'd	The worship's scarce divine
The people's bless'd	Whose table's bread and wine
He's but an ass	Who their communion flies
Who shuns the Mass	Is Catholic and wise.

Such verses gave equivoques their alternative name of 'Jesuitical verses'. Similarly ambiguous loyalties are found in this poem, which is patriotic as it stands but revolutionary if the lines are read in the numbered order:

1. I love my country—but the King
3. Above all men his praise I sing,
2. Destruction to his odious reign
4. That plague of princes, Thomas Paine;
5. The royal banners are displayed
7. And may success the standard aid
6. Defeat and ruin seize the cause
8. Of France, her liberty, and laws.
       (C. C. Bombaugh, *Gleanings for the Curious*, 1890)

Another set of equivoques has nothing to do with religion or politics but it expresses a cynical view of marriage, unless one reads the alternate lines only:

That man must lead a happy life
Who's free from matrimonial chains,
Who is directed by a wife
Is sure to suffer for his pains

Adam could find no solid peace
When Eve was given for a mate;
Until he saw a woman's face
Adam was in a happy state.

In all the female race appear
Hypocrisy, deceit, and pride;

Truth, darling of a heart sincere,
In woman never did reside.

What tongue is able to unfold
The failings that in woman dwell;
The worths in woman we behold
Are almost imperceptible.

Confusion take the man, I say,
Who changes from his singleness,
Who will not yield to woman's sway,
Is sure of earthly blessedness.

(W. S. Walsh, *Handy-Book of Literary Curiosities*, 1892)

Finally, here is an equivoque in prose. It was supposedly written by Cardinal Richelieu to the French ambassador in Rome but was probably composed at a later date. Its ambiguous form might be useful today for anyone who has to write a testimonial for someone they dislike.

First read the letter across, then double it in the middle, and read the first column.

SIR,— Mons. Compigne, a Savoyard by birth, is the man who will present to you this letter. He is one of the most meddling persons that I have ever known He has long earnestly solicited me to give him a suitable character, which I have accordingly granted to his importunity; for, believe me, Sir, I should be sorry that you should be misinformed of his real character; as some other gentlemen have been, and those among the best of my friends; I think it my duty to advertise you to have especial attention to all he does, nor venture to say any thing before him, in any sort; for I may truly say, there is none whom I should more regret to see received and trusted in decent society. And I well know, that as soon as you shall become acquainted with him you will thank me for this my advice. Courtesy obliges me to desist from saying any thing more on this subject. a Friar of the order of Saint Benedict, as his passport to your protection, discreet, the wisest and the least or have had the pleasure to converse with. to write to you in his favor, and together with a letter of credence; his real merit, rather I must say, than to his modesty is only exceeded by his worth. wanting in serving him on account of being I should be afflicted if you were misled on that score, who now esteem him, wherefore, and from no other motive that you are most particularly desired, to show him all the respect imaginable, that may either offend or displease him no man I love so much as M. Compigne, neglected, as no one can be more worthy to be Base, therefore, would it be to injure him. are made sensible of his virtues, and you will love him as I do; and then The assurance I entertain of your urging this matter to you further, or Believe me, Sir, &c.   RICHELIEU.

(C. C. Bombaugh, *Gleanings for the Curious*, 1890)

PROSE POEMS

Critics of some modern poetry claim that it is merely prose cut up into lines made to look like poetry. Indeed, in editing *The Oxford Book of Modern Verse*, W. B. Yeats printed as the first poem a passage from Pater's prose essay on Leonardo da Vinci, which Yeats himself had cut up into a poem. Poetry has been found in the prose of such writers as Dickens and Dr Johnson, and these discoveries are called 'prose poems' or 'found poems'.

Respectable poems have been made by John S. Barnes from the prose work of Thomas Wolfe (in *A Stone, A Leaf, A Door*) and by John Updike from one of Dr Johnson's notebooks (in *Telephone Poles and Other Poems*). In his *Abracadabra* (1967), J. R. Colombo even found poems in extracts from the *Encyclopaedia Britannica* and Sax Rohmer's *The Insidious Dr Fu-Manchu*.

Poetry has also been discovered in such apparently unpoetic works as a nineteenth-century treatise on Mechanics by Dr William Whewell, Master of Trinity College, Cambridge. He was annoyed when people pointed out the poetry in: 'There is no force, however great, can stretch a cord, however fine, into a horizontal line, which is accurately straight.' Such accidental verse is quite common. Addison wrote: 'What I am going to mention, will perhaps deserve your attention' (recalling the old joke, 'I'm a poet, and I don't know it'). In his second inaugural address, Abraham Lincoln temporarily lapsed into poetry:

> Fondly do we hope,
> Fervently do we pray,
> That this mighty scourge of war
> May speedily pass away.
> Yet if it be God's will
> That it continue until . . .

Prose writers often fall into verse when they are trying to be 'poetic', as in this awful piece of near-verse from Disraeli's *Wondrous Tale of Alroy*:

Why am I here? are you not here? and need I urge a stronger plea? Oh, brother dear, I pray you come and mingle in our festival! Our walls are hung with flowers you love; I culled them by the fountain's side; the holy lamps are trimmed and set, and you must raise their earliest flame. Without the gate my maidens wait to offer you a robe of state.

While some people eagerly search prose writings to find pieces of unconscious poetry, others delight in concealing poems in their prose. In a letter to John Newton in 1781, William Cowper wrote:

My very dear friend,

I am going to send, what when you have read, you may scratch your head, and say, I suppose, there's nobody knows, whether what I have got, be verse or not—by the tune and the time, it ought to be rhyme, but if it be, did you ever see, of late or of yore, such a ditty before?

The letter continues in this style at some length.

In his *Fable for Critics* (1848), James Russell Lowell included doggerel verse not only in his preface but also facing the title-page (see p. 149).

Perhaps the neatest example of hidden verse is in Lewis Carroll's 'Hiawatha's Photographing'(1857). The poem uses the well-known rhythm of Longfellow's *Hiawatha* to tell a story about a photographer but Carroll's preface to the poem also has something of Longfellow about it:

In an age of imitation, I can claim no special merit for this slight attempt at doing what is known to be so easy. Any fairly practised writer, with the slightest ear for rhythm, could compose, for hours together, in the easy running metre of 'The Song of Hiawatha'. Having, then, distinctly stated that I challenge no attention in the following little poem to its merely verbal jingle, I must beg the candid reader to confine his criticism to its treatment of the subject.

RHOPALICS

Last, and almost certainly least, in this chapter come rhopalic verses, in which each line consists of words having one more syllable than the preceding word in the line. So the first word of a line will have one syllable, the second word will have two syllables, and so on. These are called 'rhopalic' from the Greek word *rhopale* meaning a club, because a club is thin at one end and thick at the other.

Sir Thomas Browne pointed out rhopalic lines in Homer's *Iliad*, and in a poem by Ausonius: 'Spes Deus aeternae stationis con-

READER ! *walk up at once (it will soon be too late) and buy
at a perfectly ruinous rate*

A

FABLE FOR CRITICS;

OR

Better—

*I like, as a thing that the reader's first fancy may strike,
an old fashioned title-page,
such as presents a tabular view of the volume's contents—*

A GLANCE
AT A FEW OF OUR LITERARY PROGENIES

(*Mrs. Malaprop's word*)

FROM

THE TUB OF DIOGENES;

A VOCAL AND MUSICAL MEDLEY

THAT IS,

A SERIES OF JOKES

By A Wonderful Quiz,

*who accompanies himself with a rub-a-dub-dub, full of spirit and grace,
on the top of the tub.*

SET FORTH IN

October, the 21st day, in the year '48.

G. P. PUTNAM, BROADWAY.

ciliator.' But few poets have actually written rhopalics deliberately. Here is a short attempt by W. R. Espy:

> May eagles lacerate eternally
> Your liver, overproud Prometheus!
> Your fiery offering, predictably,
> Has rendered humankind vainglorious.

Dmitri Borgmann describes prose rhopalics in which each word has one *letter* more than the preceding word. He gives this example:

I do not know where family doctors acquired illegibly perplexing handwriting; nevertheless, extraordinary pharmaceutical intellectuality, counterbalancing indecipherability, transcendentalizes intercommunications' incomprehensibleness.

A contributor to *Word Ways* in November 1981 supplied the following example of rhopalic prose with the words increasing by one *syllable* each time:

Some people completely misunderstand administrative extemporization— idiosyncratical antianthropomorphism undenominationalizing politico- ecclesiastical honorificabilitudinity.

Concrete Poetry

Early in the 1950s, people in Brazil, Switzerland, and Sweden began experimenting with a new form of poetry. Each was unaware that similar experiments were being made in other countries. In Brazil, the Noigandres group of poets (Decio Pignatari, Augusto de Campos, and Haraldo de Campos) decided to call their invention *poesia concreta*. In Switzerland, Eugen Gomringer independently chose a similar name: *die konkrete Dichtung*. And in Sweden, Öyvind Fahlström published a *Manifesto for Concrete Poetry* in 1953. When the Swiss and Brazilian experimenters met at Ulm in 1955, they agreed to call their invention CONCRETE POETRY.

Concrete poetry is half way between literature and art. It uses words and letters to create patterns, shapes, or pictures. Normal sentence-construction takes second place to the way the letters are arranged on the page. Concrete poets 'play' with words in a way that is nearer the work of sculptors and painters than poets: they invite us to look at a piece of text as if it were a picture or a piece of sculpture. Typical of the early experiments is this poem from Eugen Gomringer's *Constellations* (1953):

```
silencio   silencio   silencio
silencio   silencio   silencio
silencio              silencio
silencio   silencio   silencio
silencio   silencio   silencio
```

Concrete poetry seemed to be something radically new, but it had been anticipated several decades earlier. In *Un Coup de Dés* (1897), the French poet Mallarmé scattered words about the page with large spaces between. The Italian futurist Filippo Tommaso Marinetti wrote in 1914 that words should be set free from their 'scientific and photographic perspective, [which is] absolutely contrary to the rights of emotion'. He believed that words should illustrate their own meanings. In his *Les Mots en Liberté* (1919), capital and small printed letters were jumbled together with handwritten letters.

Apollinaire's *Calligrammes* (1918) includes a poem about rain in which the words are arranged in long, slanting lines. Other writers who anticipated the methods of concrete poetry were Gerard Manley Hopkins, James Joyce, and the American poet e.e. cummings, who arranged letters in special ways to add an extra dimension to his poems:

```
                    n
                    OthI
                    n

                    g can

                    s
                    urPas
                    s

                    the m

                    y
                    SteR
                    y

                    of

                    s
                    tilLnes
                    s
```

The Swiss painter Paul Klee made pictures by combining several capital letters. And the *lettrists* of the 1940s treated letters as isolated units, making poems out of meaningless combinations and even inventing new letters of the alphabet.

These pioneers might have been surprised to learn that experiments with concrete poetry had been made more than 2,000 years earlier. Simmias of Rhodes, a Greek poet who flourished about 324 BC, wrote three poems in the shape of an egg, a hatchet, and a pair of wings. The ancient Romans and Persians also wrote shaped poems. The medieval Latin poet Mellin de Saint-Gellais (1481-1558) followed Simmias in writing verses shaped like wings, as did the seventeenth-century English poet George Herbert in his 'Easter Wings':

Lord, who createdst man in wealth and store,
　　Though foolishly he lost the same,
　　　Decaying more and more,
　　　　Till he became
　　　　　Most poor:
　　　　　With thee
　　　　O let me rise
　　　As larks, harmoniously,
　　And sing this day thy victories:
Then shall the fall further the flight in me.

My tender age in sorrow did begin:
　　And still with sicknesses and shame
　　　Thou didst so punish sin,
　　　　That I became
　　　　　Most thin.
　　　　　With thee
　　　　Let me combine,
　　　And feel this day thy victory:
　　For, if I imp my wing on thine,
Affliction shall advance the flight in me.

George Herbert also wrote a poem shaped like an altar:

The Altar

A broken ALTAR, Lord, thy servant rears,
Made of a heart, and cemented with tears:
　Whose parts are as 'hy hand did frame;
　No workman's tool hath touch'd the same.
　　　　　A　HEART　alone
　　　　　Is　such　a　stone,
　　　　　As　nothing　but
　　　　　Thy pow'r doth cut.
　　　　　Wherefore each part
　　　　　Of my hard heart
　　　　　Meets in this frame,
　　　　　To praise thy name.
　　That if I chance to hold my peace,
　　These stones to praise thee may not cease.
O let thy blessed SACRIFICE be mine,
And sanctifie this ALTAR to be thine.

In his *Gleanings for the Curious* (1890), C. C. Bombaugh wrote:

The quaint conceit of making verses assume grotesque shapes and devices, expressive of the theme selected by the writer, appears to have been most fashionable during the seventeenth century. Writers tortured their brains in order to torture their verses into all sorts of fantastic forms, from a flower-pot to an obelisk, from a pin to a pyramid. Hearts and fans were chosen for love-songs; wine-glasses, bottles, and casks for Bacchanalian songs; pulpits, altars, and monuments for religious verses and epitaphs.

Other writers confirm that the seventeenth century was a time of great popularity for all kinds of shaped poetry. Ben Jonson refers to:

> those finer flames
> Of eggs, and halberds, cradles, and a hearse,
> A pair of scissors and a comb in verse . . .
>
> (*The Underwood, a.* 1637)

while Samuel Butler has this to say about the poet Samuel Benlowes:

As for altars and pyramids in poetry, he has outdone all men that way; for he has a made a gridiron and a frying-pan in verse, that, beside the likeness in shape, the very tone and sound of the words did perfectly represent the noise that is made by those utensils.   (*Characters, a.* 1680)

Shaped poems were also found in other countries of Europe. The French writer Pannard wrote two drinking-songs in the shape of a wine-glass and a bottle. H. B. Wheatley used the wine-glass shape shown overleaf on the title-page of his book about anagrams and other word play.

Serious writers tended to regard such verses with contempt. In *The Spectator* for 7 May 1711, Addison was as ironical about shaped poetry as he was about all other forms of 'false wit':

It was impossible for a man to succeed in these performances who was not a kind of painter, or at least a designer. He was first of all to draw the outline of the subject which he intended to write upon, and afterwards conform the description to the figure of his subject. The poetry was to contract or dilate itself according to the mould in which it was cast. In a word, the verses were to be cramped or extended to the dimensions of the frame that was prepared for them; and to undergo the fate of those persons whom the tyrant Procrustes used to lodge in his iron bed; if they were too short, he

OF ANAGRAMS,

A MONOGRAPH TREATING OF THEIR
HISTORY FROM THE EARLIEST AGES
TO THE PRESENT TIME; WITH AN
INTRODUCTION,   CONTAINING
NUMEROUS   SPECIMENS   OF
MACARONIC   POETRY,
PUNNING   MOTTOES,
RHOPALIC,   SHAPED,
EQUIVOCAL,   LYON,
AND ECHO VERSES,
ALLITERATION,
ACROSTICS,
LIPOGRAMS,   CHRONOGRAMS,
LOGOGRAMS,   PALINDROMES,
BOUTS
RIMÉS.
BY

H. B. WHEATLEY.

PRINTED
FOR THE
AUTHOR
BY STEPHEN AUSTIN, HERTFORD;
AND SOLD BY WILLIAMS & NORGATE,
HENRIETTA STREET; J. R. SMITH, SOHO SQUARE;
T. & W. BOONE, NEW BOND STREET, LONDON. MDCCCLXII.

stretched them on a rack, and if they were too long, chopped off a part of their legs, till they fitted the couch which he had prepared for them.

Perhaps such disapproval accounted for shaped poems going out of fashion after the seventeenth century. However, one of the best-known examples dates from Victorian times: the 'Mouse's Tale' from Lewis Carroll's *Alice in Wonderland*:

'Mine is a long and sad tale!' said the Mouse, turning to Alice, and sighing.

'It *is* a long tail, certainly,' said Alice, looking down with wonder at the Mouse's tail; 'but why do you call it sad?' And she kept on puzzling about it while the Mouse was speaking, so that her idea of the tale was something like this: ——

```
                    'Fury  said  to
                        a mouse, That
                            he  met  in  the
                                house,    "Let
                                    us  both  go
                                        to   law:   I
                                        will  prose-
                                        cute you.—
                                        Come,  I'll
                                        take  no  de-
                                    nial:    We
                                must  have
                            the  trial;
                        For   really
                    this   morn-
                ing  I've
            nothing
            to  do."
            Said  the
                mouse  to
                    the   cur,
                        "Such    a
                            trial, dear
                                sir,  With
                                    no  jury
                                    or judge,
                                    would
                                be wast-
                            ing  our
                        breath."
                    "I'll   be
                    judge,
                I'll be
            jury,"
            said
            cun-
              ning
                old
                    Fury:
                        "I'll
                        try
                        the
                        whole
                        cause,
                        and
                    con-
                demn
            you to
        death".'
```

Shaped poetry was enduringly popular in the Orient. W. T. Dobson wrote in his *Literary Frivolities* (1880):

Both in China and Japan such literary feats are held in great esteem even in the present day; in the latter country the poet not unfrequently arranges his verses in the shape of a man's head—thus perhaps giving a facial outline of the subject of his verse; and though the Chinese may not make so good a choice, taking perhaps a cow or some other animal for the design, they display greater ingenuity by so doing.

William Alger confirmed this, in his *The Poetry of the East* (1856):

I have seen an erotic triplet composed by a Hindu poet, the first line representing a bow, the second its string, the third an arrow aimed at the heart of the object of his passion:

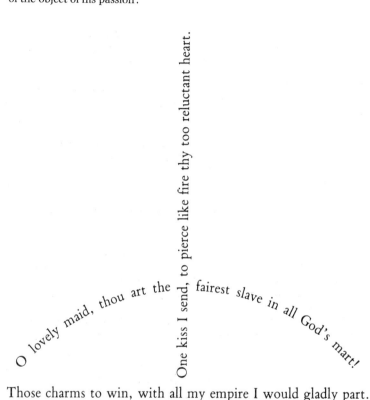

Those charms to win, with all my empire I would gladly part.

The creation of concrete poetry in the 1950s brought a renaissance in enthusiasm for shaped poems, although the new movement went much further than simply producing poems in the shapes of objects. Experiments included writing poetry by computer, transforming one word gradually into another, using the signs on the typewriter to build up pictures, and even the creation of three-dimensional 'poems' resembling sculptures. Here are examples from the work of Ian Hamilton Finlay and Edwin Morgan (from Scotland), and Emmett Williams (from the United States).

```
                              pair g
                            rl au pair
                           )air girl au
                           au pair girl
                          au pair girl a
                         rl au pair girl a
                        )air girl au pair gir
                       girl au pair girl au pair
                      )air girl au pair girl au pa
                     air girl au pair girl au pair
                     pair girl au pair girl au pa
                    lu pair girl au pair girl au
   (Ian Hamilton Finlay)     irl au pair girl au pair
                          girl au pair girl
```

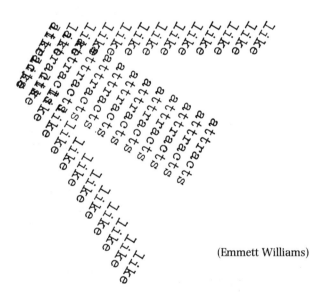

(Emmett Williams)

```
Pool.
Peopl
 e plop!
Cool.
```

(Edwin Morgan, 'Summer
Haiku')

```
jollymerry
hollyberry
jollyberry
merryholly
happyjolly
jollyjelly
jellybelly
bellymerry
hollyheppy
jollyMolly
marryJerry
merryHarry
hoppyBarry
heppyJarry
boppyheppy
berryjorry
jorryjolly
moppyjelly
Mollymerry
Jerryjolly
bellyboppy
jorryhoppy
hollymoppy
Barrymerry
Jarryhappy
happyboppy
boppyjolly
jollymerry
merrymerry
merrymerry
merryChris
ammerryasa
Chrismerry
asMERRYCHR
YSANTHEMUM
```

(Edwin Morgan, 'The Computer's
first Christmas card')

Tongue-Twisters and Cumulative Games

TONGUE-TWISTERS arose from the human tendency to alliterate—putting together words with the same sounds, usually those at the beginning of each word. Alliteration is a natural habit, as can be seen in such familiar phrases as 'good as gold', 'fit as a fiddle', and 'pretty as a picture'. The tendency to alliterate even leads people to misquote the last line of Milton's *Lycidas* ('Tomorrow to fresh woods and pastures new') as 'Tomorrow to fresh fields and pastures new'.

Alliteration has always been an important element in poetry. It was an essential feature of ancient Celtic and Germanic verse, in which rhyme was less common than today. Anglo-Saxon poems like *The Battle of Maldon* used a great deal of alliteration, as did Langland's Middle English poem *Piers Plowman*, which begins:

> In a summer season when soft was the sun,
> I shope [dressed] me in shrouds, as I a sheep were.

The last fully alliterative poem in English is generally agreed to be *Scottish Field*, written soon after 1515 about the Battle of Flodden. Perhaps the nineteenth-century versifier Henry Weber was imitating it in his 'Battle of Flodden Field', which is full of excruciating alliteration:

> Most fierce he fought at Thallian Field,
> Where Martin Swart on ground lay slain;
> Where rage did reign he never reel'd,
> But like a rock did still remain.

Rhyme took the place of alliteration as the accepted unifying ingredient of verse, but poets continued to use what Charles Churchill called 'apt alliteration's artful aid'. Thus in Spenser's *Faerie Queene* we find: 'He used to slug, or sleep in slothful shade', while Coleridge in the *Ancient Mariner* has,

> The fair breeze blew, the white foam flew,
> The furrow followed free.

Swinburne was notorious for his use of alliteration:

> O swallow, sister, O fair swift swallow,
> Why wilt thou fly after spring to the south,
> The soft south whither thine heart is set?   ('Itylus')

He was good-humoured enough to recognize his own failing, which he parodied in a poem called 'Nephelidia' that began:

> From the depth of the dreamy decline of the dawn through a notable nimbus of nebulous moonshine,
> Pallid and pink as the palm of the flag-flower that flickers with fear of the flies as they float . . .

Shakespeare made fun of such excessive alliteration when he gave Quince in *A Midsummer Night's Dream* these tongue-twisting lines:

> Whereat, with blade, with bloody blameful blade,
> He bravely broach'd his boiling bloody breast.

It was a short step from here to the tongue-twister proper: a sentence or rhyme that is deliberately difficult to pronounce. These seem to have come into fashion early in the nineteenth century, when several books printed one of the most popular tongue-twisters of all:

> *Peter Piper pick'd a peck of pepper:*
> *Did Peter Piper pick a peck of pepper?*
> *If Peter Piper pick'd a peck of pepper,*
> *Where's the peck of pepper Peter Piper pick'd?*

This tongue-twister often has 'pickled' inserted before 'pepper' but the wording above is found in *Peter Piper's Practical Principles of Plain and Perfect Pronunciation* (1819), which contains one tongue-twister for each letter of the alphabet. The one for L is:

> *Lanky Lawrence lost his lass and lobster:*
> *Did Lanky Lawrence lose his lass and lobster?*
> *If Lanky Lawrence lost his lass and lobster,*
> *Where are the lass and lobster Lanky Lawrence lost?*

All the tongue-twisters in Peter Piper's book take the same stereotyped form ('Did . . . ? If . . . Where . . . ?'), but the final verse covers the last three letters of the alphabet thus:

XYZ have made my brains to crack-o,
X smokes, Y snuffs, and Z chews tobacco;
Yet oft by XYZ much learning's taught;
But Peter Piper beats them all to nought.

Mrs L. M. Child's *Girl's Own Book* (1832) has a slightly different wording for 'Peter Piper':

> *Peter Piper picked a peck of pickled peppers;*
> *A peck of pickled peppers Peter Piper picked;*
> *If Peter Piper picked a peck of pickled peppers,*
> *Where is the peck of pickled peppers Peter Piper picked?*

This became the generally accepted form for tongue-twisters of a conventional sort.

Mrs Child quotes several tongue-twisters in French, such as these:

Etánt sorti sans parapluie, il m'eut plus plu qu'il plut plus tôt.
A Frenchman having taken herb tea for a cough, his neighbour asked him, '*Ton thé, t'a t'il ôté ta toux?*'

J. A. Morgan cited an example of an even earlier French tongue-twister:

A very learned Frenchman in conversation with Dr Wallace of Oxford, about the year 1650, after expatiating on the copiousness of the French language, and its richness in derivations and synonyms, produced, by way of illustration, the following four lines on rope-making:

> *Quand un cordier, cordant, veut corder une corde;*
> *Pour sa corde corder, trois cordons il accorde,*
> *Mais, si un des cordons de la corde décorde*
> *Le cordon décordant fait décorder la corde.*

To show that the English language was at least equally rich and copious, Dr Wallace immediately translated the French into as many lines of English, word for word, using the word *twist* to express the French *corde*:

> *When a twister a twisting, will twist him a twist:*
> *For the twisting a twist, he three twines will entwist,*
> *But if one of the twines of the twist do untwist,*
> *The twine that untwisteth, untwisteth the twist.*
>
> (*Macaronic Poetry*, 1872)

J. A. Morgan also quotes 'the epigram written with a diamond on a window-pane of the hotel Sans Souci, Baden-Baden':

Venez ici, sans souci, vous
partirez d'ici sans six sous. (Ibid.)

Tongue-twisters are found in many languages besides French. Spanish has *Dijo un jaque de Jerez, con su faja y traje majo*, while Dutch has *Acht-en-tachtig glad geschuurde kacheltjes*, and Gaelic has *Cha robh reatha leathann, liath, riamh reamhar* ('a broad grey ram was never fat'). Italian boasts the following:

Se l'Archivescovo di Costantinopoli si volesse disarcivescoviscostantino politannizzare, vi disarcivescoviscostantinopolitannizzereste voi per non fare dis arcivescoviscostantinopolitannizzare lui?

('If the Archbishop of Constantinople wished to give up his archbishopric, would you do the same in order that he may not give up his arch-bishopric?')

(*Notes and Queries*, 6 June 1903)

To the outsider, the Welsh language seems to be full of natural tongue-twisters, notably the name of the village *Llanfair-pwllgwyngyllgogerychwyrndrobwllllantysiliogogogoch*, which means literally 'St Mary's Church in the hollow of the white hazel near the rapid whirlpool of Llantysilio of the red cave'. The name is usually abbreviated to 'Llanfair P. G.' in the neighbourhood.

R. H. Barham, in 'Look at the Clock' (from his *Ingoldsby Legends*), poked fun at the tongue-twisting unpronounceability of Welsh place-names:

Not far from his dwelling,
From the vale proudly swelling,
Rose a mountain; its name you'll excuse me from telling,
For the vowels made use of in Welsh are so few
That the A and the E, the I, O, and the U,
Have really but little or nothing to do;
And the duty, of course, falls the heavier by far,
On the L, and the H, and the N, and the R.
Its first syllable 'Pen',
Is pronounceable;—then
Come two LLs, and two HHs, two FFs and an N;
About half a score Rs, and some Ws follow,
Beating all my best efforts at euphony hollow:
But we shan't have to mention it often, so when
We do, with your leave, we'll curtail it to 'Pen'.

Another comic poet, Thomas Hood, used tongue-twisting words for humorous effect:

> The poor dramatist, all fume and fret,
> Fuss, fidget, fancy, fever, funking, fright,
> Ferment, fault-fearing, faintness—more f's yet:
> Flush'd, frigid, flurried, flinching, fitful, flat,—
> Add famish'd, fuddled, and fatigued, to that;
> Funeral, fate-foreboding—sits in doubt,
> Or rather doubt with hope, a wretched marriage,
> To see his play upon the stage come out.
>
> ('Ode to Perry', *a.* 1845)

The best-known tongue-twisters in verse are probably the patter songs written by W. S. Gilbert for his operas with Arthur Sullivan. In *The Pirates of Penzance*, the Major-General sings:

> I know our mythic history, King Arthur's and Sir Caradoc's,
> I answer hard acrostics, I've a pretty taste for paradox.
> I quote in elegiacs all the crimes of Heliogabalus,
> In conics I can floor peculiarities parabolous.

And in *The Mikado*, the trio of Ko-Ko, Pooh-Bah, and Pish-Tush sings:

> To sit in solemn silence in a dull, dark dock,
> In a pestilential prison, with a life-long lock,
> Awaiting the sensation of a short, sharp shock,
> From a cheap and chippy chopper on a big black block!

Nowadays, tongue-twisters are generally regarded as childish, or at least as a form of amusement suitable for children. Iona and Peter Opie say that ' "Peter Piper", "The Leith Police", "Unique New York", "A proper copper coffee pot", "A stewed sow's snout", "Three grey geese in a green field grazing", and "She sells sea shells on the sea shore" continue to be favourites as they were fifty years ago.'

Other popular tongue-twisters listed by the Opies include the following:

Of all the felt I ever felt, I never felt a piece of felt which felt the same as that felt felt, when I first felt the felt of that felt hat.

Your Bob owes our Bob a bob. If your Bob doesn't give our Bob the bob your Bob owes our Bob, our Bob will give your Bob a bob in the eye.

Our Dicky wants to know if your Dicky will lend our Dicky your Dicky's Dicky-bow; if your Dicky won't lend our Dicky your Dicky's Dicky-bow, then our Dicky won't lend your Dicky our Dicky's Dicky-bow when our Dicky has a Dicky-bow.

There's no need to light a night-light
On a light night like tonight,
For a night-light's a slight light
On a night like tonight.

How much wood could a woodchuck chuck
If a woodchuck could chuck wood?
As much wood as a woodchuck would chuck
If a woodchuck could chuck wood.

The Opies add that this last tongue-twister is attractive because it can suggest many variations, like *How much oil can a gumboil boil, if a gumboil can boil oil?* and *How many cans can a cannibal nibble, if a cannibal can nibble cans?*

In the nineteenth century, children played a round game in which the first child pronounced a tongue-twister that had to be repeated by all the others in turn. The leader then gave a second tongue-twister, followed by the first, and both had to be said by everyone. The whole thing built up to a tremendous test, not only of memory (like 'The House That Jack Built' or 'Old Macdonald had a Farm') but also of enunciation:

One old ox opening oysters.
Two toads totally tired trying to trot to Tewkesbury.
Three tame tigers taking tea.
Four fit friars fishing for frogs.
Five fairies finding fireflies.
Six soldiers shooting snipe.
Seven salmon sailing in Solway.
Eight elegant engineers eating excellent eggs.
Nine nimble noblemen nibbling nectarines.
Ten tall tinkers tasting tamarinds.
Eleven electors eating early endive.
Twelve tremulous tale-bearers telling truth.

(Notes and Queries, 2 January 1915)

Of course, this sequence is found in many variant forms. The last line, for instance, occurs as *Twelve typographical typographers typically translating types* and *Twelve twittering tomtits trembling on twisted twigs.*

There are countless games in which players have to remember and repeat an ever-increasing list of things that are difficult to say. One of the oldest is GRANDMOTHER'S TRUNK, in which the first player says: 'My grandmother keeps an apple in her trunk' (or any other object beginning with 'A'). The second player has to add an article beginning with 'B'—for example, 'My grandmother keeps an apple and a buzzard in her trunk.' The objects can be as ridiculous as players wish. Anyone who cannot remember the whole list is out of the game. This pastime is also called 'I PACKED MY BAG', 'I WENT ON A TRIP', 'I WENT TO THE STORE', and 'PORTMANTEAU'. In some versions, the objects listed do not have to be in alphabetical order (cf. alphabet games, q.v.).

A game called ASSOCIATIONS, FREE ASSOCIATION, or PELMANISM has been made from the psychiatrists' technique of asking people what word comes into their mind when another word is spoken. It makes an amusing round game for several players if each person has to say the word that immediately comes to mind as a result of the preceding one. There need be no apparent connection between the words: the fun is in the hints they may give about someone's character.

A more formalized version of the game is called the TENNIS–ELBOW–FOOT game. In this case the players have to say a word that has some definite connection with the previous word. The sequence might go something like this: *tennis, elbow, foot, shoe, horse, chestnut, joke*, etc. Any player drops out who fails to think of a word immediately or who cannot explain its connection with the preceding word.

STEPPING STONES presents players with the problem of moving from one word to another, by way of specified categories. For example, the problem may be to move from *drinks* to *cricket*, by way of *transport* and *Christmas*. This could be done as follows: *drinks, whisky, Scotch, Annie Laurie, lorry* (this is *transport*), *container, box, Boxing Day, Christmas, stocking, leg, leg before wicket, cricket.*

Perhaps the best of these cumulative games are those in which the confusion is raised to its greatest height. In MY NAME IS MARY, an object like a doll or toy animal is passed around the circle. The first player gives his own name and the name of the object: 'My name is Fred and this is Gladys.' The second player hands the object to the third player, saying: 'My name is Mary and Fred says that this is Gladys.' And so on round the circle.

One of the funniest games is called A WHAT? or THE CAT AND THE DOG. The players sit in a circle and the first player hands the second an object, saying 'This is a cat.' The second player, somewhat surprised, asks the first player: 'A what?' and the first player repeats: 'A cat'. The second player then passes the object to the third player, saying 'This is a cat' and the third player asks 'A what?' When the object has gone round the circle at least once, the first player starts another object moving in the opposite direction, saying: 'This is a dog' (or 'wombat', or whatever) and both objects proceed around the circle in opposite directions, causing some complications when they meet.

An old story tells of a military commander who sent an urgent message to his headquarters: 'Send reinforcements: we're going to advance.' The message was passed from soldier to soldier and, by the time it reached headquarters, it had changed into: 'Send three-and-fourpence: we're going to a dance.'

This is the basis for a game which 'Professor Hoffmann' in his *Drawing-Room Amusements* (1879) calls RUSSIAN GOSSIP (also known as Chinese Whispers). The participants are arranged in a circle, and the first player whispers a story or message to the next player, and so on round the circle. The original story is then compared with the final version, which has often changed beyond recognition.

Lewis Carroll described a similar situation when a tutor tries to examine a pupil who is in the quadrangle. The tutor sits in his own room and shouts the questions to a scout (servant) who is outside his door, who passes on the questions to a sub-scout and a sub-sub-scout who are positioned between him and the pupil. The conversation goes like this:

TUTOR: What is twice three?
SCOUT: What's a rice tree?
SUB-SCOUT: When is ice free?
SUB-SUB-SCOUT: What's a nice fee?
PUPIL (*timidly*): Half a guinea!
SUB-SUB-SCOUT: Can't forge any!
SUB-SCOUT: Ho for Jinny!
SCOUT: Don't be a ninny!
TUTOR (*looks offended, but tries another question*): Divide a hundred by twelve!
SCOUT: Provide wonderful bells!
SUB-SCOUT: Go ride under it yourself!
SUB-SUB-SCOUT: Deride the dunder-headed elf!
PUPIL (*surprised*): Who do you mean?
SUB-SUB-SCOUT: Doings between!
SUB-SCOUT: Blue is the screen!
SCOUT: Soup-tureen!

'Professor Hoffmann' also describes a game called CROSS QUESTIONS AND CROOKED ANSWERS:

The players sit round in a circle, and the first, in a whisper, asks a question and receives an answer from the second. The second person then (also in a whisper) asks a question of the third, and so on, the last person asking a question of the first. Each person then states aloud the *question he or she was asked*, and the *answer he or she received*, which of course have no connection the one with the other.

In Louisa M. Alcott's *Little Women* (1871), a story-telling game was played which is still encountered today:

They all adjourned to the drawing-room to play 'Rigmarole'. One person begins a story, any nonsense you like, and tells as long as they please, only taking care to stop short at some exciting point, when the next takes it up and does the same. It's very funny when well done, and makes a perfect jumble of tragical, comical stuff to laugh over.

Children's counting-out rhymes (like 'Eeny, meeny, myny, mo') may have developed from old forms of counting which are still used today as tongue-twisters. In East Anglia and the North Country, shepherds and fishermen often counted up to twenty with a strange set of words. This was one form, used in Lincolnshire:

Yan, tan, tethera, pethera, pimp, sethera, lethera, hovera, covera, dik, yan-a-dik, tan-a-dik, tethera-dik, pethera-dik, bumfit, yan-a-bumfit, tan-a-bumfit, tethera-bumfit, pethera-bumfit, figgit (20).

Although tongue-twisters may seem childish, they have been used for serious purposes. Elocutionists and speech-therapists have employed them to improve pronunciation. *The Standard Elocutionist* (1883) by D. C. and A. M. Bell contains several 'difficult words and sentences' which the reader is exhorted to 'repeat several times, quickly, and with firm accentuation'. These include:

> *Such pranks Frank's prawns play in the tank.*
> *A knapsack strap.*
> *She sells sea-shells.*
> *Some shun sunshine.*
> *Truly rural.*
> *A laurel-crowned clown.*

One poem used by elocutionists was turned into a song for the film *Singin' in the Rain*, in which Gene Kelly and Donald O'Connor made fun of these ridiculous words:

> *Moses supposes his toeses are roses,*
> *But Moses supposes erroneously;*

> For Moses he knowses his toeses aren't roses
> As Moses supposes his toeses to be.

(The third line sometimes occurs as *For nobody's toeses are posies of roses*.)

Tongue-twisters are said to have been used to test the sobriety of a person suspected of drunkenness. The words allegedly used most often for this purpose are *The Leith police dismisseth us*, a sentence which is only the first line of a complex and clever tongue-twister:

> The Leith police dismisseth us,
> I'm thankful, sir, to say;
> The Leith police dismisseth us,
> They thought we sought to stay.
> The Leith police dismisseth us,
> We both sighed sighs apiece,
> And the sigh that we sighed as we said goodbye
> Was the size of the Leith police.

Tongue-twisters formed the basis for several songs during the heyday of the music-hall. The comedian Wilkie Bard became famous for 'She Sells Sea-Shells', which he sang in the Drury Lane pantomime *Dick Whittington* in 1908:

> She sells sea-shells on the sea-shore,
> The shells she sells are sea-shells, I'm sure,
> For if she sells sea-shells on the sea-shore,
> Then I'm sure she sells sea-shore shells.

World War I brought the song 'Sister Susie's Sewing Shirts for Soldiers', which, according to the sheet-music, was 'sung by Jack Norworth in the highly successful revue "Hullo, Tango!" at the London Hippodrome'. The chorus went:

> Sister Susie's sewing shirts for soldiers.
> Such skill at sewing shirts our shy young sister Susie shows!
> Some soldiers send epistles, say they'd sooner sleep in thistles
> Than the saucy, soft, short shirts for soldiers sister Susie sews.

The 1925 song 'I Miss My Swiss' included the words:

> I miss my Swiss, my Swiss miss misses me,
> I miss the bliss that Swiss kiss gives to me.

Dion Titheradge wrote a revue sketch in 1928 for Cicely Court-neidge in which she tries to order *two dozen double damask dinner napkins* but keeps getting the words twisted and eventually says: 'Oh, hell! Give me twenty-four serviettes!'

One of the favourite children's tongue-twisters, quoted by Iona and Peter Opie, is:

> *A tutor who tooted the flute*
> *Tried to tutor two tooters to toot.*
> *Said the two to the tutor:*
> *Is it harder to toot, or*
> *To tutor two tooters to toot?*

This reminds us that tongue-twisters sometimes appear in the form of limericks, such as these:

> *A flea and a fly in a flue*
> *Were imprisoned, so what could they do?*
> *Said the fly, 'Let us flee,'*
> *Said the flea, 'Let us fly,'*
> *So they flew through a flaw in the flue.*

> *There was a young person named Tate*
> *Who went out to dine at 8.8,*
> *But I will not relate*
> *What that person named Tate*
> *And his tête-à-tête ate at 8.8.*

> *A canner, exceedingly canny,*
> *One morning remarked to his granny,*
> *'A canner can can*
> *Anything that he can,*
> *But a canner can't can a can, can he?'*
> (C. Wells, *Book of American Limericks*, 1925)

Such verses are unlikely to be published in *The Oxford Book of English Verse* but the following poem was included in the 1939 edition of that book, in the section of anonymous songs:

> *O would I were where I would be!*
> *There would I be where I am not:*
> *For where I am would I not be,*
> *And where I would be I can not.*

This verse dates back to 1784, when it was published (in a slightly different form) in *Gammer Gurton's Garland*.

Finally, here is a selection of some of the best-known and most difficult tongue-twisters:

What noise annoys a noisy oyster? A noisy noise annoys a noisy oyster.
Red leather, yellow leather.
A proper cup of coffee from a proper coffee pot.
'Are you copper-bottoming 'em, my man?' 'No, I'm aluminiuming 'em, Mum!'
Which switch, Miss, is the right switch for Ipswich, Miss?
She was a thistle sifter and sifted thistles through a thistle sieve.
The sixth sheikh's sixth sheep's sick.
Lemon liniment.
I can think of six thin things and of six thick things too.
Mixed biscuits.

19

Spoonerisms

The Revd William Archibald Spooner was Warden of New College in Oxford from 1903 to 1924. He is best remembered not for being head of an Oxford college but for his supposed habit of transposing letters at the beginning of words, producing what have come to be called SPOONERISMS.

E. L. Woodward remembers him thus:

I think that the most curious figure in my early time at New College was Warden Spooner. He was a shrewd, humorous man, of very considerable personal dignity, in spite of his smallness and his peering, short-sighted eyes. There was no doubt about his Spoonerisms. He made scores of them. There were many types, of which the misplacement of initial syllables was the least whimsical. There were Spoonerisms in writing and Spoonerisms in act. I have a letter from him beginning with the words 'My dear Woodhead'. I remember him asking my wife what she thought of Synge's play *The Ploughboy of the Western World*, or, at another time, talking, in a college meeting, about the Rugby cricket match at Twickenham. I have heard him ask an undergraduate whether he had 'formed up a fill'. The first time I saw him he made one of the more interesting Spoonerisms. I was introduced to the Warden before we sat down to dessert in the common room. We sat at small tables in a half-circle round the fire. The Warden, who had a guest of his own, wanted to sit with his guest on his right and to invite me to sit on his left. So he moved to take his seat, pointed to the chairs on either side of him, and said to me, 'Mr Woodward, will you sit in these two chairs?' I sat. Then he turned to me, and following a Spoonerist train of thought which it takes a moment or two to understand, began a conversation with the words, 'What proportion of cricketers do you think are left-handed?'

Spooner's biographer, Sir William Hayter, said: 'There is in fact very little doubt that Spooner did on occasion fall into metaphasis, the technical term for this transposition of sounds (*Punch* once referred to him as "Oxford's great metaphasiarch").' But Hayter doubted if Spooner created all the spoonerisms attributed to him, and Spooner obviously resented being connected with this strange habit. C. M. Bowra remembers:

Once after a bump-supper we serenaded him and stood outside his window calling for a speech. He put his head out and said, 'You don't want a speech. You only want me to say one of those things,' and immediately withdrew.

Sir William Hayter stated that it was commonly believed in New College that Spooner admitted giving out a hymn in chapel as '*Kinquering Kongs*' but denied all the rest. Yet other witnesses claim to have heard him say '*In a dark, glassly*' and '*The weight of rages will press harder and harder upon the employer.*'

Certainly there is good evidence that William Spooner often confused *ideas*, if not *words*, as Sir Julian Huxley recalls:

After a discussion about our expedition to Spitsbergen, in which I had stressed its easy accessibility in spite of its high latitude, he remarked to his wife: 'My dear, Mr Huxley assures me it is no further from the north coast of Spitsbergen to the North Pole than it is from Land's End to John of Gaunt.' Mrs Spooner, a large and majestic woman, fixed me with a stony look: I didn't even smile.

R. F. Horton recorded that, at a board-meeting organizing charity work, Spooner said: 'The case of this boy came before us, you remember, *next* week.' On meeting Stanley Casson in the college quadrangle, Spooner said, 'Do come to dinner tonight, to meet our new Fellow, Casson.' Casson answered 'But, Warden, I *am* Casson,' to which Spooner replied 'Never mind, come all the same.'

Perhaps the strangest story of all concerning Spooner's mental transpositions is told by Arnold Toynbee:

The acted 'spoonerism' was witnessed by my mother's old friend Eleanor Jourdain. At a dinner-party in Oxford, she saw Dr Spooner upset a salt-cellar and then reach for a decanter of claret. He poured claret on the salt, drop by drop, till he had produced the little purple mound which would have been the end-product if he had spilled claret on the table-cloth and had then cast a heap of salt on the pool to absorb it.

The undergraduates of Oxford enthusiastically took up the idea of spoonerisms in the 1890s, when Spooner was a Fellow of New College. They probably created most of the spoonerisms which have subsequently been attributed to Warden Spooner:

I have in my bosom a half-warmed fish.
A toast which needs no commendation from me—our queer Dean.
A well-boiled icicle.

A blushing crow.
The Lord is a shoving leopard.
Please sew me to another sheet; someone is occupewing my pie.
You have hissed my mystery lectures; you have tasted a whole worm. You will
    leave Oxford on the next town drain.
You were fighting a liar in the quadrangle.
Is the bean dizzy?

When a cartoon of Spooner by 'Spy' appeared in *Vanity Fair* for
April 1898, 'Jehu Junior' wrote:

His chief flaim to came lies in his genius for metathesis, for he is the inventor
of 'Spoonerisms'. The half-warmed fish has risen to his breast; he knows all
about Kinquering Kongs; his cat has popped on its drawers; he has un-
wearily addressed beery wenches; and he will doubtless be grattered and
flatified by his appearance in *Vanity Fair*.

The following 'Lines by an Oxford Don' appeared in *The Globe* in June
1895:

> My brain was filled with rests of thought,
> No more by currying wares distraught,
> As lazing dreamily I lay
> In my Canoodian canay.
>
> Ah me, methought, how leaf were swite
> If men could neither wreak nor spite;
> No erring bloomers, no more slang
> No tungles then to trip the tang!
>
> No more the undergraddering tits
> Would exercise their woolish fits
> With tidal ales (and false, I wis)
> Of my fame-farred tamethesis!

Oxford students may have got the inspiration for spoonerisms from
Warden Spooner, but the habit is found in a novel about Oxford life
written when Spooner was a boy—Cuthbert Bede's *Further Adventures of Mr Verdant Green* (1854), in which Mr Bouncer says: 'Will
you poke a smipe?' Indeed, the tendency is even older, as Henry
Peacham recounts in his *Complete Gentleman* (1622):

A melancholy gentleman sitting one day at table, where I was, started up
upon a sudden, and meaning to say, 'I must go buy a dagger,' by transposition of the letters, said: 'Sir, I must go dye a beggar.'

In Shakespeare's *Taming of the Shrew*, Grumio makes a transposition worthy of William Spooner: he says, 'The oats have eaten the horses.'

Baron Nicholson, in his *Autobiography of a Fast Man* (1863) refers to 'Fanny King, or as Bill Leach, in the interesting language called *Marouski*, termed her, Kanny Fing.' J. C. Hotten explains this spooneristic language in the second edition of his *Dictionary of Modern Slang* (1860):

Medical Greek, the slang used by medical students at the hospitals. At the London University they have a way of disguising English, described by Albert Smith as the *Gower-street Dialect*, which consists in transposing the initials of words, e.g., '*poke a smipe*'— smoke a pipe, '*flutter by*'— butterfly, etc. This disagreeable nonsense is often termed marrowskying.

From being an accidental human tendency, spoonerisms developed into a deliberate game or form of word play. When George S. Kaufman's daughter told him that a friend of hers from Vassar College in New York had eloped, he said: 'Ah! She put her heart before the course.' Oscar Wilde said that 'Work is the curse of the drinking classes.' When Adlai Stevenson was campaigning in St Paul, Minnesota, in 1960, a clergyman named Norman Peale made some unfortunate remarks, whereupon Stevenson told the press that he found St Paul appealing and Peale appalling.

Robert Morse wrote a poem ending:

> I'll hash my wands or shake a tower,
> (a rug of slum? a whiskey sour?)
> water my pants in all their plots,
> slob a male hairy before I seep—
> and dropping each Id on heavy lie,
> with none to sing me lullaby,
> slop off to dreep, slop off to dreep.

As a game, spoonerisms take two main forms. One game offers clues to phrases which, when spoonerized, give new phrases. Torquemada, the great deviser of crossword puzzles, included several of these in his *Torquemada Puzzle Book* (1934):

When spoonerized,
What chain of shops suggests that bald birds are beating up scientists?
Boots Cash Chemists (coots bash chemists)

What famous public house suggests an unkind puppy?
  Welsh harp (harsh whelp)
What light opera suggests the Flying Squad?
  The Yeoman of the Guard (The Go Men of the Yard)
What thing carried by females suggests a coven of witches?
  handbag (hag band)
What aid to illumination suggests a slim sorceress?
  light switch (slight witch)
What wall embellishment suggests a French author?
  dado (Daudet)

The other main form of spooneristic puzzle is the SPOONERGRAM, a poem containing blanks to be filled by spoonerisms, such as:

> His pretty love was young, petite.
> Her *first* adorned by silken bow;
> They shared sauternes, their joy complete;
> Their kisses had a *last*, you know.

(The missing words are *tiny waist* and *winey taste*.)

> It was raining *one* today,
> And that is nothing new.
> My little car exploded, though,
> And it started raining *two*.

(The missing words are *cats 'n' dogs* and *Datsun cogs*.)

Spooner's verbal habit has ensured him a place in the English dictionary, if not in the history books, as this versified obituary, written by V. Ernest Cox for a *New Statesman* competition, makes clear:

> Born in London in 1844,
> 'Twas not until young Spooner spurned to leak
> That his dum and mad grew puzzled
> For all his boyish chatter sounded Greek.
>
> At Oswestry he passed exams,
> And down to Oxford went,
> Kew Knowledge was to be his home
> From youth to ancient gent.
>
> As student, fellow, tutor, dean,
> Rev. Spooner said he always got around
> Upon 'a well boiled icicle',
> A claim for which he's still renowned.

He thighed in nineteen-dirty;
Folk forget his classics brain,
It's his transposition habit
That the reference books explain.

20

Lapsus Linguae

A subject of perennial fascination is the overlapping of English with other languages, especially French and Latin. Poor attempts by the English to use foreign languages, and almost equally bad attempts by foreigners to speak English, give rise to outlandish mixtures of two languages which cause amusement or are used as the basis for games or word play.

Most people, for example, have heard of those strange advertisements purporting to promote the amenities of foreign hotels. Gerard Hoffnung immortalized several in a speech at the Oxford Union in 1958, such as 'Here you shall be well fed up'; 'Sorrowfully I cannot abide your auto'; and 'There is a French widow in every bedroom affording delightful prospects.'

Laughter is always aroused by stumbling attempts to teach an unfamiliar language, as in foreign phrase-books which tell us how to say 'My postilion has been struck by lightning.' The most notorious phrase-book of this kind was published in Paris in 1855 by José da Fonseca, with the title *O Novo Guia da Conversação, en Portuguez e Inglez* or *The New Guide of the Conversation, in Portuguese and English*. The Portuguese author compiled this work by translating a book of French dialogues word for word into English with a dictionary.

The Preface reads:

A choice of familiar dialogues, clean of gallicisms and despoiled phrases, it was missing yet to studious portuguese and brazilian youth; and also to persons of others nations. . . . We expect then, who the little book (for the care what we wrote him, and for her typgraphical correction) that may be worth the acceptation of the studious persons, and especialy of the Youth, at which we dedicate him particularly.

The 'English' phrases recommended by the author include: 'Do you cut the hairs?'; 'It knock one's the door, go to and see who is it'; 'Take attention to cut you self'; 'I have put my stockings outward'; and 'These apricots and these peaches make me and to come water in mouth'.

The book also gives typical conversations, such as this one on 'The Walk':

Will you and take a walk with me?
It is very hot.
Wait for that the warm be out.
Where we sall go?
Go to the public garden.
How will you that we may go it? in the coach, or on foot?
On foot, that is good for the health.
Go through that meadow. Who the country is beautiful! who the trees are thick!
That side is pretty well for to study.
Look the walk that it present a good perspective.
Sit down us to the shade.
Take the bloom's perfume.
Make a nosegay.
Do you know these ladies who come from our side?
It seem me who they look where to sit down one's.
Leave them this bench.
Go the country's side.
It seems me that the corn does push already.
You hear the bird's gurgling?
Which pleasure! which charm!

If foreigners misuse our language, we torture theirs just as much. The English have been mangling foreign languages for centuries, as Chaucer indicates in describing the Prioress who spoke French 'After the school of Stratford atte Bow [i.e. Stratford in East London], For French of Paris was to her unknown.'

W. S. Walsh tells of an English preacher who exhorted a French audience to seek the water of life, translating it literally as '*eau de vie*' which is French for brandy.

In *The Innocents Abroad*, Mark Twain quotes a letter from one of his American friends to a hotel-keeper in Paris:

Monsieur le Landlord—Sir: *Pourquoi* don't you *mettez* some *savon* in your bedchambers? *Est-ce que vous pensez* I will steal it? *La nuit passée* you charged me *pour deux chandelles* when I only had one; *hier vous avez* charged me *avec glace* when I had none at all; *tout les jours* you are coming some fresh game or other on me, *mais vous ne pouvez pas* play this *savon* dodge on me twice.

Savon is a necessary *de la vie* to anybody but a Frenchman, *et je l'aurai hors de cet hôtel* or make trouble. You hear *me. Allons.*

BLUCHER.

This strange mixture of French and English has come to be called *franglais*, both by the French (who apply it to the excessive use of English words in French) and by the English (who also use it for a kind of stumbling French spoken or written by English people with an insecure grasp of the language). Miles Kington has made himself an expert in the latter type of *franglais*, of which he says in the preface to *Let's Parler Franglais!* (1979): 'Si vous êtes un fluent English speaker, et si vous avez un 'O' level français, Franglais est un morceau de gâteau.' Kington's *franglais* consists mainly of using English words whenever one does not know the correct French ('Pourquoi vous avez laissé entrer ce nutter?') and translating English idioms literally into French ('C'est un merveilleux matin pour cette sorte de chose').

FRACTURED FRENCH also uses literal translations to create comical definitions, such as these from F. S. Pearson's *Fractured French* (1951):

coup de grâce, lawn mower.
pas du tout, father of twins.
entrechat, let the cat in.
mise en scène, there are mice in the river.
honi soit qui mal y pense, I honestly believe I am going to be sick.

Charles G. Leland immortalized the broken English spoken by German immigrants in America. The first of his *Breitmann Ballads* appeared in a Philadelphia magazine in 1857:

Hans Breitmann's Party

Hans Breitmann gife a barty;
Dey had biano-blayin',
I felled in lofe mit a Merican frau,
Her name was Matilda Yane.
She hat haar as prown ash a pretzel,
Her eyes vas himmel-plue,
Und vhen dey looket indo mine,
Dey shplit mine heart in dwo. . . .

Such faltering attempts at using a foreign language are found nearly two centuries earlier in William Drummond's *Polemo-Middinia,* which mixes Latin and English words with others that are half-English and half-Latin:

Hic aderant Geordy Aikenheadus, et Rob Littlejohnus,
Et Jamy Richaeus, et stout Michael Hendersonus,
Qui gillitrips ante alios dansare solebat,
Et bobbare bene, et lassas kissare bonaeas.

This poetic mixture of Latin and English is known as MACARONIC
VERSE. Boswell reported that Dr Johnson was interested in the derivation of this type of poetry:

Dr Johnson endeavoured to trace the etymology of Maccaronick verses,
which he thought were of Italian invention from Maccaroni; but on being
informed that this would infer that they were the most common and easy
verses, maccaroni being the most ordinary and simple food, he was at a
loss; for he said, 'He rather should have supposed it to import in its primitive
signification, a composition of several things; for Maccaronick verses are
verses made out of a mixture of different languages, that is, of one language
with the termination of another.' I suppose we scarcely know of a language
in any country where there is any learning, in which that motley ludicrous
species of composition may not be found. It is particularly droll in Low
Dutch. (*Life of Johnson*, 1791)

The earliest poets to mix English with Latin in this way were
probably John Skelton (*c*.1460-1529) and William Dunbar (*c*.1465-
1530). Skelton's *Colin Clout* intersperses the English lines with many
Latin words:

Religious men are fain
For to turn again
In secula seculorum,
And to forsake their quorum
And *vagabundare per forum*. . . .

Here the Latin can be translated straightforwardly to fit in with
the sense, as it can in Holofernes' English-Latin speeches in Shakespeare's *Love's Labour's Lost*. However, other writers composed verses
which were apparently in Latin but only made sense if read as
English words. Jonathan Swift sent this sort of thing to his friends:

A Love Song

Apud in is almi des ire,
Mimis tres I ne ver re qui re.
Alo veri findit a gestis,
His miseri ne ver at restis.

Thus the last line should be read as 'His misery never at rest is.' One
of the best poems of this kind is called 'Mi Molle Anni: An Irish
Ballad'. It begins:

O pateo tulis aras cale fel O,
Hebetis vivis id, an sed, 'Aio puer vello!'
Vittis nox certias in erebo de nota olim,—
A mite grate sinimus tonitis ovem.

(*Notes and Queries*, 27 March 1852)

This can be translated as:

O Patty O'Toole is a rascally fellow,
He beat his wife's head, and said, 'I hope you are well, O!'
With his knocks, sir, she has in her body not a whole limb,—
A mighty great sin I must own it is of him.

The same sort of humour is still current today, if we can believe a modern schoolboy—Molesworth of St Custard's—writing in *Down with Skool!* (1958) by Geoffrey Willans and Ronald Searle:

All latin masters hav one joke.
Caesar adsum jam forte
or
Caesar had some jam for tea.

Molesworth also notes that French teachers 'hav a joke too if they manage to shout it loud enuff'

Je suis I am a pot of jam
Tu es thou art a clot etc.

Molesworth was not the first schoolchild to note this kind of macaronic humour. In his *Handy-Book of Literary Curiosities* (1892), W. S. Walsh comments that:

A favourite kind of school-boy humour is that which takes the form of evolving sentences like the following: *Forte dux fel flat in gutture*, which is good Latin for 'By chance the leader inhales poison in his throat', but which read off rapidly sounds like the English 'Forty ducks fell flat in the gutter'. A French example is *Pas de lieu Rhône que nous*, which it is hardly necessary to explain makes no sense in French at all, though every word be true Gallic, but by a similar process of reading reveals the proverbial advice, 'Paddle your own canoe'.

Sometimes macaronics mix together more than two languages, as in the following, quoted in W. T. Dobson's *Poetical Ingenuities* (1882):

In tempus old a hero lived,
Qui loved puellas deux;
He ne pouvait pas quite to say
Which one amabat mieux.

In his *Literary Frivolities* (1880), W. T. Dobson quotes a macaronic version of a well-known nursery rhyme:

Little Jack Horner

Parvus Jacobus Horner
Sedebat in corner,
Edens a Christmas pie:
Inseruit thumb,
Extraxit a plum—
Clamans, 'Quid sharp puer am I!'

{ 21 }

The Games of Lewis Carroll

DOUBLETS is the best-known game invented by that great word-game enthusiast, Lewis Carroll. He explained its origin in an article published in *Vanity Fair* on 29 March 1879:

Doublets—a verbal puzzle

Just a year ago last Christmas, two young ladies—smarting under that sorest scourge of feminine humanity, the having 'nothing to do'—besought me to send them 'some riddles'. But riddles I had none at hand, and therefore set myself to devise some other form of verbal torture which should serve the same purpose. The result of my meditations was a new kind of Puzzle— new at least to me—which, now that it has been fairly tested by a year's experience and commended by many friends, I offer to you, as a newly-gathered nut, to be cracked by the omnivorous teeth which have already masticated so many of your Double Acrostics.

The rules of the Puzzles are simple enough. Two words are proposed, of the same length; and the Puzzle consists in linking these together by interposing other words, each of which shall differ from the next word in *one letter only*. . . . As an example, the word 'head' may be changed into 'tail' by interposing the words 'heal, teal, tell, tall'. I call the two given words 'a Doublet', the interposed words 'Links', and the entire series 'a Chain', of which I here append an example:

HEAD
HEAL
TEAL
TELL
TALL
TAIL.

. . . The easiest 'Doublets' are those in which the consonants in one word answer to consonants in the other, and the vowels to vowels; 'head' and 'tail' are a Doublet of this kind. Where this is not the case, as in 'head' and 'bare', the first thing to be done is to transform one member of the Doublet into a word whose consonants and vowels shall answer to those in the other member (e.g., 'head, herd, here'), after which there is seldom much difficulty in completing the 'Chain'.

I am told that there is an American game involving a similar principle. I have never seen it, and can only say of its inventors, '*pereant qui ante nos nostra dixerunt!*' [i.e. 'Death to those who voiced our ideas before we did!']

Lewis Carroll then gave three doublets for *Vanity Fair* readers to solve:

1. Drive PIG into STY. 2. Raise FOUR to FIVE. 3. Make WHEAT into BREAD. The answers were:

PIG	FOUR	WHEAT
WIG	FOUL	CHEAT
WAG	FOOL	CHEAM
WAY	FOOT	CREAM
SAY	FORT	BREAM
STY	FORE	BREAD
	FIRE	
	FIVE	

The game proved so popular with readers that the magazine soon made it into a weekly competition with prizes. Lewis Carroll was proud of his invention (which he had started by calling 'Word-links'), and his letters for the next few years contain many references to the game. Writing to Arthur Lewis in May 1879, Carroll referred to the first doublets printed in *Vanity Fair*:

You will see that 'Cheam' was accepted by the Editor. *I* would have rejected it, I confess, as not sufficiently well known.
   'Ship–Dock' is easy.
   'Watch–Clock' seems to be a very long one. I see on looking at your second letter that you take 13. I will send you mine, but can't recall it just now.
   We are getting into terrible difficulties about 'admissible' words. Only yesterday the Editor sent me a batch of remonstrances to read. The only way out of it seems to be to issue a glossary, which I am now preparing.

Carroll included such a glossary in the first edition of his pamphlet, *Doublets*, published in 1879. And in *Vanity Fair* for 17 May 1879 he wrote a humorous piece about the sort of words that he thought ineligible for his game:

Choker humbly presents his compliments to the four thousand three hundred and seventeen (or thereabouts) indignant Doubleteers who have so strongly shent him, and pre to being soaked in the spate of their wrath, asks for a fiver of minutes for reflection. Choker is in a state of complete pye.

He feels that there must be a stent to the admission of spick words. He is quite unable to sweal the chaffy spelt, to sile the pory cole, or to swill a spate from a piny ait to the song of the spink. Frils and the mystic Gole are strangers in his sheal: the chanceful Gord hath never brought him gold, nor ever did a cate become his ain. The Doubleteers will no doubt spank him sore, with slick quotations and wild words of yore, will pour upon his head whole steres of steens and poods of spiles points downwards. But he trusts that those alone who habitually use such words as these in good society, and whose discourse is universally there understood, will be the first to cast a stean at him.

Lewis Carroll had discovered the sad truth experienced by many people involved in such games as Scrabble and crosswords—that hell hath no fury like a word-gamer who uses an unfamiliar word to score a point.

Carroll's own rules for Doublets excluded proper names, most abbreviations, and nouns formed from verbs (like 'trader' from 'trade')—which explains his use of the word 'Choker' in the piece quoted above. His method of scoring was typical of his mathematical approach. He explained it in a letter of 8 March 1896 to Elisabeth Bury:

The rule for scoring is 'Take the square of the number next above the number of letters in each word, and deduct 2 for every Link.'

Here, for instance, is a Chain for 'Turn CAT into DOG'. The score is '16 less 4': i.e. '12'.

> CAT
> COT
> DOT
> DOG

In 1892, Carroll changed the rules to allow the use of anagrams:

The new Rule is that you may, at any step, re-arrange the letters of the word, instead of introducing a new letter: but you may not do both in the *same* step.

> IRON
> ICON
> COIN
> CORN
> CORD

LORD
LOAD
LEAD

Lewis Carroll was still playing Doublets in 1897, as Ursula Mallam recalled:

He invited me to tea in his rooms at Christ Church. . . . After tea we played writing games. We turned *Pig* into *Sty* and put *Pen* into *Ink*, sitting in two groups and changing the letters, racing with each other to finish first, all of it very noisy.

Doublets became a popular game which is still played today. It has often appeared under different names. For instance, in *Puzzles Old and New* (1893), 'Professor Hoffmann' calls it 'Transformations' and gives these examples:

SIN	HATE	MORE	HAND	BLACK
SON	HAVE	LORE	HARD	SLACK
WON	LAVE	LOSE	LARD	STACK
WOE	LOVE	LOSS	LORD	STALK
		LESS	FORD	STALE
			FORT	SHALE
			FOOT	WHALE
				WHILE
				WHITE

A magazine called *The Golden Penny* described the game as 'Passes' and its issue for 2 November 1895 gave the following example:

Transmute dust into gold in five passes—
dust–gust–gist–gilt–gild–gold.

J. E. Surrick and L. M. Conant called them 'laddergrams' in a book of that title published in 1927. Some of their examples need fifteen steps to transform the word:

SMALL	SEVEN
STALL	SEVER
STILL	SAVER
SPILL	SAVED
SPILE	PAVED
SPINE	PALED

SEINE	PILED
SEISE	RILED
SENSE	RELED
TENSE	RELET
TERSE	REGET
VERSE	BEGET
VERGE	BEGOT
MERGE	BIGOT
MARGE	BIGHT
LARGE	EIGHT

Other names for Doublets have included Stepwords, Transitions, Word Chains, Word Ladders, Word Links, Word Ping-Pong, and Word Golf. The last of these names is used by Vladimir Nabokov in his novel *Pale Fire*, where the narrator says that he likes playing word golf and 'some of my records are: hate–love in three, lass–male in four, and live–dead in five (with "lend" in the middle)'. Nabokov may have made these transitions in the following ways:

HATE	LASS	LIVE
HAVE	MASS	LINE
HOVE	MAST	LIND
LOVE	MALT	LEND
	MALE	LEAD
		DEAD

All these examples illustrate one of the constant principles of Doublets: that the words being joined should either be opposites (*hate*, *love*) or otherwise connected in some way (*seven*, *eight*).

H. E. Dudeney observed this rule in 1925 when his anti-German feeling showed itself in this doublet:

KAISER
RAISER
RAISED
RAILED
FAILED
FOILED
COILED
COOLED
COOKED
CORKED
CORKER
PORKER

Another common aim in Doublets is to use only as many steps as there are letters in the words that are being transformed. Yet even three-letter words may take twice as many steps, and Lewis Carroll took six steps to change *ape* into *man*:

APE
ARE
ERE
ERR
EAR
MAR
MAN

The best that subsequent solvers have achieved is to reduce Carroll's six moves to five:

APE
APT
OPT
OAT
MAT
MAN

The scientist John Maynard Smith drew a parallel between Doublets and the process of evolution. 'Ape' may actually have changed into 'Man' by step-like changes in the evolution of the DNA molecule, the prime transmitter of life. Another scientist who recalled playing Doublets as a child was Sir Julian Huxley. His mother was Julia Arnold, one of the two little girls for whom Lewis Carroll invented the game when they had 'nothing to do'.

Carroll invented several other games but they never became as widespread as Doublets. When he offered his game SYZYGIES to *Vanity Fair*, it was rejected. So the first published syzygy appeared in another magazine—*The Lady*—in July 1881. The idea had occurred to Carroll a dozen years earlier, when he noted in his diary: 'Invented a new way of working one word into another. I think of calling the puzzle "syzygies".' The word 'syzygy' comes from the Greek and means 'yoke' or 'conjunction'. In answer to an enquiry about the word's pronunciation, Carroll said: '*I* pronounce it "sizzijiz" leaning on the first syllable so as to rhyme to "fizzy fizz". '

Less than three weeks after he had invented it, Carroll sent the rules to Helen Feilden, saying in the covering letter:

You thought so favourably of my former puzzle *Doublets*, that I am sending you a new one while still in an experimental and unsettled state, and would be really obliged if you would try it, and let me know how you think it works. You may work it, I believe, with *any* two words whatever, taken at random: it will *always* be possible to link them with a 3-letter Chain— sometimes also with a 4-letter Chain—and so on.

Syzygies uses the same principle as Doublets in changing one word into another by steps. In Syzygies, the steps are words that have some letters in common with the preceding word. Lewis Carroll recorded his first syzygies in his diary on 12 December 1879:

Send MAN on ICE.	MAN
	permanent
	entice
	ICE

RELY on ACRE.	ACRE
	sacred
	credentials
	entirely
	RELY

Prove PRISM to be ODIOUS.	PRISM
	prismatic
	dramatic
	melodrama
	melodious
	ODIOUS

Carroll preferred Syzygies to Doublets because he thought they were 'more varied, and likely to be more interesting'. But they never became popular because they were too complex, and Carroll's system of scoring made the game incomprehensible to the average person, with complicated methods of giving extra points for shared letters and deducting points for unshared letters.

The idea of Syzygies survives in WORD CHAINS, of which H. E. Dudeney described three kinds: (1) take a word of four letters, add two so that the last four spell a word, then add another two so that

Lewis Carroll's Syzygies (in his own handwriting) on the name of Beatrice Earle.

the final four spell a word (e.g. *west* to *east*: west-star-area-east); (2) make a chain of words in which the last letter of one word is the first letter of the next (e.g. AdverBasiCarDinE . . .); (3) cut off the head of each successive word and add extra letters to form new words (e.g. bag-age-gem-emu-mug).

Nowadays, 'word chains' usually refers to a game in which you take a combination of two words and then think of another combination which starts with the second of these two words. Thus, if the first player says *race-horse*, the second player might say *horse-box* and the next player *box-office*, and so on until one of the players loses by being unable to think of a suitable word.

Lewis Carroll invented yet another game—MISCHMASCH— in 1880. He introduced it to many of his child-friends and was still playing it in 1897. In some ways it resembles Superghosts (q.v.). Here is his own explanation of the rules:

The essence of this game consists in one player proposing a 'nucleus' (i.e. a set of two or more letters, such as 'gp', 'emo'', 'imse'), and in the other trying to find a 'lawful word' (i.e. a word known in ordinary society, and not a proper name), containing it. Thus, 'magpie', 'lemon', 'himself', are lawful words containing the nuclei 'gp', 'emo', 'imse'.

Carroll said that one advantage of this game was that 'it needs no counters or anything: so you can play it out walking, or up in a balloon, or down in a diving-bell, or anywhere!'

To his godson Willy Wilcox, Carroll sent these 'nuclei': *mfi, ols, vv, ngu, ewh,* and *sten.* His answers were: *comfit, bolster, navvy, tongue, somewhere,* and *listen.* When he sent the letters *eon* for Elisabeth Bury to solve, she could not think of an answer. He wrote to her:

It is a gratifying fact to fall back on, in an age of so much greediness and over-eating, that there is at least *one* young lady in Oxford, who not only never *takes* luncheon, but has never even *heard* of such a meal. No doubt you only allow yourself *breakfast,* and *dinner.* Do not, however, my dear young friend, carry on such rigorous habits too long. You are not yet 40, and so may safely keep to 2 meals *at present.* But when you reach the age of 80 or 90 (*I* am getting on for 90), you will find that luncheon, and even afternoon-tea (a meal with which you are no doubt unacquainted), may occasionally be taken with advantage to the health.

Consequences

The game of CONSEQUENCES was foreshadowed by a pastime described in Ben Jonson's *Cynthia's Revels* (1600) as 'A Thing Done, and Who Did It'. One of the characters in the play describes the game:

I imagine, a thing done; Hedon thinks who did it; Moria, with what it was done; Anaides, where it was done; Argurion, when it was done; Amorphus, for what cause it was done; you, Philautia, what followed upon the doing of it; and this gentleman, who would have done it better.

Ben Jonson's characters then proceed to play the game by saying their pieces in reverse order ('this gentleman' starting, followed by Philautia etc.), and then reciting the resulting story in its correct sequence. In this way, a nonsensical tale is created from the random contributions of several people.

One of the earliest descriptions of Consequences occurs in *Parlour Pastime for the Young* by 'Uncle George', published in 1857. He described the game as follows:

This game requires paper and pencils. And each player is to write according to the directions given by the leader. The first player is told to write one or more terms descriptive of a gentleman. He does so, and then folds down the paper so as to conceal what is written, and hands it to the next player, who, after receiving the order, writes, folds the paper down as before, and passes it on to the next, and so on until the directions are exhausted. The leader then reads the contents of the sheet aloud, which from its inconsistencies and absurdities will cause much amusement.

Let us suppose these to be the directions of the leader:
'Begin by writing a term descriptive of a gentleman.'
'A gentleman's name; someone you know or some distinguished person.'
'An adjective descriptive of a lady.'
'A lady's name.'
'Mention a place and describe it.'
'Write down some date or period of time when an event might happen.'
'Put a speech into the gentleman's mouth.'
'Make the lady reply.'
'Tell what the consequences were.'

'And what the world said of it.'

The paper being opened, we will suppose it to read as follows:

'The handsome and modest Napoleon, met the graceful and accomplished Miss Norton, at Brighton, that fashionable place of resort, on the 10th of November, 1890. He said, "Dear lady, my respect for you is unbounded," and she replied, "Yes, I am very fond of it." The consequences were, that they were united in matrimony, and the world said, "It is so very silly." '

As 'Uncle George' describes it, the game differs in some respects from its normal modern form. Note that only one slip of paper seems to be used, instead of several circulating at once, and that the items include categories (like a description of the place) which are seldom used nowadays.

A later description of the game—about the year 1870 in *Indoor Games and Family Pastimes*, published as one of 'Bennett's Penny Every-day Books'—has several pieces of paper circulating:

Each player has before him a long, narrow piece of writing-paper and a pencil. At the top of the paper each writes the quality of a gentleman. 'The frivolous', for instance, or 'the witty', or 'the plausible', or any quality, in fact, that may occur to the mind at that moment.

As before, the examples given may not strike the modern reader as particularly hilarious:

The amiable John Bright and the objectionable Mrs Grundy met on the sands at Margate. He said to her 'How do I look?' She said to him, 'Sour apples'; the consequence was 'a secret marriage', and the world said, 'We knew how it would be.'

Cassell's Book of Indoor Amusements (1881) adds a new category— after 'where they met', one has to write 'what he gave her'. Writing seventeen years later, the games expert Alice Bertha Gomme, omits the descriptive adjectives and stipulates that 'Names of fictitious people may be used instead of those of persons present, but absent friends' names should not.' And in 1912, E. M. Baker in *Indoor Games for Children and Young People* added several new categories to the list, making a much longer story:

Pugnacious Captain Swift, who was dressed in flannels, patent boots, and a silk hat, met dainty Mrs Kruger in a mauve satin petticoat and bathing slippers paddling by moonlight, when he would much rather have met the Duchess of York. They met at Southminster. What he thought was, 'How charming she looks with that delicate flush on her fresh young cheeks', but he said, 'Madam, I'm surprised at you.' She thought, 'I wish I'd put on my best hat', but she merely said, 'I'd no idea you were in earnest.' They went for a ride on the Twopenny Tube, and learnt to love one another very dearly. The consequence was she wrote a long letter of complaint to the Queen, and the world said, 'What else could you expect under the circumstances?'

One suspects that Consequences was an appealing game in Victorian times because it enabled young people to flirt with one another under the guise of a harmless recreation. The game is played today simply for its ability to create nonsensical juxtapositions. The rules still vary—in three of his books, Gyles Brandreth gives three different lists of categories for the game. The generally accepted form of Consequences seems to be: an adjective; a man's name; an adjective; a woman's name; where they met; what he said to her; what she said to him; the consequence; what the world said. The traditional quality of games like this is exemplified by the man still preceding the woman (despite our modern awareness of male chauvinism) and the continuance of the delightfully old-fashioned phrase 'and the world said'.

One of the nice things about Consequences is that it is not a competitive game: everyone co-operates. Dan Rosenberg has pointed out some of the other delights of such games:

They are definitely participation games. The actual playing of them is more important than the literary or artistic result. The social situation which they reflect, the interaction of the participants, the fun at the time are their justification. . . . Not the least of the fun comes from hearing your own jokes suddenly made very funny by the random contexts in which they are embedded.

Consequences is a real game of chance.

{ 23 }

Twenty Questions

TWENTY QUESTIONS was the first broadcast 'panel game' in Britain to achieve mass appeal. It started on the BBC's Home Service (now Radio 4) in 1947 and soon had an audience of fifteen million, the most popular programme on British radio. As Jonathan Dimbleby describes in his biography of his father:

The team of Richard Dimbleby, Daphne Padel (though she was soon replaced by Joy Adamson), Jack Train and Anona Winn, with Stewart MacPherson in the Chair, and Norman Hackforth as the Mystery Voice, soon became famous radio 'personalities'. . . . Hard-pressed producers spent much time denying that the programme was rigged; that question-master and team were in league to provide faked drama; that Anona Winn (who talked much more than the others) did not know the answers in advance.

The programme's chairman, Stewart MacPherson, had discovered the game when he was on holiday in Canada and heard it broadcast on American radio. Yet, like many such games on radio and television, Twenty Questions is an old game that dates back to well before the twentieth century. Hannah More, in a letter to her sister on 17 February 1786, wrote:

Mrs Fielding and I, like pretty little Misses, diverted ourselves with teaching Sir Joshua and Lord Palmerston the play of twenty questions, and thoroughly did we puzzle them by picking out little obscure insignificant things which we collected from ancient history. Lord North overhearing us, desired to be initiated into this mysterious game, and it was proposed that I should question him: I did so, but his twenty questions were exhausted before he came near the truth. As he at length gave up the point, I told him my thought was the earthen lamp of Epictetus. 'I am quite provoked at my own stupidity,' said his lordship, 'for I quoted that very lamp last night in the House of Commons.' (*The Letters of Hannah More*, ed. R. Brimley Johnson, 1926)

Twenty Questions is a very simple game. One person thinks of something and tells the other players whether it is 'animal, vegetable, or mineral'. They then have to guess the mystery object by asking up to twenty questions, which must be answered simply by 'yes' or 'no' (although Stewart MacPherson was more talkative in the radio version!). The person who guesses the object normally thinks up the next mystery item. A guess usually counts as one of the twenty questions. 'Animal' means any living creature or anything of animal origin; 'vegetable' refers to plants, fruits, fibres, and so on; and 'mineral' embraces inorganic things like stones, metals, chemicals, etc. Sometimes the fourth category, 'abstract', is allowed, to cover anything that is neither animal, vegetable, or mineral.

The game has sometimes been called ANIMAL, VEGETABLE, AND MINERAL or YES AND NO. The latter was the name used in Dickens's *Christmas Carol*:

It was a game called Yes and No, where Scrooge's nephew had to think of something, and the rest must find out what; he only answering to their questions yes or no, as the case was. The brisk fire of questioning to which he was exposed, elicited from him that he was thinking of an animal, a live animal, rather a disagreeable animal, a savage animal, an animal that growled and grunted sometimes, and talked sometimes, and lived in London, and walked about the streets, and wasn't made a show of, and wasn't led by anybody, and didn't live in a menagerie, and was never killed in a market, and was not a horse, or an ass, or a cow, or a bull, or a tiger, or a dog, or a pig, or a cat, or a bear. At every fresh question that was put to him, this nephew burst into a fresh roar of laughter, and was so inexpressibly tickled, that he was obliged to get up off the sofa and stamp. At last the plump sister, falling into a similar state, cried out:

'I have found it out! I know what it is, Fred! I know what it is!'

'What is it?' cried Fred.

'It's your Uncle Scro-o-o-o-oge!'

Which it certainly was.

CLUMPS is a variation of Twenty Questions that requires two teams of several members. One member from each side goes out of the room and these two agree on an object. When they return, each side gathers in a 'clump' around the member from the other side and tries to find out what the mystery object is, by asking questions which are met by 'yes' or 'no' answers.

Clumps was a favourite game for house-parties in the earlier part of this century and John Betjeman remembered it in 'Indoor Games near Newbury':

Oh but Wendy, when the carpet yielded to my indoor pumps
There you stood, your gold hair streaming,
Handsome in the hall-light gleaming
There you looked, and there you led me off into the game of clumps.

A. A. Milne liked the game:

In 'clumps' two people go into the hall and think of something, while the rest remain before the fire. Thus, however long the interval of waiting, all are happy; for the people inside can tell each other stories (or, as a last resort, play some other game) and the two outside are presumably amusing themselves in arranging something very difficult. Personally I adore clumps; not only for this reason, but because of its revelation of hidden talent. There may be a dozen persons in each clump, and in theory every one of the dozen is supposed to take a hand in the cross-examination, but in practice it is always one person who extracts the information required by a cataract of searching questions. Always one person and generally a girl. I love to see her coming out of her shell. . . . In a moment she discovers herself as our natural leader, a leader whom we follow humbly.

How, When, and Where is a similar game in which one person leaves the room while the others decide on a word, preferably one with several meanings. When he returns, the lone person asks each player in succession, 'How do you like it?', 'When do you like it?', and 'Where do you like it?' If the word is *glass*, for instance, the answers to 'How do you like it?' might be: *full* or *polished* or *clear*. If the person succeeds in guessing the word, he indicates who gave the answer that suggested it, and then that person goes out of the room for the next round of the game.

Another guessing game with resemblances to this is What is my Thought Like? One player thinks of something and asks the other players one after another 'What is my thought like?' Each has to answer with the name of something different, for example: *a sausage*, *a traffic-light*, *a bicycle*, etc. Then the first player reveals what he was thinking of, saying 'My thought was a banana. Why is a sausage like a banana?' The person who named a sausage has to think quickly of some connection, such as 'They both have skins.' The person who said a traffic-light might say: 'They are both yellow' and the person who named a bicycle might say (in desperation) 'Neither of them has an engine.' The players may disallow any of these answers: if they do, that person is out of the game or has to pay a forfeit.

Two other games use the name of a person as the mystery word. In Who Am I?, each player has the name of a famous person written on a piece of paper and pinned to his back. He then has to find out who he is by asking questions which elicit 'yes' or 'no' answers.

A more adult game is Botticelli, a development of Crambo (q.v.), in which one player thinks of a famous person, real or fictitious, and tells the other players the first letter of that person's surname. For example, he might say 'J', thinking of Dr Jekyll. Every other player has to think of someone whose name begins with 'J' and ask an indirect question which would lead to that name. Thus, one might ask 'Did you write a dictionary? and the first player would have to reply: 'No, I am not Dr Johnson.' The next player might ask: 'Are you a pop singer?' and the first player would reply: 'No, I am not Mick Jagger' (or Elton John, or Michael Jackson).

If the first player cannot think of a suitable answer to anyone's question, that person is entitled to ask a direct question, such as 'Are you real or fictitious?' The first person to guess the mystery name is able to choose the next personality.

Another game is COFFEEPOT, which is sometimes known as TEAPOT and TEAKETTLE. In an article on Christmas games in *The Tatler* in 1958, Hubert Phillips said that it was once his favourite indooor game, and described it as follows:

One player thinks of a word—or, rather, of a word-sound—which has a number of different meanings. The others, in turn, ask him questions; in his reply to each of them he must introduce his word-sound, substituting however the word *Coffeepot*. Suppose his 'coffeepot' is *Fair* (*Fare*):

Q. 'Can you play Contract Bridge?'
A. 'Yes, I play a coffeepot game.'
Q. 'What sort of girls do you like?'
A. 'Plump girls with coffeepot complexions.'
Q. 'Are you going to Switzerland this winter?'
A. 'No: the coffeepot's too much for me.'

Any player who has just put a question can have a shot at guessing the word, scoring a point for his team. Bad guesses are penalized.

This game provides amusement not only in the attempts to guess the word but also in the incongruous answers created by using the word 'coffeepot' or 'teakettle'. Another game called SAUSAGES depends entirely on this incongruity. One or more of the players ask one or more of the others a series of questions, which must only be answered with the word 'sausages'. If the answerer laughs or smiles, he is out of the game. Gyles Brandreth updates the game by substituting the word 'knickers', but players can choose any word that they find particularly funny.

STINKY PINKY—also known as HINKY PINKY and HANKY PANKY—is a guessing game in which clues are given to rhyming phrases.

One player gives the clues and the other players have to guess the rhyming phrase. Thus, if the clue is 'angry father', the answer would be 'mad dad'. If the clue is 'uncle's fat relation', the answer would be 'obese niece'.

CALL MY BLUFF has been popularized as a television game, devised by the Americans Mark Goodson and Bill Todman. There are two teams, each of three members. Each member of one team gives a definition of a strange word, and the other team has to guess which is the correct definition. Only one of the three definitions is true— the other two are 'bluffs'.

The words are taken from the complete *Oxford English Dictionary*. A typical round of the game might use the word *grimthorpe*. Is it: (1) a throw at Cumberland wrestling; (2) to restore an old building with more money than taste; or (3) a strong, rich-looking silk fabric used for making ceremonial garments? The correct definition is the second one.

When played at home, the game may be called DICTIONARY or THE DICTIONARY GAME or FICTIONARY DICTIONARY. The home version usually involves one person at a time acting as the leader, and choosing an unusual word from the dictionary. He or she reads out the word and the other players have to write down their imagined definitions of it. The leader writes down the true definition, and then collects in the papers and reads out the definitions one by one. Each player in turn tries to decide which is the correct definition. Points are awarded to any player who guesses the true meaning, and sometimes to any player whose definition is chosen as the correct one by any of the other players.

The game can also be played with paragraphs from an encyclopaedia instead of words from a dictionary: the players then have to write paragraphs on such subjects as Fritz Todt or Turkey Buzzards. Another variation is to choose a sentence from a book and read out the first letters of each word. Players then have to write sentences using those letters as the initials for each word. When the sentences are read out, each player tries to choose the genuine one.

For children, the *Concise Oxford Dictionary* contains plenty of words suitable for The Dictionary Game. Advanced players will need the larger *OED*, which includes such gems as: *acersecomic* (someone whose hair has never been cut); *agnification* (representing people as sheep or lambs); *artolatry* (the worship of bread); and *hippocrepiform* (shaped like a horse-shoe).

{ 24 }

Hangman

HANGMAN—also called GALLOWS and HANGING THE MAN—is a very easy game but it is found in various forms. In *Victorian Parlour Games for Today* (1974), Patrick Beaver describes the game thus:

One player, the hangman, having chosen a word (any word) announces how many letters it contains and marks on a piece of paper the same number of 'blanks'. Suppose the word to be 'Capricorn' (nine letters) the nine blanks are indicated thus: - - - - - - - - -. The condemned man (or men), desperately seeking reprieve, asks the hangman whether the word contains any Es. The answer, in this case, is 'no' and the hangman starts to build his gallows. On next being asked, for example, if there are any Cs, the hangman is compelled to place the Cs on the first and sixth blanks, where they belong and he must postpone the erection of his gallows. The game continues in this manner until the condemned man either wins a reprieve by discovering the word before the gallows is built and the hanging takes place or, until the execution is carried out. The sequence of gallows construction and the 'turning off' is effected as follows.

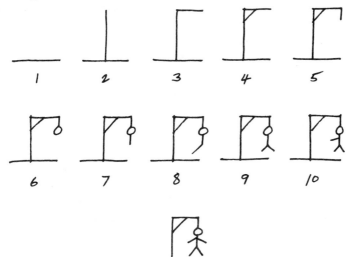

The number of guesses is reduced to seven in the version described by Hubert Phillips and B. C. Westall in their *Book of Indoor Games* (1933), as the hangman starts by drawing the upright of the gallows, and the guesses add the arm of the gallows, its support, rope, and the person's head, body, and two legs. Phillips and Westall suggest using the titles of novels for the concealed words, preferably those that contain uncommon letters or unfamiliar combinations, like *Jew Suss*, *Lalla Rookh*, or *They and I*.

Andrew Pennycook's *Indoor Games Book* (1973) allows thirteen guesses but 'some people start with the gallows complete and you only have six chances before being hanged'. Others add fingers, feet, eyes, nose, mouth, and hair to the hanged man. Some people limit the word to five, six, or seven letters; others allow one or more words of any length. However, short words may be the hardest to guess, since a word like *way* can use up a large number of guesses, even if the victim has already guessed the last two letters.

A similar game in which a word has to be guessed is called CRASH. One player thinks of a word, usually of five or six letters. The other player suggests words of the same length and is told if any of the letters in this word are the same as letters in the same position in the mystery word. Thus, if the mystery word is *crash*, the player might suggest *break* and is told that the second letter is the same in both words. He then tries more words in an attempt to build up an idea of the mystery word.

In a variation of this called JOTTO or GIOTTO, the guesser is told when *any* of the letters in his word is the same as *any* of the letters in the mystery word. So that, if the mystery word is *crash*, the guesser will be told he has two letters the same in *break*.

Yet another form of the game is called WILD CRASH, in which the mystery word can be changed as the game proceeds, so long as it fits the number of 'crashes' or correspondences that have already occurred.

Crash and Jotto are, of course, based on the same principle as the popular game of Mastermind, in which players have to guess the order of a series of coloured pegs. Keen Jotto players have tried to conserve their energies by finding a set of five five-letter words which could be used as guesses one after the other, thus eliminating most of the possible letters. However, it is difficult to discover five words that eliminate twenty-five letters, and Jotto players usually have to be content with covering twenty-four letters by using such series as *blown-fixed-gravy-jumps-ketch.* If you find yourself up against a player who knows such a series by heart, suggest playing with six-letter words instead!

In THE FOREHEAD GAME or FOREHEADS, a game devised by Dave Silverman, each player writes a four-letter word on a slip of paper and sticks it on the forehead of the person on his right. Each player sees the words of all his opponents but not his own. The players in turn announce a word composed of letters in their opponents' words, or else guess their own word. A player can build up an idea of the word on his forehead by noting which letters are mentioned that do not occur in any of the words that he can see on other people's foreheads.

{ 25 }

Puns

When Henry Erskine heard someone say that punning was the low-est form of wit, he replied: 'It is, and therefore the foundation of all wit.' In one of his lectures on Shakespeare, Coleridge said: 'Pun-ning . . . may be the lowest, but at all events is the most harmless, kind of wit, because it never excites envy.' Oscar Levant was perhaps more truthful when he said: 'A pun is the lowest form of humour—when you don't think of it first.'

Sigmund Freud explained that 'Puns . . . pass as the lowest form of verbal joke, probably because they are the "cheapest"—can be made with the least trouble.' PUNS are easy to make because they depend simply on finding two words which sound similar. One of these words is substituted for the other, as when a man discovers the fish-shop and says: 'This must be the plaice.' Often puns are linked together in long strings: 'He mustard his soldiers to pepper the enemy in a salt.'

A pun is sometimes called a 'play on words' but some authorities restrict this term to word play based on only one word which hap-pens to have two meanings. To illustrate the difference, the following ancient joke depends on a pun:

> *First man*: 'My wife's gone to the West Indies.'
> *Second man*: 'Jamaica?'
> *First man*: 'No—she went of her own accord.'

On the other hand, these lines from Pope's *Dunciad* exemplify a play on words because they use one word (*port*) which has two distinct senses:

> Where Bentley late tempestuous wont to sport
> In troubled waters, but now sleeps in port.

Henri Bergson tried to make the distinction clear:

In the pun, the same sentence appears to offer two independent meanings, but it is only an appearance; in reality there are two different sentences made up of different words, but claiming to be one and the same because both have the same sound. We pass from the pun, by imperceptible stages, to the true play upon words. Here there is really one and the same sentence through which two different sets of ideas are expressed, and we are confronted with only one series of words; but advantage is taken of the different meanings a word may have, especially when used figuratively instead of literally.

Many people groan at puns but an equal number of people enjoy them and approve of them. Aristotle, for example, in his *Rhetoric*, stated that puns were acceptable in some kinds of writing. Jesus used a pun when he said: 'Thou art Peter (Greek *Petros*), and upon this rock (Greek *petra*) I will build my Church.' Pope Gregory made a famous pun when he supposedly commented that the English slaves were 'Non Angli, sed angeli'—'Not Angles, but angels'.

Addison noted that 'Cicero was an inveterate punster'. When a man ploughed up the field where his father was buried, Cicero said: 'Hoc est vere colere monumentum patris', that is: 'This is truly to cultivate a father's memory.'

According to M. M. Mahood's estimate in *Shakespeare's Wordplay*, Shakespeare uses about 3,000 puns in his plays, often in the most serious scenes. In *King Henry IV, Part Two*, when Henry Percy hears that his son Hotspur has been killed, he says:

> Said he young Harry Percy's spur was cold?
> Of Hotspur, Coldspur?

After the first terrible murder in *Macbeth*, Lady Macbeth says:

> If he do bleed,
> I'll *gild* the faces of the grooms withal;
> For it must seem their *guilt*.

Dr Johnson said that for Shakespeare a pun was 'the fatal Cleopatra for which he lost the world, and was content to lose it'. But Coleridge thought that Shakespeare's punning was justitifed: 'A pun, if it be congruous with the feeling of the scene, is not only allowable in the dramatic dialogue, but oftentimes one of the most effectual intensives of passion.' (*Shakespearean Criticism*, 1811-12)

Queen Elizabeth I joined the ranks of the punsters when she said: 'You may be burly, my Lord of Burleigh, but ye shall make less stir in my realm than the Lord of Leicester.' An unlikely pun is attributed to Sir Francis Drake, who is said to have reported the defeat of the

Spanish Armada by sending the Queen one word—'*Cantharides*', which is the name of an aphrodisiac otherwise known as '*The Spanish fly*'.

A single word was again used to report a victory when General Sir Charles Napier defeated the Indian province of Sind in 1843, and sent the British War Office a message of one Latin word—'*Peccavi*'—which means '*I have sinned*'.

Most of the Elizabethan playwrights were fond of puns, and so were the Metaphysical poets like John Donne and Andrew Marvell. The sermons of Bishop Lancelot Andrewes (1555–1626) were full of puns and word play, such as the following:

If this child be *Immanuel*, God with us; then, without this child, this Immanuel, we be without God. Without Him, in this world (saith the Apostle); and, if without Him in this, without Him in the next. And, if without Him there, it will be *Immanu-hell*; and that, and no other place, will fall (I fear me) to our share. Without Him, this we are: what, with Him? Why, if we have Him; and God, by Him; we need no more: *Immanu-el*, and *Immanu-all*.

When Charles I's jester Thomas Killigrew said he could make a pun on any subject, the King said: 'Make one on me.' But Killigrew replied that he could not do that, 'for the king is no subject'.

The mottoes and coats of arms of noblemen often contained puns. In his notes for *Waverley*, Sir Walter Scott mentions as 'a perfect pun' the motto of the Vernons—'*Ver non semper vivet*' ('*The spring will not last for ever*')—and that of the Onslows—'*Festina lente*' ('*Make haste slowly*').

In the eighteenth century, Jonathan Swift and his friend Thomas Sheridan were notorious punsters. Swift wrote *A Modest Defence of Punning* (1716) and Sheridan followed with *Ars Pun-ica* or *The Art of Punning* (1719) which laboriously defined the pun and gave examples of punning dialogue:

Q. Who were the first bakers?
A. The Crustumenians. (Masters of the Rolls, quoth Capt. Wolseley.)
Q. Where did the first hermaphrodites come from?
A. Middlesex.
Q. What part of England has the most dogs?
A. Barkshire.

Sheridan gives thirty-four rules for the use of puns, such as:

Rule 8. *The Rule of Interruption.* Although the company be engaged in a discourse of the most serious consequence, it is and may be lawful to interrupt them with a pun. . . .

Rule 9. *The Rule of Risibility.* A man must be the first that laughs at his own pun.

The Jacobites invented a silent pun. When drinking a toast to 'The King' they would pass their glasses over the water-bottle before drinking the toast. Thus, without saying a word, they proclaimed their allegiance to 'The King over the water'.

Puns in Greek also flourished in the eighteenth century. William Hogarth invited a friend to dinner with a picture of a pie, knife, and fork accompanied by the Greek letters *Eta, beta, pi*. In recounting this, the *Gentleman's Magazine* in 1781 added:

This reminds us of a pun by Garth to Rowe, who making repeated use of his snuff-box, the Doctor at last sent it to him with the two Greek letters written on the lid, *Φ P* (Phi Rho—i.e. 'Fie, Rowe!'). At this the sour Dennis was so provoked as to declare that 'a man who could make so vile a pun would not scruple to pick a pocket'.

Despite such disapproval, puns flowed just as wildly in the nineteenth century from the pens of such incorrigible punsters as Charles Lamb, Theodore Hook, and Thomas Hood. Lamb said: 'I never knew an enemy to puns who was not an ill-natured man' and that 'the last breath he drew in he wished might be through a pipe and exhaled in a pun'.

Lamb believed that the worst puns were the best:

A pun is not bound by the laws which limit nicer wit. It is a pistol let off at the ear; not a feather to tickle the intellect. . . . The puns which are most entertaining are those which will least bear an analysis. (*Popular Fallacies*, 1826)

One of his favourite puns occurs in the story of the Oxford student who met a porter carrying a hare through the streets and asked him, 'Is that your hare, or a wig?'

Theodore Hook committed equally atrocious puns, such as this stream of them on the subject of a strike among the working-men of Paris:

The bakers, being ambitious to extend their *do*-mains, declared that a revolution was *needed*, and though not exactly *bred* up to arms, soon reduced their *crusty* masters to terms. The tailors called a council of the *board* to see what *measures* should be taken, and, looking upon the bakers as the *flower* of chivalry, decided to follow *suit*; the consequence of which was, that a *cereous* insurrection was *lighted up* among the candle-makers, which, however *wick*-ed it might appear in the eyes of some persons, developed traits of character not unworthy of ancient *Greece*. (C. C. Bombaugh, *Gleanings for the Curious*, 1890)

Theodore Hook and Thomas Hood were great friends. Hood once said to Hook: 'They call us "the inseparables"; but, after all, it's only natural that Hook and I should always be together.' When Hood found that an undertaker was taking too much interest in him, he said that the undertaker was 'trying to urn a lively Hood'.

Hood's poems are full of puns and plays on words, such as the opening verses of 'Faithless Nelly Gray':

> Ben Battle was a soldier bold,
> And used to war's alarms:
> But a cannon-ball took off his legs,
> So he laid down his arms!
>
> Now as they bore him off the field,
> Said he, 'Let others shoot,
> For here I leave my second leg,
> And the Forty-second Foot!'

Hood's poem about 'Faithless Sally Brown' ends with the lines:

> His death, which happened in his berth,
> At forty-odd befell:
> They went and told the sexton, and
> The sexton toll'd the bell.

G. K. Chesterton said of Hood that 'He knew that the most profound and terrible and religious thing in literature was a profound and terrible and religious pun. . . . In the long great roll that includes Homer and Shakespeare, he was the last great man who really employed the pun.' Chesterton pointed to the humanity that could best find its expression in a pun, in such lines as these by Hood:

> So each one upwards in the air
> His shot he did expend.
> And may all other duels have
> That upshot at the end.

Chesterton said: 'In a primary sense puns are the perfect type of art. That is, they briefly embody the chief essence of art; that completeness of form should confirm completeness of idea.'

Oliver Wendell Holmes was less charitable. In *The Autocrat of the Breakfast-Table* (1858), he said that killing a punster could be justifiable if the pun is bad enough. 'People that make puns are like wanton boys that put coppers on the railroad tracks. They amuse themselves and other children, but their little trick may upset a freight train of conversation for the sake of a battered witticism.'

Holmes might have been anticipating such collections of puns as Hugh Rowley's *Puniana* (1867) and *More Puniana* (1875), which are crammed with creaking conundrums and paltry puns:

Why is a deceptive woman like a seamstress? Because she is not what she seems! ('Not bad,' the friendly reader may remark, button the hole perhaps it's sewnly sew-sew; a-hem! and a needles(s) addition to our work.)

Sam Weller in Dickens's *Pickwick Papers* and *Master Humphrey's Clock* gave his name to a kind of saying which often includes a pun— the WELLERISM. Sam Weller was given to saying things like 'Out with it, as the father said to the child, when he swallowed a farden.' Such wellerisms became popular during the nineteenth century, although they had been used before Sam Weller was invented. In *The Proverb* (1931), Archer Taylor quotes examples from classical Greek and Latin, and from Chaucer. In Samuel Beazley's farce *The Boarding-House* (1811), a character called Samuel Spatterdash says such things as 'She's off with a whisk, as the butcher said to the flies.'

Wellerisms were a craze in nineteenth-century America. *The Spirit of the Times* for 1840 included: 'I guess he'll re-wive, as the gentleman said when his friend fainted away at his wife's funeral.' (Note the Welleristic pronunciation of *revive*.) And in an American book of 1896—*House on the Styx* by J. K Bangs—we find: 'That isn't the point, as the man said to the assassin who tried to stab him with the hilt of a dagger.'

Wellerisms can be made into a game, by getting players to write a sentence as far as the word 'as' and then swopping their pieces of paper and adding a humorous ending, e.g. 'Meet you at the corner, as one wall said to another.' Perhaps the best-known wellerism is 'Ere we go, as the earwig said when it fell off the wall.'

Nowadays puns are still reviled, yet many of us cannot resist making them when the opportunity arises. Famous twentieth-century punsters include James Joyce and many Americans: Groucho Marx, Ogden Nash, Dorothy Parker, S. J. Perelman, James Thurber, and Peter De Vries. When Groucho Marx went to dinner with T. S. Eliot,

I discovered that Eliot and I had three things in common: (1) an affection for good cigars and (2) cats; and (3) a weakness for making puns—a weaknss that for many years I have tried to overcome. T.S., on the other hand, is an unashamed—even proud—punster. For example, there's his Gus, the Theater Cat, whose 'real name was Asparagus'.

Groucho Marx once said 'Time wounds all heels', a punning phrase that uses a kind of inversion rather like a spoonerism (q.v.). We find it again in Mae West's 'It's not the men in your life that count—it's the life in your men.'

Personal names are often the basis for puns. Anybody with an unusual name is subjected to endless punning. The author of this book has lost count of the number of times he has been addressed as 'Augarde our help in ages past'. In 'A Hymn to God the Father', John Donne punned on his own name:

> And, having done that: Thou hast done,
> I fear no more.

Lord Baden-Powell, the founder of the Scouts, was nicknamed 'bathing towel' when he was a boy. W. S. Walsh noted that:

The poor man born with a punnable name suffers untold agony against which he is absolutely defenceless. When Mr Garrison has been told for the hundredth time to hold the fort, when Mr Younghusband for the thousandth time has been twitted on the fact that he is an old bachelor, when Mr Archer has been repeatedly warned not to draw the long bow . . . it would be justifiable homicide in any of these gentlemen to slay their oppressors. (*Handy-Book of Literary Curiosities*, 1892)

Some people have given themselves punning names (like the singer Sandie Shaw), perhaps imitating such cartoon characters as Andy Capp and Olive Oyl. Punning names form the basis for an amusing game in which you have to think of suitable authors for particular books. The best known is probably '*The Broken Window* by Eva Brick' but there are hundreds of others. The following are from *Foulsham's Fun Book* (1933):

Cutting it Fine by Moses Lawn.
The Corn by Honor Foot.
The Antiques by Fay Kingham.
The Cliff Tragedy by Eileen Dover.
Knighted by Watts E. Dunn.
Wine and Women by Rex Holmes.
The Woman Who Sang by Topsy Sharp.
The Housing Problem by Rufus Quick.
The Song of the Shirt by Dryden Aird.

The Queen is said to have played a similar game, called the NAME GAME. Helen Cathcart describes it in *The Queen in her Circle* (1977):

Take the name of a racing sire and dam and suggest an appropriate new name for their offspring. Ingenuity, brain-cudgelling and speed are essential. The match of Pinza and Open Country led to the foaling of Prairie Song. By Court Martial from Above Board came Above Suspicion, by Court Martial from Avila came Spanish Court, and again the offspring of Court Martial out of Choral and was named to perfection Martial Music. The foal of Fair Copy and Carmen evoked the name Opera Score.

Another game using names is KNOCK, KNOCK, a kind of conundrum (q.v.). One person says 'Knock, knock.' The other asks 'Who's there?' The first person might then say 'Amos.' If the second person cannot guess the answer, he has to say 'Amos who?' and the punning reply is 'A mosquito.' Here are some other examples:

Knock, knock.
Who's there?
Ken.
Ken who?
Ken I come in?

Knock, knock.
Who's there?
Ivor.
Ivor who?
Ivor you let me in the door or I'll climb in the window.

Knock, knock.
Who's there?
Sarah.
Sarah who?
Sarah doctor in the house?

Knock, knock.
Who's there?
Howard.
Howard who?
Howard you like a punch on the nose?

Knock, Knock has become so familiar that it is no longer restricted
to personal names: almost anything can be at the door:

Knock, knock.
Who's there?
A little old lady.
A little old lady who?
I didn't know you could yodel.

Knock, knock.
Who's there?
Butcher.
Butcher who?
Butcher right arm in . . .

Knock, knock
Who's there?
Ammonia.
Ammonia who?
Ammonia little boy who can't reach the doorbell.

Knock, Knock was so popular that the *Sun* newspaper started a
daily strip-cartoon in the early 1980s, consisting simply of Knock,
Knock jokes. But they date back to at least forty years ago, when
Torquemada devised crossword puzzles in which some of the clues
were Knock, Knock jokes. For instance, his clue, 'Blank who?
Blank'd love to' leads to the name *Obadiah*, and 'Blank who? Blank
fool and caught a cold' leads to *Abinadab*.

Knock, Knock jokes depend on finding a phrase in which the first
word or words sound the same as other words. In an American book
called *Anguish Languish* (1956), Howard L. Chace took this principle
further by writing whole stories in words that sound the same as
the original words. His version of *Little Red Riding Hood* begins like
this:

Ladle Rat Rotten Hut

Wants pawn term dare worsted ladle gull hoe lift wetter murder inner ladle
cordage honour itch offer lodge, dock florist.

This sort of rewriting is found in a passage attributed to Victor Hugo:

Gall, amant de la reine, alla, tour magnanime,
Galamment, de l'arène à la Tour Magne, à Nîmes.

This has been translated into English as:

Gall, doll-lover, 'ghost' to royalty at right hour,
Galled all over, goes to royal tea at Rye Tower.

A book by Luis d'Antin Van Rooten called *Mots d'heures: gousses, rames* (1967) appears to consist of French verse but, when read aloud in the style of old-fashioned French actors, the poems sound suspiciously like nursery rhymes or—as the book's title suggests—Mother Goose rhymes:

Oh, les mots d'heureux bardes
Où en toutes heures que partent.
Tous guetteurs pour dock à Beaune.
Besoin gigot d'air.
De que paroisse paire.
Et ne pour dock, pet-de-nonne.

Once you start thinking about sounds in this way, you soon find yourself changing *mince pie* into *Mint spy, grey day* into *Grade A, a nice cold shower* into *an ice-cold shower, the stuff he knows* into *the stuffy nose,* and *for he's a jolly good fellow* into *freeze a jolly good fellow.*

One can also look for unusual word-divisions that create new phrases, so that *nowhere* becomes *now here, therapist* becomes *the rapist,* and *legend* becomes *leg end.* Other suitable words for this treatment include: *allowed, candied, Chicago, comedies, cornice, crumbled, earnest, forego, heathen, island, modesty, notice, panties, pantry, unclean,* and *yeasty.* Some words can be divided into more than two separate words—for example, *altogether, significant,* and *toreador.*

New languages have been created by following the way that words are pronounced rather than the way they are written. The language 'Strine' was developed (by a man calling himself 'Afferbeck Lauder') from the pronunciation particular to Australians. It includes such words and phrases as *air fridge* meaning 'ordinary, not extreme'; *dimension* used as a response to 'thank you'; *ebb tide* meaning 'hunger, desire for food'; and *flesh in the pen* for something momentarily brilliant or startling.

WHAT IS THE QUESTION? is a punning game which reverses a conundrum. One player gives an answer; the other player or players must supply an appropriate question. For example, 'Edwin Drood' might be supplied with the question, 'What did Edwin do with his crayons?' 'Kiss me, Hardy' might be matched with 'Have you got one last wish, Laurel?' And '9 W' could be the answer to the question, 'Wagner, do you spell your name with a V?'

Another punning game is TOM SWIFTIES, also known as ADVERBIAL PUNS. The first name is said to derive from the kind of sentence used by a character called Tom Swift in some 1920s books by Edward Stratemeyer. The aim in Tom Swifties is to make a pun on an adverb or adverbial phrase, as in the following sentences:

> 'I can't find the oranges,' said Tom, fruitlessly.
> 'I'll try to dig up a couple of friends,' said Tom gravely.
> 'I work at the quarry,' answered Tom, stonily.
> 'Let's trap that sick bird,' said Tom illegally.
> 'I got the first three wrong,' she said forthrightly
> 'The bacon is burnt,' he said with panache.
> 'That's a very large whale,' said Captain Ahab superficially.

A similar game, invented by Laurence Urdang, poses the names of people from particular trades and professions, and asks how we can get rid of them. For example, chiropodists can be 'defeated', hairdressers can be 'distressed', feudal barons can be 'demoted', ninth-century Scots can be 'depicted', and Superman can be 'dismantled'.

DAFFY DEFINITIONS is a game in which one tries to think of punning definitions for words, such as 'a dug-out canoe' for *travelogue*, 'a fake diamond' for *shamrock*, and 'a man whose career lies in ruins' for *archaeologist*. Some fairly daffy definitions are found in Dr Johnson's *Dictionary of the English Language* (1755), although he did not use puns but irony, as in his definition of *oats*: 'a grain, which in England is generally given to horses, but in Scotland supports the people'.

Gustave Flaubert wrote a *Dictionnaire des Idées reçues* ('Dictionary of Accepted Ideas') in which he defined words in the overworked senses used in everyday conversation, for example:

> *Architects*, all idiots; they always forget to put in the stairs.
> *Lord*, wealthy Englishman.
> *Rabbit pie*, always made of cat.

The American Ambrose Bierce wrote *The Devil's Dictionary* which defined words in a similarly ironical way:

> *Cab*, a tormenting vehicle in which a pirate jolts you through devious ways to the wrong place, where he robs you.
> *Faith*, belief without evidence in what is told by one who speaks without knowledge, of things without parallel.
> *Harangue*, a speech by an opponent, who is known as an harangue-outang.

Only the last of these definitions depends on a pun, which is the mainstay of modern Daffy Definitions. Here is a selection of a few more such gems:

> *urchin*, the lower part of a lady's face.
> *eavesdropper*, an icicle
> *violin*, a bad hotel
> *archaic*, what you can't have, and eat.
> *boomerang*, what you say when you frighten a meringue.

As Daffy Definitions try to explain words in new ways, so MY WORD does the same thing with well-known quotations or phrases. This game was popularized by Frank Muir and Denis Norden in the BBC radio series of the same name. Frank and Denis ended each programme by providing unusual explanations for sayings like *Too many cooks spoil the broth* and *Here today, gone tomorrow*, although their explanations usually turned the sayings into something quite different, like *Too many kirks spoil Arbroath* and *Hyères today, Ghent tomorrow*.

It often happens that apparently modern games originated much earlier than most people realize, and this is true of My Word. It was anticipated in the stories which Flann O'Brien wrote for *The Irish Times* under the pseudonym of Myles na Gopaleen. The stories tell of two characters that the author calls Keats and Chapman. Each story leads to a punning version of a familiar phrase. Thus, when Keats and Chapman go to the circus and see a lion-tamer reading a newspaper in the lion's cage, Keats explains that 'He's reading between the lions.' When a painter called Franz Huehl wastes all his money in gambling, Keats tell Huehl's wife: 'You have been living in F. Huehl's pair o' dice' and Chapman adds: 'F. Huehl and his Monet are soon parted.'

{ 26 }

Postscript: The Longest Word

Finding (or trying to create) the longest word in the English language is a tantalizing quest.

An old joke says that the longest word is *smiles* because there is a mile between the first and last letter. The longest words that most people know are *antidisestablishmentarianism* (twenty-eight letters—allegedly coined by Gladstone, with the sense 'opposition to the idea that the Church should cease to be formally recognized by the State') and *supercalifragilisticexpialidocious* (thirty-four letters—popularized by a song in the 1964 film version of *Mary Poppins*). James Murray, editor of the *Oxford English Dictionary*, noted in 1897 that:

The quotation from a newspaper of 1894 in the 'New English Dictionary', under the word 'Disproportionableness', to the effect that 'a correspondent has submitted the word "disproportionableness' as the longest in the English language', has awakened the interest of persons fond of such statistics. One of these submits that 'anthropomorphologically', which is quoted from a theological work of 1850, has two letters more, and is the longest word that has as yet appeared in the 'Dictionary'. He thinks that it will hold the 'record' for some time to come at least.

This, of course, does not reckon names of chemical compounds and their derivatives, such as 'trioxymethylanthraquinonic' or 'dichlorhydro-quinonedisulphonic', which outstrip all reckoning. (*Notes and Queries*, 10 April 1897)

Other long words in the *Oxford English Dictionary* include the following, ranging from nineteen to twenty-five letters:

> *extraterritoriality* (19)
> *anti-tintinnabularian* (20)
> *salpingo-oöphorectomy* (20)
> *indistinguishableness* (21)
> *de-anthropomorphization* (22)
> *honorificabilitudinity* (22)
> *incircumscriptibleness* (22)
> *historico-cabbalistical* (22)

historico-philosophical (22)
theologico-metaphysical (22)
transubstantiationalist (23)
philosophico-psychological (25)

The longest word in the *OED* seems to be *floccinaucinihilipilification* (29), which means 'the action or habit of estimating something as worthless'. In a letter of 1741, William Shenstone wrote: 'I loved him for nothing so much as his flocci-nauci-nihili-pili-fication of money.' Sir Walter Scott, in a diary entry for 18 March 1829, changed the spelling slightly: 'Segars in loads. Whiskey in lashings; but they must be taken with an air of contempt, a flocci-paucinihilipilification of all that can gratify the outward man.'

The 1982 *Supplement* to the *OED* added the word *pneumono-ultramicroscopicsilicovolcanoconiosis* (45). It supposedly means 'a lung disease caused by the inhalation of very fine silica dust' but its inventor, Francis Joseph Xavier Scully, probably used it as a joke when he introduced it into his book *Bedside Manna* (1936), spelling it '-koniosis'.

The longest word used by Shakespeare has twenty-seven letters and comes in *Love's Labour's Lost*, where Costard says:

They have lived long on the alms-basket of words. I marvel thy master hath not eaten thee for a word; for thou art not so long by the head as *honorificabilitudinitatibus*: thou art easier swallowed than a flap-dragon.

Honorificabilitudinitatibus is a Latin ablative plural and literally means 'with honourablenesses'. The word is also interesting for its long regular succession of alternate consonants and vowels.

Other long words in literature include one of a hundred letters near the beginning of James Joyce's *Finnegans Wake*: 'The fall (bababadalgharaghtakamminarronnkonnbronntonnerronntuonnt-hunntrovarrhounawnskawntoohoohoordenenthurnuk!) of a once wallstrait oldparr is retaled early in bed and later on life down through all christian minstrelsy.' François Rabelais' *Gargantua and Pantagruel* is full of similarly nonsensical words, which are reproduced in the translation by Thomas Urquhart and Peter Le Motteux:

Was it not enough thus to have morcocastebezasteverestegrigeligosco-papopondrillated us all in our upper members with your botched mittens, but you must also apply such morderegripippiatabirofreluchambure-lurecaquelurintimpaniments on our shin-bones . . . ?

In Aristophanes' *Ecclesiazusae* there is a word of 170 Greek letters which makes 182 letters when it is transliterated into English. It describes a stew made of all kinds of meat and fish.

The names of real people and places can also provide us with long words. An American-Indian village in the state of New York is called *Kowogoconnughariegugharie* (25), while there is a lake in Massachusetts named *Chargoggagoggmanchauggagoggchaubunagunga-maugg* (45).

New Zealand has a place-name of fifty-seven letters: *Taumatawhaka-tangihangakoauauotamateapokaiwhenuakitanatahu*. It names the hill where the legendary traveller, Tamatea-pokai-whenua, played his flute. It was made familiar in Britain by being sung as the background to a hit record called 'The Lone Ranger' by the British band Quantum Jump in 1979.

As for the British Isles, there is the famous Welsh place-name beginning *Llanfair—* (for which see Chapter 18 on tongue-twisters). And *Brewer's Dictionary of Phrase and Fable* for 1894 mentions a place in the Isle of Mull called *Drimtaidhvrickhillichattan*.

In 1935, a Greek man living in Michigan announced that he had decided to change his name to 'Pappas', as a simpler form of his surname *Pappatheodorokomoundoronicolucopoulos* (37). Dmitri Borg-mann tells of an inhabitant of Pennsylvania whose surname has 666 letters. To save time, he sometimes signs his name as 'Hubert B. Wolfe + 666, Sr.'

The middle names of Hawaiian women are sometimes remarkably long as well as beautifully poetic. Gwendolyn K. Kekino gave her middle name as: *Kuuleikailialohaopiilaniwailauokekoaulumahiehie-kealaomaonaopiikea* (65). But a girl baptized in Honolulu in 1967 was given this middle name of a hundred letters: *Napaumohalaen-aenaamekawehiwehionakuahiwiamenaawawakehoomakehoaalakeeaonaai-nananiakeaohawaiiikawanaao*. It means: 'The fragrant abundant beautiful blossoms begin to fill the air of hills and valleys throughout the length and breadth of these glorious Hawaiian Islands at dawn.'

As James Murray pointed out, the longest words of all are scientific names. Words like *trinitrophenylmethylnitramine* (29) and *hepa-tocholangiocystoduodenostomy* (32) are overshadowed by many longer words invented in the worlds of science and medicine. In *Headlong Hall* (1816), Thomas Love Peacock describes the human body as '*osseocarnisanguineoviscericartilaginonervomedullary*' (51). Dr Edward Strother (1675-1737) characterized the spa waters of Bristol as '*aqueosalinocalcalinoceraceoaluminosocupreovitriolic*' (52).

As more is discovered about medical complications and chemical combinations, scientists concoct longer and longer words by splicing verbal elements together. *Word Ways* for May 1980 printed the full name for the protein bovine glutamate dehydrogenase: it consists of 3,641 letters. Another protein is said to have 4,059 letters in its abbreviated form and more than 8,000 letters in full!

At the other end of the spectrum, it seems easier to find the shortest words in the language. Several letters of the alphabet—such as A, I, O, and even U (as in 'U and non-U') are acceptable as one-letter words, with I arguably being the shortest because it is the narrowest.

As for place-names, Ross Eckler has discovered a town called Y in Michigan. In the same American state, a newspaper reported in 1931 the death of 'H. P. Re, reputed to have the shortest surname of any man in the United States. . . . A newsdealer in Coldwater, he spent a good deal of his time explaining to strangers that his name was really Re.' One wonders if anyone in the world has a surname of only one letter.

Select Bibliography

This bibliography lists some of the most useful books for the study of word games.

E. M. Baker, *Indoor Games for Children and Young People* (1912)
S. Bann, *Concrete Poetry* (1967)
D. St P. Barnard, *Anatomy of the Crossword* (1963)
Patrick Beaver, *Victorian Parlour Games for Today* (1974)
Howard Bergerson, *Palindromes and Anagrams* (1973)
C. C. Bombaugh, *Facts and Fancies for the Curious from the Harvest-Fields of Literature* (1905)
—— *Gleanings for the Curious from the Harvest-Fields of Literature* (1890)
Dmitri A. Borgmann, *Language on Vacation* (1965)
Gyles Brandreth, *Indoor Games* (1977)
William Camden, *Remains* (1605)
Lewis Carroll, *Complete Works* (Nonesuch ed., 1939)
—— *Letters* (ed. M. N. Cohen, 1979)
Cassell's Book of Indoor Amusements, Card Games and Fireside Fun (1881)
Delights for the Ingenious (1711)
Isaac d'Israeli, *Curiosities of Literature* (1824)
W. T. Dobson *Literary Frivolities* (1880)
—— *Poetical Ingenuities and Eccentricities* (1882)
H. E. Dudeney, *World's Best Word Puzzles* (1925)
A. Ross Eckler, *Word Recreations* (1979)
Willard R. Espy, *An Almanac of Words at Play* (1975)
—— *Another Almanac of Words at Play* (1981)
—— *The Game of Words* (1971)
John Fisher, *The Magic of Lewis Carroll* (1973)
Darryl Francis, *Puzzles and Teasers for Everyone* (1974)
Games and Puzzles (magazine, 1972–81)
Uncle George, *Parlour Pastime for the Young* (1857)
A. B. Gomme, *Games for Parlour and Playground* (1898)
—— *Traditional Games* (1894)
Paul Hammond and Patrick Hughes, *Upon the Pun* (1978)
Darwin A. Hindman, *Handbook of Indoor Games and Contests* (1957)
Professor Hoffmann, *Drawing-Room Amusements* (1879)
The Late Tom Hood and his Sister, *Excursions into Puzzledom* (1879)
Helene Hovanec, *The Puzzler's Paradise* (1978)
Logophile (magazine, 1977–)

Select Bibliography

J. A. Manson, *Indoor Games* (1906)

The Masquerade (1797)

Roger Millington, *The Strange World of the Crossword* (1974)

James Appleton Morgan, *Macaronic Poetry* (1872)

Notes and Queries (journal, 1850-)

Iona and Peter Opie, *Children's Games in Street and Playground* (1969)

—— *The Lore and Language of Schoolchildren* (1959)

—— *Oxford Dictionary of Nursery Rhymes* (1951)

David Parlett, *Penguin Book of Word Games* (1982)

Hubert Phillips, *Word Play* (1945)

F. Planche, *Guess Me* (1872)

Peter Puzzlewell, *A Choice Collection of Riddles, Charades, Rebusses, etc.* (1796)

—— *Home Amusements* (1859)

Sid Sackson, *A Gamut of Games* (1974)

M. E. Solt, *Concrete Poetry* (1970)

John Taylor (the Water Poet), *Works* (1872)

Verbatim (magazine, 1974-)

William S. Walsh, *Handy-Book of Literary Curiosities* (1892)

H. B. Wheatley, *Of Anagrams* (1862)

W. T. Williams and G. H. Savage, *The Strand Problems Book* (1935)

Word Ways (magazine, 1968-)

Acknowledgements

The author and publishers acknowledge with thanks permission to reprint the following copyright material:

Michael Alexander: from *Old English Riddles* (1980). Reprinted by permission of Anvil Press Poetry Ltd.

Dmitri Borgmann: from *Language on Vacation*, copyright © 1965 Dmitri A. Borgmann. Reprinted by permission of Charles Scribner's Sons.

Lewis Carroll: extracts from *The Diaries of Lewis Carroll* (Cassell, 1954), ed. R. Lancelyn Green; from *Lewis Carroll, Letters*, vol. i, ed. M. N. Cohen (Macmillan, 1979), copyright © The Executors of the Estate of C. L. Dodgson, 1979. Reprinted by permission of The Executors of the Estate of C. L. Dodgson and of A. P. Watt Ltd; 'Syzygies on the name of Beatrice Earle' is from p. 185 of E. M. Hatch, *A Selection from the Letters of L. Carroll to his Child Friends* (1933). Reprinted by permission of The Executors of the Estate of C. L. Dodgson and A. P. Watt Ltd.

Noël Coward: from *Hay Fever*. Reprinted by permission of Ernest Benn Ltd.

e. e. cummings: 'n/ /OthI', © 1963 by Marion Morehouse Cummings, from *Complete Poems 1913-1962* (MacGibbon & Kee, 1968. Reprinted by permission of Granada Publishing Ltd., and of Harcourt Brace Jovanovich, Inc.

W. R. Espy: 'May eagles lacerate eternally . . .' from *Almanac of Words at Play* (Crown Publishers Inc). 'It was raining *one* today, . . .' from *Another Almanac of Words at Play* copyright © 1980 by Willard R. Espy. Reprinted by permission of André Deutsch and Clarkson N. Potter, Inc.

Ian Hamilton Finlay: 'Au Pair Girl' from *Concrete Poetry*, ed. S. Bann. Reprinted by permission of London Magazine Editions.

Myles na Gopaleen: 'My grasp . . . Ezra £' from *Literary Criticism* by Myles na Gopaleen, ed. Kevin O'Nolan (MacGibbon & Kee, 1968). Reprinted by permission of Granada Publishing Ltd.

William Hayter: from *Spooner: A Biography*. Reprinted by permission of W. H. Allen & Co., Ltd.

A. P. Herbert: from *Misleading Cases in the Common Law* (Methuen). Reprinted by permission of A. P. Watt Ltd., on behalf of Lady Gwendolyn Herbert and Methuen, England Ltd.

H. Hovanec: 'His pretty love was young, petite . . .' from *Puzzler's Paradise*, p. 144 (Paddington Press).

A. A. Milne: from *Not That It Matters*. Reprinted by permission of Curtis Brown Ltd., London on behalf of the Estate of A. A. Milne.

Edwin Morgan: 'Summer Haiku' and 'The Computer's first Christmas card' from *Concrete Poetry*, ed. S. Bann. Reprinted by permission of London Magazine Editions.

Robert Morse: 'I'll hash my wands or shake a tower . . .', in W. H. Auden, *A Certain World* (Faber, 1970).

Ogden Nash: 'What'll we do now, or, I'm afraid I know, or, good old just plain charades, farewell' ('The Game') from *Good Intentions* by Ogden Nash, copyright 1942 by Ogden Nash. Reprinted by permission of Curtis Brown, London, on behalf of the Estate of Ogden Nash and by Little, Brown and Company.

Luis d'Antin Van Rooten: poem 4 from *Mots d'heures: gousses, rames*, copyright © 1967 by Courtlandt H. K. Van Rooten. Reprinted by permission of Angus & Robertson (UK) Ltd., and Viking Penguin, Inc.

Roger Scruton: 'Night, whispering to Morning, said . . .' from *Fortnight's Anger*, copyright © Roger Scruton 1981. Reprinted by permission of Carcanet Press, Manchester.

James Thurber: from *Do You Want To Make Something Out Of It* © 1963 Helen W. Thurber, from *Vintage Thurber*, vol. i, ed. Helen Thurber, © The Collection 1963 Hamish Hamilton. Reprinted by permission of Hamish Hamilton Ltd., and Mrs James Thurber.

Emmett Williams: 'Like attracts like' from *Concrete Poetry*, ed. S. Bann. Reprinted by permission of London Magazine Editions.

Clement Wood: 'Death of a Scrabble Master' from *Another Almanac of Words at Play* by Willard R. Espy. Copyright © 1980 by Willard R. Espy. Used by permission of Clarkson N. Potter, Inc.

Sir Llewellyn Woodward: from *Short Journey* (Faber, 1942).

While every effort has been made to secure permission, we may have failed in a few cases to trace the copyright holder. We apologize for any apparent negligence.

Index